Beyond Likes and Shares: The Semantic Web Revolution

Nimra

Contents

Contents

1 Introduction

Collaborating and exchanging information are deep-seated phenomena
that have long been part of our culture. A recent result of this world
wide collaboration of humankind is the World Wide Web or just the
Web. The Web was invented by Tim Berners-Lee as "a collaborative
medium, a place where we can all meet and read and write."[1] In its first
iteration, the Web was a network of interlinked hypermedia documents.
The Web 2.0 is known as the participative Social Web, and although
it enables and promotes user contribution, it has converged to more
centralized services controlled by globally dominating companies. Now
with the evolution toward the Web 3.0, we can see a paradigm shift to
a Giant Global Graph,[2] where distributed structured knowledge bases
enriched with links to each other and semantic descriptions are gaining
more attention. This newly evolving advancement of the Web and the
usage of the Web as a global Knowledge Graph is also known as the
Semantic Web. In particular, the interlinking of structured data on
the Semantic Web and its publication as Linked Data have led to the
success apparent as the Linked Open Data Cloud[3] with 1,239 datasets
and 16,147 links between the datasets (as of March 2019). Collaboration of globally distributed parties is the major aspect that has led
to this success of the Web and the Semantic Web. With its emphasis on links, the Semantic Web is organized in a collaborative manner
and supports the trend toward re-decentralization of the Web. This effort for re-decentralization is particularly apparent in the attention for
the Solid platform[4] for decentralized social Web applications [Man+16]
and its recent commercial inception with the foundation of the company
Inrupt.[5]

On the Semantic Web knowledge bases and ontologies are used to
formulate a common understanding of people in the distributed architecture. According to the definition by Gruber [Gru09]: "In the context
of computer and information sciences, an ontology defines a set of rep-

---

[1] *Tim Berners-Lee: Weaving a Semantic Web.* A report on the keynote of Tim

resentational primitives with which to model a domain of knowledge or discourse."[6] In the field of computer science, knowledge engineering, and data science methods and processes are developed to structure this collaboration and discourse. Studer, Benjamins, and Fensel [SBF98] give a historical overview on the development of methods to organize this collaborative process in the field of knowledge engineering. We can also observe the emergence of further models that are developed to structure the creation of data, data discovery, reuse, and maintenance of quality as a process of recurring tasks. Higgins [Hig08] proposes the Curation Lifecycle Model,[7] which targets general digital objects and databases. The *Linked Data Lifecycle* with specific regard to Linked Data has been extensively studied by Auer et al. [Aue+12] and Ngonga Ngomo et al. [Ngo+14]. Besides the immediate collaborative creation of individual knowledge bases, the knowledge engineering process is embedded in the overall process of creating, consuming, and publishing information [Aue+12]. To foster collaboration, wiki systems have been very successful in gathering and curating common knowledge; Wikipedia[8] is the most prominent example here. This approach can also lead to structured data as can be seen with the DBpedia as the nucleus of the Linked Open Data Cloud [Aue+07] and the WikiData project.[9] The wiki approach with its collaborative and agile principles[10] led to agile data engineering models, such as Semantic Media Wiki [KVV06], Powl [Aue07], and OntoWiki [ADR06]; [Fri+15]; [FAM16].

Studer, Benjamins, and Fensel draw a parallel from *software engineering* to the construction of knowledge base systems:

> In the same way as the software crisis resulted in the establishment of the discipline software engineering, the unsatisfactory situation in constructing knowledge base systems made clear the need for more methodological approaches [SBF98].

From this Studer, Benjamins, and Fensel reason that it is necessary to "[turn] the process of constructing knowledge base systems from an art into an engineering discipline" [SBF98]. They call this discipline *knowledge engineering* which "requires the development of appropriate methods, languages and tools specialized for developing knowledge base systems" [SG92]; [SBF98]. Besides knowledge engineering, which is concerned with the development of information systems, the discipline of knowledge management is concerned with the use of "knowledge

---

[6] This definition is also available online:

as a key asset and resource in modern organizations" [Sch+99]. Bhatt defines knowledge management as a process of knowledge creation, validation, presentation, distribution, and application [Bha01].

Taking a look at software engineering we can observe the success of the distributed collaborative version control system Git.[11] Git allows distributed teams to organize the software engineering process with various workflows.[12] Also a number of companies provide platforms for collaborating and hosting Git repositories, such as GitHub,[13] GitLab,[14] and Bitbucket.[15] The setup of self-hosted repositories can be supported by using tools like GitLab and Gitolite.[16] The Git hosting platform GitHub manages over 100 million projects[17] and was recently bought by Microsoft.[18] The success of Git in the domain of software engineering motivated the company GitLab to the plan to extend its infrastructure to also support data scientists in collaboration.[19]

1.1 Motivation

Companies, in general organizations, collaborate in a specific business field, while each company operates independently in its core business. For instance in supply chains information is available at different stages of the chain while the raw-material supplier is not in contact with the manufacturing company. Also in research projects collaboration has to be performed across separated organizational and technical infrastructures. In research projects the collaboration is often organized in a geographically distributed manner and depends on information technology similar to Virtual Organizations [Tra97]; [AC99]. The distributed collaboration of various corporate and academic research units is called Virtual Research Organization [AC99]. The infrastructure of each participant is separated for instance to protect corporate secrets or intellectual property and a common central point of exchange might not exist.

Parts of this section were first published in Arndt and Martin: "Decentralized Collaborative Knowledge Management using Git (Extended Abstract)" [AM19].

---

[11] *Git*. Homepage of Git, the free and open source distributed version control system:
[12] *Git: About: Distributed*: eb:Gitc];

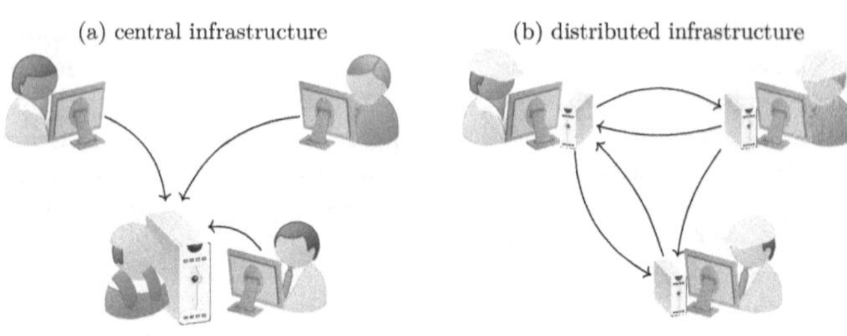

Figure 1.1: Collaboration of knowledge engineering teams on the internet can be performed in a centralized (a) or distributed (b) setup. In a centralized setup the maintenance workload is concentrated at the operator of the infrastructure in a distributed setup the maintenance workload can be distributed among collaborators.

To collaborate in a geographically distributed team in general it can be distinguished between two setups of the information technology infrastructure as depicted in fig. 1.1. In scenario (a) all collaborators are communicating through a central server system that is maintained by one of the collaborating units. But this central infrastructure might not always exist or non of the collaborating parties is willing to assume the responsibility and high workload for its maintenance. The responsibility and workload is depicted by an extra person. In scenario (b) the infrastructure is organized in a distributed manner. The workstations of the collaborators form a shared network. In this scenario the maintenance workload is distributed among the collaborators and reduced as each collaborator is only responsible for its own workstation.

To collaborate in a knowledge engineering process a shared knowledge base needs to be established. A common way to establish a shared knowledge base is to follow the wiki approach [ADR06]; [Fri+15]; [FAM16]; [KVV06]. The wiki approach assumes a commonly accessible central setup of the platform system as it is depicted in scenario (a) in fig. 1.1. The wiki establishes a shared workspace which supports a high level of social interaction [DGR14]. In a shared workspace the collaborators commonly have to decide on the installed functionalities, it is not up to an individual contributor to select a new tool to work on the knowledge base within the workspace. Within the workspace also the knowledge base is shared. In a multi-user setup collaborators simultaneously edit the same version of the dataset. The approach is reliant on expressing a consensus of all collaborators which can not always be reached due to different paradigms, ideology, opinions, perspectives, or interests. This can in particular be understood by following the discussions in the Wikipedia about notability, cleanup, and the deletion policy.[20] In the WikiData a lot of discussion is going on with regard to

---

[20] *Wikipedia:Notability.* Rules to judge the notability of articles to be added

data modelling issues.[21] Even though wikis to collaborate on structured data exist, the discussions are limited to a textual form which does not allow to express complex issues of the data modeling and its schema. This limitation hinders a process of direct contributions to a knowledge base including automatic validation of proposed submissions.

Looking at the collaborative features of the wiki approach and the setup of its infrastructure we can make the observation that: a wiki is a shared workspace; one common version of the shared artifacts exists at a time; and dissent is expressed using the discussion mechanism which is limited to the text form. From these observations we can come to the following conclusions:

- the shared workspace limits the freedom in selecting the tools to perform a task,

- the single version of the artifacts requires a consensus among the collaborators,

- dissent expressed as text does not allow to express contradictions, suggestions, and opinions in the same format as the shared artifacts as structured data.

For collaborators to perform their work independently from others but still to be able to contribute the results back to the team we establish a distributed infrastructure of workspaces which constitutes a *distributed workspace*. Each individual workspace shall support its user to organize and perform a certain task and is under the full control of the user By keeping the workspaces independent each user can freely decide on their tool set and individual workflow, which involves when to share artifacts. In a distributed collaborative setup additional aspects have to be considered as depicted in fig. 1.2. In this book we want to establish a distributed workspace with support for these aspects which requires a specific emphasis on dissent and reconciliation, and asynchrony and synchronization. The notion of a *shared workspace* is subject of research in the field of Computer Supported Cooperative Work (CSCW) where it has the intention to provide group awareness for collaborators in a team. Shim, Prakash, and Lee [SPL07a] state: "A shared workspace provides a sense of place where collaboration takes place. It is generally associated with some part of the screen real estate of the user's computer where the user 'goes' to work on shared artifacts, discovers work status, and interacts with his/her collaborators." Even though each collaborator is working at their personal computer the workspace is shared virtually as is the subject of work, the shared artifacts. In the Encyclopedia of Systems Biology Lloyd [Llo13] introduces a workspace as follows: "A workspace is a folder, or directory, in a Mercurial repository that allows a user to gather together various source code files and

---

[21] *Wikidata talk:WikiProject Books*. Discussion about the introduction, change,

resources and work with them as a cohesive unit." This description of a workspace is going in the direction of distributed collaborative work but targets a specific use case from the b ioinformatics. B oth descriptions, by Shim, Prakash, and Lee [SPL07a] and by Lloyd [Llo13], highlight different aspects of a workspace for collaboration while they leave other aspects out of consideration. In this book the concept of a workspace is divided into:

- the *workspace* as the place "where the user 'goes' to work,"

- the *workspace* as a means to participate in a *distributed workspace*,

- the *distributed workspace* as the "place where the collaboration takes place."

In the following, definitions for *workspace* and *distributed workspace* are given. The definitions are complemented with definitions of the closely related concepts of *dissent and reconciliation* as well as *asynchrony and synchronization*.

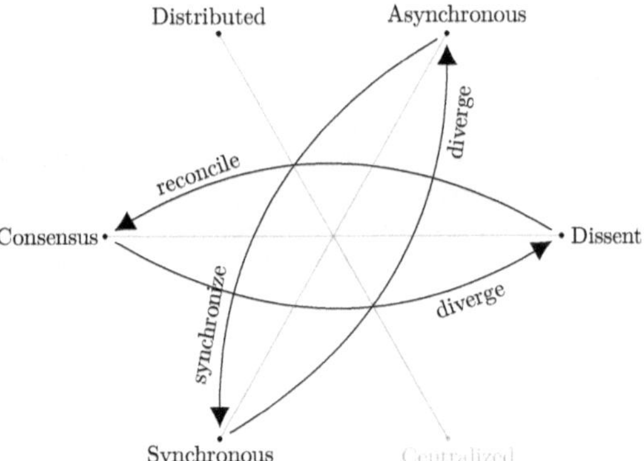

Figure 1.2: Collaboration can be organized *centralized* or *distributed*. When dealing with distributed collaboration, workspaces can *diverge* and the aspects *dissent* and *asynchrony* have to be considered. Contributions need to be *synchronized* among workspaces workspaces. Dissent needs to be *reconciled* to reach *consensus*.

Definition 1 (Workspace) *A workspace is a set of tools, databases, files, and directories to aid a user to organize and perform a specific task on artifacts. A workspace is embedded in a collaborative setup and allows to discover the work status and other shared artifacts from collaborators.*

Definition 2 (Distributed Workspace) *The distributed workspace is a network of individual workspaces used by multiple collaborators. The workspaces are geographically or topologically distributed and interconnected by a temporary or permanent computer network. Each workspace within the network remains as independent environment under the control of its user. The workspaces can exchange shared artifacts among the network in order to jointly generate a set of artifacts as a result of the collaboration.*

From a discursive perspective, collaborators might *dissent* due to different paradigms, ideology, opinions, perspectives, or interests while a collaborative process strives to reach eventual *consensus*. While a consensus is not yet reached it is necessary to express multiple viewpoints. The presentation of a dissent can provide valuable support for a discussion. It enables participants in a discussion to give examples of their point of view or present suggestions for changes.

Definition 3 (Dissent and Reconciliation) *Within a workspace dissent between contributions is expressed by storing multiple diverging versions of the shared artifacts next to each other. To incorporate contributions from diverging versions of the shared artifacts a* reconciliation *is performed. During the reconciliation the differences between the diverging artifacts are taken into account and a new consolidated version of the shared artifacts is created.*

The versions of the shared artifacts can be compared to depict the differences. Dissent or diverging versions of the shared artifacts do not necessarily need to be created by different users. A single user can decide to create multiple dissent versions. The reconciliation represents the "technical" consensus of the dissent versions, it can be a copy of one of the versions or some combination of them.

When dealing with a distributed infrastructure also the technical problem of asynchrony arises. From a technical perspective, workspaces of collaborators can become *asynchronous* while *synchronous* states are intended for a common view on the state of work. Asynchrony might happen due to technical limitations of the infrastructure, such as in mobile usage scenarios, in rural areas, or on the high seas. If concurrent changes are performed while the workspaces are asynchronous, the knowledge shared artifacts will even diverge and dissent.

Definition 4 (Asynchrony and Synchronization) *During the work on the distributed workspace the workspaces get* asynchronous *as users perform their tasks and produce differing versions of the shared artifacts. To* synchronize*, a workspace requests the versions of the shared artifacts from other workspaces, this includes dissent of shared artifacts. In the same way a workspace can transmit its shared artifacts including dissent to selected other workspaces within the distributed workspace.*

The asynchrony is intended to allow each workspace to remain under the full control of its user. As this produces diverged versions of the shared artifacts in remote locations it is similar to expressing dissent but across a distributed workspace. By sharing the asynchronously created diverged versions among workspaces it can be treated similar to dissent. While in turn the synchronization also needs to include the synchronization of dissent not the full equalization of the workspaces in order to maintain the dissent as basis for discussion.

In comparison to the conclusion we could draw from the wiki approach, for the distributed workspace we can come to the conclusion:

- on a workspace each user can freely select the tools to perform a task,

- multiple version of the artifacts can exist in the distributed workspace as well as in an individual workspace,

- dissent can be expressed as various versions of the shared artifacts which can be reconciled to a consensus version.

1.2 Requirements to the Methodology

Parts of this section were first published in Arndt and Martin: "Decentralized Collaborative Knowledge Management using Git (Extended Abstract)" [AM19].

The aim of this book is to devise a methodology that allows to perform knowledge engineering on the Semantic Web in a distributed collaborative setup. A system to provide distributed collaborative knowledge engineering needs to provide a distributed workspace. Following from the problems depicted in fig. 1.2 and based on the conclusion with regard to the distributed workspace we define the following requirements for the methodology to devise. It has to provide (a) a *distributed workspace* with support for (b) *dissent* and (c) *asynchrony*. A collaborative process strives to reach eventual consensus as the result of the collaboration. Thus a method to (d) *synchronize* asynchronous workspaces and a method to (e) *reconcile* dissent knowledge bases is required. Besides the immediate collaborative creation of individual knowledge bases the knowledge engineering process is embedded in the overall process of creating, consuming, and publishing information [Aue+12]. This embedding adds the requirements for appropriate methods to (f) *create and author* data, (g) *publish and explore* data, and track and publish (h) *provenance information*. Requirements (a-e, h) are addressed in chapters 4 and 5, (f) in chapter 6, and (g) in chapter 7.

1.3 Approach

In the field of software engineering the Distributed Version Control System (DVCS) methodology is broadly used and successful in implementing a distributed workspace to collaborate throughout the software development process. The approach of this book is to examine how to apply DVCS to the Semantic Web in order to perform knowledge engineering. To achieve this goal, a distributed knowledge engineering methodology based on the standards of the Semantic Web is devised. To support and verify the methodology, a tool collection is being developed.

In order to understand in which way this methodology interferes with the Semantic Web we need to take a closer look at the tasks within the Semantic Web. A common model to describe the relationship and dependencies between the various tasks and concepts of the Semantic Web is the Semantic Web Layer Cake. Figure 1.3 depicts a version of the Semantic Web Layer Cake with a categorization based on a version presented by Gandon.[22] The standards of the Semantic Web and the layer model are described in depth in chapter 2. The main categories of

---

[22] *An introduction to Semantic Web and Linked Data.* W3C tutorial at WWW

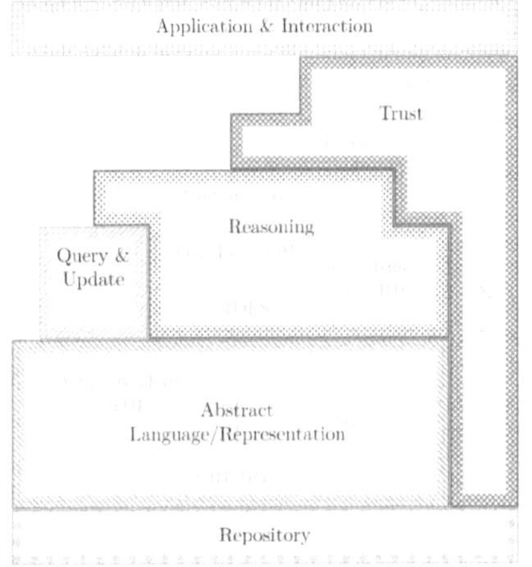

Figure 1.3: The Semantic Web Layer Cake is a model, commonly used to describe the relationship and dependencies between the tasks and concepts of the Semantic Web. In this book the model is extended by the repository layer. [Web:Gan14]

layers in the model are: *Application & Interaction, Trust, Reasoning, Query & Update*, and *Abstract Language/Representation*; in this thesis the additional *Repository* layer is introduced. Looking at software engineering the repository plays a fundamental role to persist contributions in a workspace and exchange it between collaborators' workspaces. This concept is adopted to the newly devised methodology in order to persist and exchange data and added as *Repository* layer to the bottom of the layer model. The standardized *Abstract Language/Representation* to express and exchange knowledge on the Semantic Web is the Resource Description Framework (RDF). Instead of source code files the subject of collaboration are RDF statements which have to be represented in the DVCS. To handle the RDF graph within the Git system we provide a canonical representation. On the Semantic Web SPARQL was standardized as *Query & Update* interface for RDF data. The standardized SPARQL Update operations are executed and translated to Git commits for persistence. To access the data in the repository for each stored Git commit a virtual SPARQL Query endpoint is provided. Next to the query and update operations it is important to assess trust in the data which is represented by the *Trust* layer. To build trust our approach involves provenance tracking and the possibility to query the provenance data throughout the collaboration process. The *Application & Interaction* layer provides an interface to allow the application of the underlying data and the interaction with the underlying data and systems. In software engineering an Integrated Development Environment (IDE) is used to support the creation of source code and continuous integration and delivery to combine and build the resulting software artifacts. With the Quit methodology these concepts are transferred to support the creation, maintenance, and application of data throughout the data life-cycle. The Quit methodology does not interfere with the *Reasoning* layer. This layer represents vocabularies and logical models which vary between the domains of application and are subject to a community process. With the Quit methodology we do not want to put restrictions on the usage of vocabularies and logic.

1.4 Scientific Contribution

In order to perform the Quit methodology individual modules according to the relevant tasks of the Semantic Web Layer Cake are necessary. These modules were devised to fulfill the requirements (a-h) that were formulated in section 1.2. The ideas, figures, and results presented in this book were previously published at peer-reviewed international workshops, conferences, and a journal. The modules can be categorized according to the following topics, that are contributed by this book:

Quit Methodology The Quit methodology to build a distributed workspace is presented in chapter 4. It defines the paradigms, processes, people, models, and tools involved in the methodology and the specification of their interplay. The methodology is situated at the intersection between the two paradigms software engineering and Semantic Web. The integration of the two paradigms is depicted in a combined cyclic layer model where the repository plays a central role. As a foundation for the evolutionary processes a conceptual versioning model is defined and the atomic evolutionary operations to construct a nonlinear transaction log are specified. On the distributed workspace multiple independent and thus possibly asynchronous transaction logs exist (cf. requirements *distributed workspace*, a; and *asynchrony*, c). Between the workspaces the independent transaction logs can be replicated for synchronization (cf. requirement *synchronize*; d). Within a workspace new diverging independent transaction logs can be created at any time. Dissent is expressed by updating the independent transaction logs with diverged states of the knowledge base (cf. requirement *dissent*; b). Diverged states of the knowledge base respective independent transaction logs can be reconciled with a merge operation (cf. requirement *reconcile*; e). The initial versioning concept of the Quit system was first published at the SEMANTiCS 2016 conference [ARM16]. The formalized conceptual versioning model of atomic operations together with a comparative performance evaluation was presented at the ICWE 2017 conference [AM17]. The method of distributed collaboration on the Web using the Quit system was presented at the LEDSPLaY workshop at the INFORMATIK 2017 conference [AR17]. A comprehensive article presenting the complete Quit methodology was published in the Journal of Web Semantics [Arn+19a]. This article was also invited for a presentation at the MEPDaW workshop at The Web Conference and selected for the publication of an extended abstract in the Companion Proceedings of the 2019 World Wide Web Conference [AM19].

Provenance Tracking and Exploration The provenance system as part of the Quit methodology is presented in detail in section 4.3. It allows for a fully automatic tracking of provenance information of the distributed collaboration and evolution process (cf. requirement *provenance information*; h). Contributors can attach additional meta-data to their evolution operations if required. The aggregated provenance information is made available through a provenance query interface. The query interface is following the SPARQL 1.1 Query standard [HS13] and makes the provenance information available as Linked Data. The data model of the resulting provenance graph is using the widely accepted and standardized PROV Data Model [Mor+13b] respective the PROV Ontology [Leb+13]. The provenance interface was published at the MEPDaW workshop at the ESWC 2017 conference [ANM17]. To trace back changes and in addition to the provenance data get a view on the changes performed on the data the Quit Diff method was developed, it is described in detail in section 4.4. The Quit Diff method [AR16] was first published at the SEMANTiCS 2016 conference and was awarded with the *Best Poster Award*.

Quit Store With the Quit Store ("Quads in Git") we implement the conceptual versioning model of the Quit methodology. It provides a reference implementation of the workspace (cf. requirement *distributed workspace*; a) and is presented in detail in chapter 5. It is based on the Git implementation to support the versioning system of the Quit methodology. To represent the evolution operations of an RDF knowledge base in the Git storage structure the graph is stored in a canonical representation. The evolution operations are recorded on the data structure level which allows for a generic usability. Consistency is solely interpreted with regard to the data model according to the RDF specification. To allow a good interoperability with other applications on the Semantic Web the workspace provides standardized update and query interfaces for the data. The query interfaces follow the SPARQL 1.1 Query and SPARQL 1.1 Update standards [HS13]; [GPP13]. Each update operation is translated to an evolution operation and creates a new version of the knowledge base as a snapshot. To access any version in the knowledge base evolution virtual query endpoints are made available for each version in the evolution history. The workspace provides various merge methods to control the reconciliation of diverged versioning logs (cf. requirement *reconcile*; e). Some reconciliation methods can identify conflicts between independent transaction logs. If conflicts are identified, appropriate steps are proposed to resolve these conflicts. The initial implementation of the Quit Store was first published at the SEMANTiCS 2016 conference [ARM16]. A comparative performance evaluation was presented at the ICWE 2017 conference [AM17]. A comprehensive article was published in the Journal of Web Semantics [Arn+19a].

Data Creation and Authoring The Quit Editing Interface and the Structured Feedback Protocol are methods to collaboratively create and author knowledge bases (cf. requirement *create and author*; f). The Quit

Editing Interface allows to avoid, detect, and resolve concurrent update operations. With the Structured Feedback Protocol a distributed protocol for crowdsourcing changes and feedback to a knowledge base is provided. The creation and authoring system to be used with the Quit methodology is presented in detail in chapter 6. The *Structured Feedback* method was presented and published at the LDOW Workshop at the WWW 2016 conference [Arn+16]. The *Quit Editor Interface Concurrency Control* method was presented and published at the MEPDaW workshop at The Web Conference 2019 [AR19].

Data Publication and Exploration For making the results of the collaborative Quit methodology accessible and available to the world wide community of the Web various methods to explore and publish the knowledge base are proposed (cf. requirement *publish and explore*; g). The publication and exploration system is presented in detail in chapter 7. The Dockerizing Linked Data method is an automated way to configure, provision, and run a microservice infrastructure of all components necessary to publish Linked Data knowledge bases on the Semantic Web. The Jekyll RDF system provides a method to create and publish knowledge bases as a collection of Web pages. This allows to make the results of a knowledge engineering process available without the need to maintain a query service which often involves high cost. Further, the provided templating system of Jekyll RDF allows a simple customization of the browsing interface on the data to create adapted interfaces for various domains and communities. The *Dockerizing Linked Data* method was presented and published at the SEMANTiCS 2015 conference [Arn+15]. The *Jekyll RDF* static site generation method was presented and published at the ICWE 2019 conference [Arn+19b].

Parts of this section were first published in Arndt and Martin: "Decentralized Evolution and Consolidation of RDF Graphs" [AM17], Arndt, Naumann, and Marx: "Exploring the Evolution and Provenance of Git Versioned RDF Data" [ANM17], and Arndt et al.: "Decentralized Collaborative Knowledge Management using Git" [Arn+19a].

Application and Evaluation The gathering of requirements as well as the application and evaluation of the Quit methodology were performed in a number of research projects for several domains in chapter 8. In the domain of e-humanities the work was performed in the projects Pfarrerbuch,[23] Catalogus Professorum[24] [Rie+10a], Héloïse – European Network on Digital Academic History[25] [RB16], and Professorial Career Patterns of the Early Modern History.[26] All of these projects are performed in an interdisciplinary constellation of historians, knowledge engineers, and computer scientists from various institutions. The projects range from informal collaboration to the constitution as a project consortium. The heterogeneous and highly collaborative setup brought the requirements for a distributed workspace with the possibility to allow

---

[23] *Pfarrerbuch.* AKSW Project page of the Pfarrerbuch project:

[24] *Catalogus Professorum.* AKSW Project page of the Catalogus Professorum: Leipzig Professors Catalog project:

[25] *Heloise - European Network on Digital Academic History:*
[26] *Research Project (PCP-on-Web): Early Modern Professorial Career Patterns:*

dissent. Also these projects are good examples of the need to explore and track provenance and the evolution of the domain data. In the context of managing historical prosopographical data, the source of the statements is relevant to evaluate their credibility and to consider the influence of their e nvironment. Also the linguistic project of a Multilingual Morpheme Ontology (MMoOn)[27] is performed in an interdisciplinary team. To involve the non-technical participants in all of these projects in the knowledge engineering process we had to build domain adapted exploration interfaces. The collaboratively created linguistic knowledge base, *The Hebrew Morpheme Inventory* was presented and published at the LREC 2016 conference [Kli+16]. A different usage scenario was to support the Federal Agency for Technical Relief. The aim is to digitalize the communication workflow i n a n implementing agency, which is standardized across emergency response forces in Germany. Among others requirements are to collaboratively work on the system and provide an inmanipulable archive for the reproducibility of the complete communication flow. I n l ibraries, m etadata o f electronic library resources are gathered and shared among stakeholders. The AMSL[28] project aims to collaboratively curate and manage electronic library resources as Linked Data [Arn+14]; [Nar+14]. In a collaborative data curation setup we need to track all changes that are performed on the data and identify the origin of any statement introduced into a dataset. This is essential in order to be able to track back the conclusion of license contracts and identify sources of defective metadata. But even enterprises have a need to manage data in distributed setups. The LUCID – Linked Value Chain Data[29] project researches the communication of data along supply chains. The *Publish and Subscribe in Enterprise Value Networks* method was presented and published at the LDOW Workshop at the WWW 2016 conference [Fro+16a]. The LEDS – Linked Enterprise Data Services[30] project applies Semantic Web technology in the areas of e-commerce and e-government. A focus of research was on how to organize and support distributed collaboration on datasets for the management of background knowledge and business procedures.

1.5 Structure of this book

The book is structured as follows. After this introduction chapter (chapter 1) preliminaries are presented in chapter 2 and the State of the Art is presented in chapter 3. The Quit methodology is presented in chapter 4 with the formalized model of our system and the provenance sub-system with its storage architecture and access interface. The software architecture of the Quit workspace and the unifying interface to interact with the workspace are presented in chapter 5. A system to support the creation and authoring process of knowledge with special regard to implications of a collaborative workspace is presented in chapter 6. For publishing the data and exploring its content to further distributed infrastructures and especially the Web, a system is presented in chapter 7. Applications of the Quit methodology and an evaluation of the workspace are presented in chapter 8. Finally, a discussion, conclusion, and a prospect to future work is given in chapter 9.

2 Preliminaries

This book is positioned at the intersection of the Semantic Web and software engineering. In this chapter important concepts from both domains are introduced. The foundation of the Semantic Web are the concepts of the Resource Description Framework, which is introduced in section 2.1. The standardized interface for read and write operations to data on the Semantic Web is SPARQL, which is introduced in section 2.2. The Linked Data principles, introduced in section 2.3, are widely adopted by the Semantic Web community and provide best practices for the publication of data on the Semantic Web. To overall architecture of the Semantic Web is still subject to research. With the Semantic Web Layer Model a widely accepted architecture of identified tasks and their interplay exists, which is introduced in section 2.4. From software engineering the concept that is fundamental for this book is a DVCS. The DVCS *Git* is described with its general architecture and technological details relevant for the distributed collaborative knowledge engineering in section 2.5.

2.1 Resource Description Framework

The Resource Description Framework (RDF) is an abstract framework defining a syntax, data structures, and concepts which can be used to represent information and data on the Web. The RDF is published as W3C Recommendation and the currently valid specification is RDF 1.1. In the *RDF 1.1 Concepts and Abstract Syntax* Recommendation document the RDF is introduced as follows:

> The Resource Description Framework (RDF) is a framework for representing information in the Web. [...] The abstract syntax has two key data structures: RDF graphs are sets of subject-predicate-object triples, where the elements may be IRIs, blank nodes, or datatyped literals. They are used to express descriptions of resources. RDF datasets are used to organize collections of RDF graphs, and comprise a default graph and zero or more named graphs. [CWL14]

In this section several concepts which are important for the RDF are introduced. This is the concept of Internationalized Resource Identifiers (IRIs) for identifying and addressing resources on the Web in section 2.1.1. The data structures of RDF are explained in section 2.1.2. To complete the RDF various additional standards were defined. With respect to a versioning system for RDF data the various possibilities for serialization of RDF is of special interest which we discuss in section 2.1.3. A special concept of the RDF are Blank Nodes which require additional attention when exchanging and versioning RDF data, this topic is discussed in section 2.1.4. The SPARQL Query Language to query RDF data structures is introduced in section 2.2. Taking a look at the complex system of standards, technologies, and applications which has established around RDF the tasks of the individual components are clarified in the Semantic Web Layer Model in section 2.4.

2.1.1 Internationalized Resource Identifiers

To define the identity of some entity is a philosophical problem of the ontology. This problem becomes tangible when dealing with databases and knowledge bases, especially if they are intended to work globally. A data engineer defines the delimitation of an entity and the entity is represented by a record or resource. The purpose of an identifier is to address an entity and to provide a handle for it.

In relational databases unique primary keys are used as local identifiers which are provided for each record in a table. To address a record across tables the identifier is used as foreign key. The scope of a foreign key has to be defined in the schema of the referring table. In relational tables the scope of the system of identifiers is per se limited to the instance of the relational database management system.

The RDF with its global scope of describing data on the Web is using Uniform Resource Identifiers (URIs) respective IRIs to identify resources. IRI is the internationalized version of URI. It extends the set of allowed characters from ASCII to a very wide range of Unicode characters [DS05]. In the remainder of this book mostly the term IRI is used, while in general URI and IRI are used interchangeably. The differences between ASCII and Unicode characters make no difference with regard to the presented concepts. The uniformity allows to use and introduce various types of resource identifiers and use them in many different contexts [BFM05]. A resource can by anything that is identified by a URI, it might be electronic documents or services but can also be human beings or abstract concepts that are not accessible via the Internet [BFM05].

> An identifier embodies the information required to distinguish what is being identified from all other things within its scope of identification. [...] These terms ["identify" and "identifying"] should not be mistaken as an assumption that an identifier defines or embodies the identity of what is referenced, though that may be the case for some identifiers. [BFM05]

IRIs are not bijectively mapped to resources. It is possible that multiple IRIs identify or address the same resources. The problem of finding multiple identifiers that refer to the same resource can be dealt with by creating *sameAs*-mappings between IRIs [VAK15].

The subset of IRIs that are identified by using a type of identifier that also allows to locate the resource is called Uniform Resource Locator (URL). IRIs are generally used to identify resources across contexts while it is due to a specific URI scheme to define if and how resources can technically be located. To identify individual parts in an IRI it is structured according to a generic syntax "of a hierarchical sequence of components referred to as the scheme, authority, path, query, and fragment" [BFM05]. The generic syntax is depicted in the two upper parts of listing 2.1, while the lower part shows two example IRIs with the depiction of their component parts.

```
URI        = scheme ":" hier-part [ "?" query ] [ "\#" fragment ]


hier-part  = "//" authority path-abempty
           / path-absolute
           / path-rootless
           / path-empty


  foo://example.com:8042/over/there?name=ferret#nose
  \_/   \______________/\_________/ \_________/ \__/
   |            |            |            |        |
scheme      authority      path        query   fragment
   |    ___________________|__
  / \ /                       \
  urn:example:animal:ferret:nose
```

Listing 2.1: The generic syntax of an IRI and two example IRIs with the depiction of their component parts (taken from [BFM05]).

2.1.2 Statements and Graphs

The RDF is using a graph model to describe resources. Resources are identified using IRIs. Further we have the concept of unidentified entities, they are called *blank nodes*. Textual information can be encoded as *literals*.

Lets define an RDF graph according to the common definition as given by [Hog15] which also corresponds to the standard [CWL14]:

Definition 5 (RDF graph) *Let I be the set of IRIs, B the set of blank nodes, and L the set of literals. The set I, B, and L are infinite and pairwise disjoint; collectively we call them RDF terms. An RDF triple $t := (s, p, o)$ is a member of the set $(I \cup B) \times I \times (I \cup B \cup L)$; s is called the subject, p the predicate, and o the object of t. An RDF graph G is a finite set of RDF triples. We denote by $terms(G)$ the set of all RDF terms in some triple of G. An RDF graph G is ground if $terms(G)$ contains no blank nodes.*

Having this set of triples the RDF standard states further:

> An RDF graph can be visualized as a node and directed-arc diagram, in which each triple is represented as a node-arc-node link. There can be three kinds of nodes in an RDF graph: IRIs, literals, and blank nodes. [CWL14]

Figure 2.1 shows the structure of a triple consisting of *subject*, *predicate*, and *object*. It is visualized as a directed graph consisting of two

Figure 2.1: An RDF triple consists of a *subject, predicate*, and *object*. It can be visualized as node-arc-node. The arc is directed and typed.

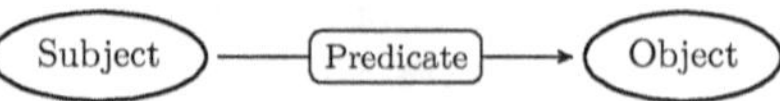

nodes and one directed and typed arc. The arc is typed by using an IRI. Using an IRI for the predicate allows to involve it in another triple to attach it to a definition.

Figure 2.2: An RDF graph consisting of three triples. The used terms are IRIs and one Literal. For the subject `https://natanael` `.arndt.xyz/#i` the graph has two outgoing edges and one incoming edge.

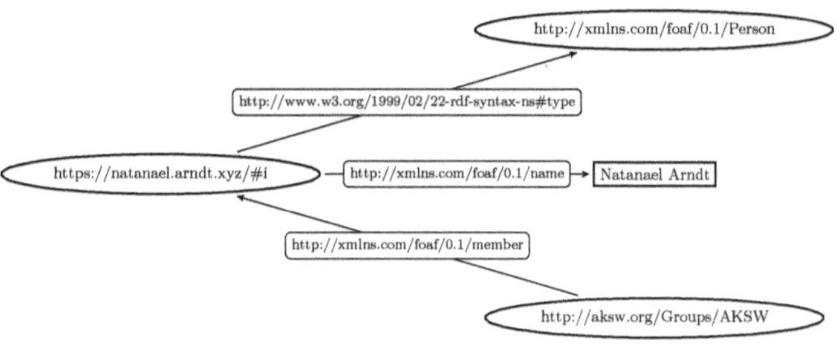

A set of triples with the same subject can be seen as a set of statements describing the subject-resource. In fig. 2.2 a graph consisting of three triples is shown. The graph relates the resource to the string `Natanael Arndt` using the predicate It can also be said: the graph is describ-ing by making statements about it. In general triples are also called statements.

Table 2.1: The tabular representation of the three triples as shown in fig. 2.2.

Besides a graph as a set of triples, RDF also specifies a *dataset* as a set of graphs. Datasets allow to use graphs to store data in separate units. Within a dataset there is exactly one default graph and further named graphs. Each named graph is identified by an IRI or a blank node. The identification of the named graphs allows to refer to a graph within a triple. The concept of named graphs and datasets is used in different applications to implement various features like provenance, access control, versioning, and domain specific organization of the data. The representation of a triple together with the identifier of the graph it belongs to is also called *quad*.

2.1.3 Serialization of RDF Data

To store data on computers, it has so far proved handy to put the data in a serial order, also called serialization. One very generic serialization format is the Extensible Markup Language (XML, cf. [Bra+06]). The XML data structure has a root element and each element can have attributes and child elements. This results in a tree-like structure of elements. XML was popular at the advent of RDF and thus was the first standardized serialization format for RDF graphs. This structure can be used to encode RDF graphs and is specified as *RDF/XML* (cf. [GS14]).

```
 1  <?xml version="1.0"?>
 2  <rdf:RDF xmlns:rdf="http://www.w3.org/1999/02/22-rdf-syntax-ns#"
 3            xmlns:foaf="http://xmlns.com/foaf/0.1/">
 4  <foaf:Person rdf:about="https://natanael.arndt.xyz/#i">
 5    <foaf:name
 6      rdf:datatype="http://www.w3.org/2001/XMLSchema#string">Natanael
           ↪ Arndt</foaf:name>
 7  </foaf:Person>
 8  <rdf:Description rdf:about="http://aksw.org/Groups/AKSW">
 9    <foaf:member rdf:resource="https://natanael.arndt.xyz/#i" />
10  </rdf:Description>
11  </rdf:RDF>
```

Listing 2.2: Example of the serialization of the RDF graph as shown in fig. 2.2 expressed in RDF/XML.

The graph as shown in fig. 2.2 is serialized in RDF/XML and is shown in listing 2.2. Like every XML document, the RDF/XML document starts with the specification of the XML version followed by the root element `rdf:RDF`. The root element has the two attributes `xmlns:rdf` and `xmlns:foaf`. The `xmlns:` attributes specify abbreviations for IRI namespace prefixes which can be used throughout a document. The tag `foaf:Person` reuses the defined namespace prefix and corresponds to With the `rdf:about` attribute the element is associated with the RDF resource IRI   The lines 4-7 correspond to the first two triples with subject   in table 2.1. The attribute `rdf:datatype` of the element `foaf:name` specifies that the value of the literal should be interpreted as string. The lines 8-10 correspond to the third triple in the same table. Because of the tree-like struc-ture of XML the syntax of RDF/XML specifies references to resources, which might be described in a different element within the document. Such a reference is shown in line 8 using the `rdf:resource` attribute.

The RDF/XML serialization can profit from a good tool and library support of XML parsers in many programming languages and frameworks. On the other hand XML introduces a lot of syntax elements which are not necessary to serialize an RDF graph and the result is often hard to read for humans. In addition to RDF/XML various other serialization formats were proposed, some of them allow the serialization of individual graphs, some of datasets. The RDF 1.1 standard besides RDF/XML (cf. [GS14]) specifies for the serialization of graphs:

Turtle (cf. [PC14]), RDFa (cf. [Adi+15]), and N-Triples (cf. [CS14a]) and for datasets TriG (cf. [CS14b]), JSON-LD (cf. [SKL14]), and N-Quads (cf. [Car14]).

The *N-Triples* and *N-Quads* formats define a syntax with one line per triple. This allows for very compact documents as shown in listing 2.3, that has three lines. In listing 2.3 we see the same graph as in listing 2.2 while each *IRI Reference* is enclosed in angle brackets (<...>) and *Literals*. *Literals* consist of a *lexical form* enclosed by quotation marks ("...") followed by a *Datatype* or *Language Tag*. The *Datatype* of Literals can optionally be attached to a lexical form using two circumflexes (^^) followed by an IRI Reference. For Literals of the datatype `xsd:string`[1] it is possible to specify the language of the string instead of the datatype by attaching an at-sign (@) followed by a language tag as specified in [PD06]; [PD09]. Each line has to consist of exactly three RDF terms of a triple in the order subject, predicate, and object followed by a dot. The *N-Quads* serialization additionally has a fourth RDF term which denotes the graph context of the triple. Providing the graph context for each triple in a document allows to store multiple graphs next to each other in one document.

```
↪ Arndt"^^<http://www.w3.org/2001/XMLSchema#string> .
```

Listing 2.3: Example of the serialization of the RDF graph as shown in fig. 2.2 expressed in N-Triples.

The *Terse RDF Triple Language* (Turtle) comprises the *N-Triples* serialization and introduces additional abbreviations. These abbreviations comprise prefix definitions and enumerations. The prefix definitions are adopted from XML and consist of a prefix name which is mapped to an IRI namespace which is abbreviated. Each prefix definition is introduced with the keyword `@prefix` and concluded with a dot. The enumerations are inspired by sentence structures as known from human languages and allow to avoid the multiple use of subjects and predicates. Listing 2.4 shows the same RDF graph as listings 2.2 and 2.3, table 2.1, and fig. 2.2. In the first three lines we can see the prefix definitions for `xsd:`, `foaf:`, and `aksw_group:`. To resolve the term `aksw_group:AKSW` we replace the prefix with the defined IRI namespaces and end up with the IRI reference `<http://aksw.org/Groups/AKSW>`. Line 5 shows a triple consisting of subject, predicate, and object similar to the N-Triples serialization, except for the used prefixes. In the lines 7 and 8 we see two triples where the triple in line 8 reuses the subject from line 7, which is denoted by the semicolon (;) at the end of line 7. Due to the grouped and abbreviated format the Turtle serialization

---

[1] This prefix notation is not allowed in N-Triples but used for brevity in the text.

has shown to be handy for human interaction with the raw RDF data model. To serialize complete datasets in one file the Turtle format is extended to the *TriG* format. The TriG format allows to enclose a set of statements with curly brackets preceded by the keyword GRAPH and the RDF term identifying the named graph.

```
1 @prefix xsd: <http://www.w3.org/2001/XMLSchema#> .
2 @prefix foaf: <http://xmlns.com/foaf/0.1/> .
3 @prefix aksw_groups: <http://aksw.org/Groups/> .
4
5 aksw_groups:AKSW foaf:member <https://natanael.arndt.xyz/#i> .
6
7 <https://natanael.arndt.xyz/#i> a foaf:Person ;
8                       foaf:name "Natanael␣Arndt"^^xsd:string .
```

Listing 2.4: Serialization example of an RDF graph with Turtle.

2.1.4 Blank Nodes in Versioning

Blank Nodes are defined as follows in the *RDF 1.1 Concepts and Abstract Syntax* [CWL14]:

> Blank nodes are disjoint from IRIs and literals. Otherwise, the set of possible blank nodes is arbitrary. RDF makes no reference to any internal structure of blank nodes.

Using RDF as an exchange format, blank nodes are still a problem we have to deal with. Blank nodes can be identified with local blank node identifiers. But, blank node identifiers only have a local scope and so might be different for each participating platform. The standard document especially notes:

> Blank node identifiers are local identifiers that are used in some concrete RDF syntaxes or RDF store implementations. They are always locally scoped to the file or RDF store and are not persistent or portable identifiers for blank nodes. [...] Implementations that handle blank node identifiers in concrete syntaxes need to be careful not to create the same blank node from multiple occurrences of the same blank node identifier except in situations where this is supported by the syntax.

The recommendation of RDF 1.1 suggests replacing blank nodes with IRIs [CWL14], which is called skolemization. Replacing all inserted blank nodes with skolem-IRIs would alter the stored dataset. Our preferred solution is thus to break down all operations on the dataset to atomic graphs, as proposed by Auer and Herre [AH06]. Since we cannot identify blank nodes across changes we thus consider isomorphic sub-graphs as identical and de-duplicate these sub-graphs during our operations. This is not exactly the same behavior as for lean-graphs [HP14], but our graphs are similar to lean-graphs regarding the aspect that we eliminate internal redundancy.

Parts of this section were first published in Arndt, Radtke, and Martin: "Distributed Collaboration on RDF Datasets Using Git: Towards the Quit Store" [ARM16] and Arndt et al.: "Decentralized Collaborative Knowledge Management using Git" [Arn+19a].

2.2 SPARQL

The SPARQL language and protocol [The13] provide standardized languages and interfaces to access and manipulate RDF graphs in an RDF dataset. The RDF dataset consists of one graph, which is called the default graph and which has no name, and zero or more RDF graphs which are identified by an IRI reference. If the RDF graph is identified by an IRI reference, we call it a *named graph*. The SPARQL standard specifies two languages, the query language is standardized as the SPARQL 1.1 Query Language [HS13] and the language to update data as SPARQL 1.1 Update [GPP13]. Besides these to languages the collection of SPARQL standards defines query result formats, the evaluation of queries with respect to inferred statements, and protocols for the interaction of SPARQL endpoints and with SPARQL endpoints. In the following the two languages are introduced by example with the necessary concepts for this book. For an extensive introduction to all concepts involved with SPARQL the standard documents [The13] are the best recommended reads.

Graph Pattern

In the SPARQL query languages a central concept for retrieving data from an RDF graph are *graph patterns*. In listing 2.5 a simple SPARQL query is given, lines 6 to 7 enclose the graph pattern to be matched. A graph pattern consist of a set of *triple patterns*. A *triple pattern* consists of three terms as already known from triples in the abstract RDF model (subject, predicate, and object). In addition to the already known term types (IRI Reference, Blank Node, and Literal) in SPARQL the fourth type *query variable* is defined. A query variable is allowed at each position in a triple pattern. To evaluate a graph pattern on a graph the individual triple patterns are matched against the triples contained in the graph. The triples are compared to the triple pattern and possible solutions are bound to the variables. This results in a set of possible solutions which match all given triple patterns on the given graph. If a query should not be evaluated on the default graph of a dataset, the graph can be specified with the GRAPH keyword, as shown in listing 2.5 line 5. The GRAPH keyword can be followed by an IRI reference or a query variable. If a query variable is given, it is evaluated as in the triple pattern and matched against the IRI references identifying the named graphs in the data set. The graph pattern enclosed by the curly brackets following the GRAPH keyword and the reference (lines 5 to 8) are evaluated on the specified graph respective the graphs bound to the given variable.

Table 2.2: Example SPARQL result set retrieved, when evaluating listing 2.5 on an RDF data with one graph http://example.org/ and the triples as give in listing 2.4.

```
1 PREFIX foaf: <http://xmlns.com/foaf/0.1/>
2
3 SELECT ?name ?group ?graph
4 WHERE {
5   GRAPH ?graph {
6     ?group foaf:member ?person .
7     ?person foaf:name ?name .
8   }
9 }
```

Listing 2.5: A SPARQL SELECT query with two triple patterns and a projection of three variables.

Query Operations

The SPARQL Query Language defines four query forms, SELECT, CONSTRUCT, ASK and DESCRIBE, which can match graph patterns and differ in the result representation. A SELECT query is used to match a graph pattern in the data and to project the result variables to a tabular result set. An example for a SELECT query can be seen in listing 2.5. In the first line a prefix definition is given similar to the format as used for the Turtle serialization. To keep the examples concise the prefix declarations are omitted in the following examples and used as specified in section 1.5. In the third line the specification of the query type and the project of the variables ?name, ?group, and ?graph is given. This query can be evaluated on an RDF dataset that consist of one graph which is identified with the IRI http://example.org/ and contains the triples as give in listing 2.4. This evaluation of the query will produce the result set containing the projected variable solutions as represented in table 2.2.

```
1 CONSTRUCT
2 FROM <http://example.org/>
3 WHERE {
4   ?person foaf:name ?name .
5 }
```

Listing 2.6: A CONSTRUCT query to retrieve a subgraph that matches the given graph pattern.

```
1 CONSTRUCT {
2   ?person ex:belongsTo ?group .
3 }
4 WHERE {
5   GRAPH <http://example.org/> {
6     ?group foaf:member ?person .
7   }
8 }
```

Listing 2.7: A CONSTRUCT query that returns a new graph based on template, which is filled with the variables bound through the graph pattern.

A CONSTRUCT query matches a graph pattern and constructs a new graph to represent the result. In listings 2.6 and 2.7 two examples for CONSTRUCT queries are given. The query in listing 2.6 specifies the default graph for the query evaluation to be http://example.org/ using the FROM keyword. On this default graph it retrieves the matched part of the graph directly as it is, this allows to specify a sub graph selection. The resulting sub graph will be only the *person to name* statement as

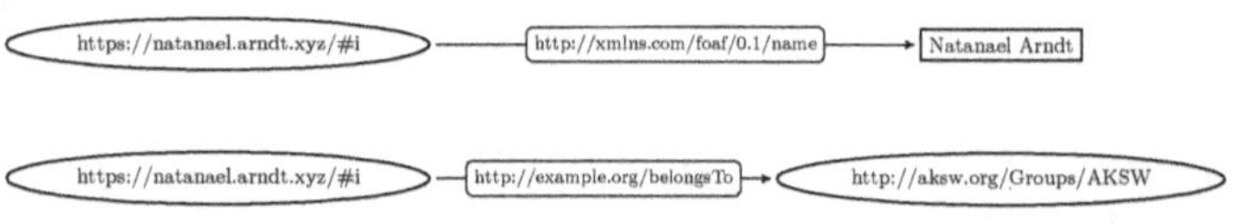

Figure 2.3: The result graphs of the CONSTRUCT operations in listings 2.6 and 2.7. The graph in the upper part results from listing 2.6, the graph in the lower part from listing 2.7.

shown in the upper part of fig. 2.3. The query in listing 2.7 has different graph patterns in the matching part, indicated by WHERE and the graph template (lines 1 to 3). By executing this query a new graph with new statements is retrieved as shown in the lower part of fig. 2.3. In this way it is also possible to specify rules to infer statements from a given graph.

```
1 ASK
2 WHERE {
3   GRAPH <http://example.org> {
4     aksw_groups:AKSW foaf:member ?person .
5     ?person foaf:name "Natanael" .
6   }
7 }
```

Listing 2.8: An ASK query to find out if a graph pattern can be matched on a given data set.

An ASK query reports whether a solution for a graph pattern exists or not by returning a boolean value. An example for an ASK query is given in listing 2.8. Evaluating this query on the previously used dataset would result in the answer *true*. The fourth query type DESCRIBE is included in an informative way in the SPARQL standard and is often not implemented by SPARQL processors. A DESCRIBE query returns an RDF graph which describes the resources given by the variables and IRIs following the keyword.

Update Operations

To update RDF Graphs and RDF Datasets the SPARQL 1.1 Update Language [GPP13] consists of a set of *graph update* operations and *graph management* operations. The *graph management* operations are CREATE, DROP, COPY, MOVE, and ADD. The exact definition of t hese o perations can be found in the specification document [GPP13] and are not further relevant for this book.

The *graph update* operations provide a write interface to the RDF data model. It consists of the query types INSERT DATA, DELETE DATA, DELETE/INSERT WHERE, LOAD, and CLEAR. The operations INSERT DATA and DELETE DATA specify concrete triples or quad data to be inserted into the dataset or removed from the dataset. Listing 2.9 shows an INSERT DATA operation that adds one statement to the graph http://example .org/ in the previously used dataset. The DELETE DATA operation works analog to the insert operation.

The DELETE/INSERT WHERE operations consist of templates in the DELETE and INSERT clauses and graph patterns in the WHERE part of the query. This is similar to CONSTRUCT but instead of retrieving the resulting graph the statements are removed or inserted into the dataset. In listing 2.10 an operation consisting of all three parts is shown. The WHERE part in lines 13-18 matches all statements with the predicate foaf:member and binds the variable ?group to the subject and ?member to the object. It also matches the property rdfs:label of the nodes bound to the variable ?group. In the DELETE part, lines 1-5, it is specified to remove the rdfs:label property from the nodes bound to ?group. In the INSERT part, lines 6-12, new statements are created that specify the rdf:type for ?member and ?group to be foaf:Agent respective foaf:Group. Also the removed label property is re-added as a foaf:name property.

```
1 INSERT DATA {
2   GRAPH ex: {
3     aksw_groups:AKSW rdfs:label "AKSW Group".
4   }
5 }
```

Listing 2.9: An INSERT DATA operation that specifies the triples to be inserted into the graph http://example.org/.

```
1 DELETE {
2   GRAPH ?graph {
3     ?group rdfs:label ?label .
4   }
5 }
6 INSERT {
7   GRAPH ?graph {
8     ?member a foaf:Agent .
9     ?group a foaf:Group ;
10          foaf:name ?label .
11  }
12 }
13 WHERE {
14  GRAPH ?graph {
15    ?group foaf:member ?member ;
16          rdfs:label ?label .
17  }
18 }
```

Listing 2.10: A DELETE/INSERT WHERE operation to remove and insert data by using templates based on variables bound with graph patterns in the WHERE part.

The LOAD operation allows to import RDF graphs from documents on the Web into the dataset. The destination of the data can be specified with the optional INTO GRAPH keyword followed by the IRI reference for a named graph in the dataset. If the INTO GRAPH keyword is not given, the imported graph is inserted into the default graph. Listing 2.11 shows a LOAD query in the first line. This query imports the document located at the URL hinto the RDF graph identified by the IRI http://example.org/. The third line shows a CLEAR query, which removes all triples from the graph http://example.org/.

```
1 LOAD <https://natanael.arndt.xyz/#i> INTO GRAPH <http://example.org/> ;
2
3 CLEAR GRAPH <http://example.org/>
```

2.3 Linked Data

RDF is a framework to represent data on the Web and the data representation follows a graph model with typed directed arcs. Untyped directed arcs were already used as hyperlinks in hypertext documents, simply called links. In the same way as hypertext documents on the Web, RDF resources are identified by IRIs. Linked Data is a subset of the Semantic Web Stack (cf. section 2.4), as also visualized by Benjamin Nowack.[2] A result of the Linked Data principles is to simplify the set of used standards to focus on and to improve interoperability. The concept of *Linked Data* defines four rules to publish data on the Web. The four rules as formulated in [Ber09] are[3]:

1. Use URIs as names for things

2. Use HTTP URIs so that people can look up those names.

3. When someone looks up a URI, provide useful information, using the standards (RDF*, SPARQL)

4. Include links to other URIs, so that they can discover more things.

When a resource is requested people expect their browser to receive an HTML page which is rendered by the browser to present information useful to the reader. On the other hand the RDF data graph is important to be accessible for software so that it can interpret the encoded semantics and even present it in appropriate ways to users. To achieve these two requirements when retrieving a resource from an IRI different methods exist to make the respective data available as needed. Such methods are a lookup of *HTML header link tags*[4] or *HTTP Link headers* [Not17] and *content negotiation* [FR14].

Following the Linked Data rules in this way allows to make data available and automatically discoverable on the Web. To discover the data an agent[5] can retrieve the data by requesting the IRI of a node and following the links to gather new knowledge. These basic rules are a foundation for distributed social networking on the Semantic Web. Individual profiles are identified by an IRI and refer to the IRI that identifies a person. Data to describe this person is attached to this IRI as well as friendship relations. These friendship relations refer to other

---

[2] *The Semantic Web - Not a piece of cake...*:
[3] IRIs here, cf. section 2.1.1
[4] *HTML 5.2: § 4.2.4. The link element*:
52-20171214/document-metadata.html#the-link-element [Web:HTM17]
[5] c

person's IRIs and thus can be retrieved following the same procedure. Besides social networking, arbitrary RDF data can be published and navigated in this way. The Linked Data Fragments standard [Ver+16] defines a protocol for making RDF data available as individual fragments of an RDF dataset. Using triples that link to other fragments (called *controls*) a network of interlinked fragmented Linked Data is produced. By publishing data as Linked Data on the Web a Web of Data is created next to the Web of documents. Because of the big emphasis on interlinking data and expressing data as links between resources (triples) the term Linked Data is often used synonymously to data expressed as RDF.

2.4 Semantic Web Layer Model

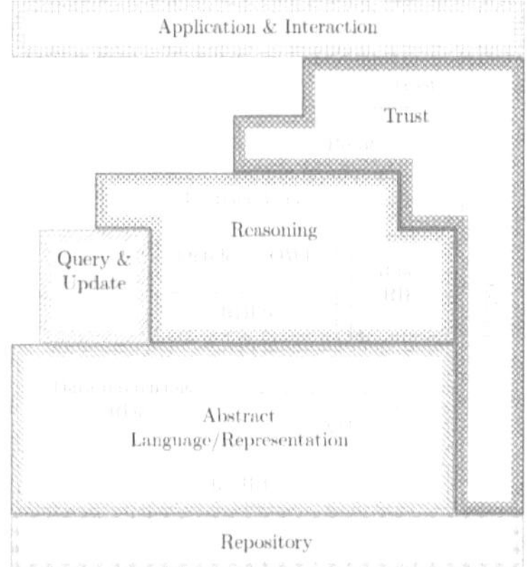

Figure 2.4: The Semantic Web Layer Cake categorized into *Application & Interaction, Trust, Reasoning, Query & Update, Abstract Language/Representation,* and extended with an additional layer *Repository.* [Web:Gan14]

Layer models are a widely used pattern for structuring software systems into individual aspects. The individual aspects describe subtasks which are abstracted from the rest of the system (cf. [Bus+96]). The probably most well known layer model is the *Open Systems Interconnection model* (OSI model) [OSI96] which specifies seven layers and their functions for operating a communication network. By separating the individual layers from each other while defining the interoperation between them, the task for each layer is clearly defined. Also for the Semantic Web several layer models were proposed, known as the Semantic Web Stack or Semantic Web Layer Cake. The first widely used and referenced model was presented by Tim Berners-Lee in 2000.[6] This model is predated by several other proposals, which have not reached the same wide audience. Based on the 2000 version of the model, a

---

[6] *Semantic Web - XML2000 - slide "Architecture"*

model was proposed in 2005-2007[7] which is widely used with small variations.[8] This Semantic Web layer model does not represent a standard but allows to gain an overview on the various tasks, their interplay, and abstraction. Figure 2.4 shows the layer cake with the individual techniques and standards used throughout the Semantic Web and in individual systems working on the Semantic Web. The individual layers can be categorized according to the tasks fulfilled by the layers. The frames in fig. 2.4 depict these categories based on a categorization by Fabien Gandon.[9] In this figure an additional layer *Repository* was added to represent the persistence of stored data and technologies for exchange of data among systems. The layers of the layer cake can thus be categorized according to the six tasks *Abstract Language/Representation*, *Query & Update*, *Reasoning*, *Trust*, *Application & Interaction*, and *Repository*.

Abstract Language/Representation   The bottom layers of the layer cake are *URI/IRI*, *XML*, and *Data interchange: RDF*. The Uniform Resource Identifier (URI) [BFM05] and Internationalized Resource Identifier (IRI) [BFM05] are concepts for identifying things, IRI is an internationalized extension of URI. This concept to identify resources is a foundation of the Web to identify Web Pages or in general Web Resources as introduced in section 2.1.1. The Extensible Markup Language (XML) [Bra+06] was used historically for the first serialization format but on a conceptional level it is now the donor of the data type and the namespace concepts as introduced in section 2.1.3. The top facing abstraction layer and heart of the Semantic Web is the Resource Description Framework (RDF) [CWL14]; [HP14] it defines the abstract syntax respective data model. This abstract syntax defines how to express statements in form of *triples* consisting of subject, predicate, and object. A set of *triples* forms a directed graph of nodes (subjects and objects) and edges (predicates). These concepts are introduced in section 2.1 and specifically in section 2.1.2.

Query & Update   The *Query and Update* layer provides access to the underlying data model. The standardized query language and protocol is SPARQL [The13]. Besides the possibility to retrieve data using the SPARQL 1.1 Query Language [HS13] it as well provides SPARQL 1.1

Update [GPP13] as a write interface to the RDF data model. The SPARQL languages and concepts are introduced in section 2.2.

Reasoning Based on the abstract model it is possible to add meaning and thus provide an interpretation for the data encoded in the data model. The meaning respective semantics of the data can be expressed in semantic extensions of RDF. The RDF Schema (RDFS) [BG14] is a semantic extension and provides a framework to define the semantics of classes and properties. On top of RDFS the *Web Ontology Language* (OWL and OWL 2) is defined which provides a language with formally defined meaning [W3C12]. Other semantic extensions are the *Simple Knowledge Organization System* (SKOS) [MB09] to express thesauri, classifications, and controlled vocabularies and the *Shape Constraint Language* (SHACL) [KK17] to define shapes of RDF data which can be used for data validation or definition of data interfaces. These semantic extensions may impose specific syntactic conditions or restrictions upon RDF graphs [HP14]. This means that some valid RDF statements might produce errors within some special semantic extension, while they remain correct with regard to the RDF data model. Besides the definition of semantics it is also possible to define rules in various rule systems e. g. first-order, logic-programming, and action rules [KB13]. Based on these semantic extensions and rules it is possible to infer additional knowledge by reasoning on the data.

Trust Statements can origin from various sources which can be rated differently by users and applications e. g. with regard to quality and trustworthiness. Provenance information and formal proofs can help to value the trustworthiness of the data. Quality assessment tools can be used on the data to decide on which statements a system should trust. With the parallel crypto layer it is possible to ensure the integrity of the data all the way through the layers of the stack, under the condition, that all layers which alter the data can be trusted.

Application & Interaction This layer adds the interface for humans to the Semantic Web Stack. Applications provide visualization of the data and other kinds of exploration and exploitation interfaces on the data. The implementations of applications are utilizing different technologies and standards which are provided throughout the whole stack. An application can but does not necessarily need to employ the full width of layers. The application layer allows various applications of other domains and technologies to integrate with the Semantic Web Stack. On this layer it is possible to provide user interfaces that transform Semantic Web data to human language or that allows for humans to add new data to the Semantic Web by speaking their language. Through human user interfaces it is also possible for collaborators to communicate and collaboratively evolve data.

Repository The additional task of the layer cake which is introduced and described in this book is the *repository*. Looking into the field of software engineering the repository plays an important role to persist and allow exchange of contributions between collaborators. But also on the Semantic Web various approaches exist to persist RDF data. The trivial strategy is to use the RDF representation in one of the standardized serialization formats. Such files can be stored in a file system and can be exchanged over the internet. Triple stores respective quad stores can help to organize the data, its storage, retrieval and exchange similar to other data base management systems. But also mapping systems exist to store RDF data in conventional relational data base management systems [UM17]; [USA12]. RDF data can be transformed to various formats and stored and transmitted through different media. The repository can be organized in a centralized manner or in various distributed ways. Repository systems inspired by the exchange of data following the Linked Data principles are *RDF Slice* [Mar+17b], *K-Box* [Mar+17a], and *Linked Data Fragments* (LDF) [Ver+16]. These systems exchange small portions of RDF datasets to distribute the work load and build repository services on top of the datasets.

2.5 Distributed Version Control System Git

Git[10] is a Distributed Version Control System (DVCS) designed for distributed software development. The main strength of Git is its support to branch the state of a source code base and to merge diverged states of the development. Also its ability to synchronize remote repositories without the need for a central instance is a good support for distributed software development teams. Based on these features and the flexibility of Git, development models with best practices were developed to organize the software engineering workflow with respect to different versions of the source code. Common development models are Gitflow[11] and the Forking Workflow.[12] By now Git is used to manage over 100 million projects on the Git repository hosting platform GitHub[13] and it is used on other hosting platforms, such as Bitbucket[14] and GitLab.[15] It is also possible to setup a self controlled hosting platform using software like

GitLab CE or GitLab EE, Gogs, Gitea, or Gitolite.[16] But a hosting platform is not necessary to use Git as it can be used just locally or repositories can be synchronized in a peer-to-peer manner.

In contrast to other Version Control Systems (VCSs) such as Subversion or CVS,[17] Git is a DVCS. As such, in Git, users work on local versions of a remote Git repository that are complete clones of the remote repository. Git operations, such as *commit*, *merge*, *revert*, as well as (*interactive*) *rebase* are executed on the local system. The repository contains commits that represent a certain version of the working directory and the file contents. Even though Git is mainly intended to work with source code respective text files, its storage system does not distinguish between text and arbitrary binary files.

Parts of this section were first published in Arndt, Radtke, and Martin: "Distributed Collaboration on RDF Datasets Using Git: Towards the Quit Store" [ARM16] and Arndt et al.: "Decentralized Collaborative Knowledge Management using Git" [Arn+19a].

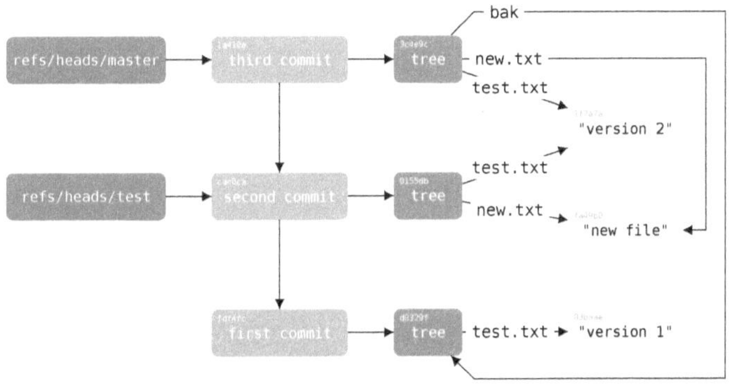

Figure 2.5: The internal structure of Git (cf. [CS14c]).

The internal structure of Git is shown in fig. 2.5. The data types used by Git are *blobs* (Binary Large Objects; in fig. 2.5 the three columns to the right) and *references* (red, left column). *Blobs* are objects to hold the data in the Git repository. *References* are used to represent organizational information, such as branches and tags, by pointing to the respective blobs. Blobs are identified and addressed by their sha1-hash[18] (blob ID; in the top left corner of the boxes). Blobs can contain raw-data like file content (grey boxes), *trees* (blue boxes) which represent directories, and *commits* (yellow boxes) which represent versions. The blob ID of a commit is also called the commit ID. The relations between the data types are shown in fig. 2.5. The *commit* is the user facing data structure. It contains meta-data like the author, committer, commit message, a reference to the preceding commits blob id, and a

---

[16] *GitLab Installation (Community Edition)*:

reference to the tree's blob id which represents the working directory's structures for this commit. A *tree* in turn can reference further trees, representing subdirectories, and blobs containing the data of a file. When a new commit is created, the blobs of files that have not changed are referenced by the new commit. In this way new storage space is only needed for files that are changed. The data of a Git repository is stored in the file system in a `.git` folder. For remote collaboration the blob object storage and the references are synchronized between the distributed repositories using the Git transfer protocol. Because each repository holds the complete commit history it is not necessary to have a central instance for the individual repository synchronization.

3 State of the Art

In a knowledge engineering process the domain experts collect knowledge in an academic discipline. In this book the subject of research is a methodology to support domain experts in distributed collaboration in a knowledge engineering process on RDF data. To allow collaboration on data and to support collaborators in their work in a distributed team various systems exist. In section 1.2 a set of requirements is formulated that a suitable collaboration methodology needs to fulfill. Currently, to our knowledge, no system exists that supports all of these aspects. Nevertheless various research and development activity is taking place to support individual aspects in part or with a related aim. In this chapter we focus on related work within topics that are close to and overlapping with the presented methodology. In table 3.1 these topics are listed and put in relation to the requirements. The cells are marked with a black dot (●) if within the respective topic an approach exists to fulfill t he r equirement a nd w ith a h alf-filled ci rcle (◐) if a partial approach exists or methods are available to be adapted.

The results presented in this chapter were first published in Arndt et al.: "Structured Feedback: A Distributed Protocol for Feedback and Patches on the Web of Data" [Arn+16]; Arndt, Radtke, and Martin: "Distributed Collaboration on RDF Datasets Using Git: Towards the Quit Store" [ARM16]; Arndt, Naumann, and Marx: "Exploring the Evolution and Provenance of Git Versioned RDF Data" [ANM17]; Arndt and Martin: "Decentralized Evolution and Consolidation of RDF Graphs" [AM17]; Arndt et al.: "Decentralized Collaborative Knowledge Management using Git" [Arn+19a]; and Arndt and Radtke: "Conflict Detection, Avoidance, and Resolution in a Non-Linear RDF Version Control System: The Quit Editor Interface Concurrency Control" [AR19].

	section	distributed workspace (a)	dissent (b)	asynchrony (c)	synchronize (d)	reconcile (e)	create and author (f)	publish and explore (g)	provenance (h)
Collaborative Knowledge Engineering on the Web	3.1	●	●	●	●	●	●	●	●
Collaboration with Groupware and in Virtual Organizations	3.2	●		●	●				
Distributed Database Systems	3.3		◐	●	●	◐	●		
Organization of distributed data in Web Application Engineering	3.4	●	●	●	●	●			
Versioning of RDF Datasets	3.5		●	◐	●	●			●

Table 3.1: Topics of the State of the Art sections and their relation to the requirements for the Quit methodology

3.1 Collaborative Knowledge Engineering on the Web

The Web was built as a place of information exchange and collaboration. Initially it was a collection of interlinked documents. The Web 2.0 also called Participative Web or Social Web highlighted the usage of the Web and its protocols for collaborative applications. Various systems were implemented on the Web to foster collaboration and provide different organizational forms. Examples are commenting systems, Online Social Networks, collaborative editors, and wiki systems but also systems specific to a field of application such as collaborative software engineering systems. The systems support collaboration on different artifacts and with different properties. Most of the collaboration platforms provided on the Web 2.0 are employing central infrastructures, while in recent time a trend for re-decentralization is perceptible.

In the following various systems are presented that support the collaborative knowledge engineering process of distributed participants. To complement the discussion of the selected systems we look into two broader fields of application for distributed collaboration. We take a look at Online Social Networks in section 3.1.1, these are systems to support overall communication between people. In this section we put an emphasis on commenting systems as they play a central role in Online Social Networks and are also applied in the mentioned document collaboration systems. This method is used to support the group awareness and to enable discussions about shared artifacts. As we are interested in collaborative engineering processes we take a closer look at the collaboration in software engineering in section 3.1.2. A field of collaboration on distributed knowledge bases is the field of Linked Data. Around the Linked Data principles and the Semantic Web Stack a knowledge engineering method was developed called Linked Data lifecycle and is presented in section 3.1.3.

Table 3.2 provides a comparison of collaboration systems for distributed participants with regard to the requirements as formulated in section 1.2. We don't limit this comparison to systems that operate on RDF datasets since we are also interested in the general properties of collaborative systems. The presented methods roughly fall into the three categories of document collaboration systems, data exchange protocols, and distributed software engineering. The methods to implement document collaboration systems are collaborative document editors that are mostly provided as Software as a Service (SaaS) setup, the wiki approach, and derived from the general wiki approach we look at data wikis. The data exchange protocols of interest on the Semantic Web are the SPARQL protocol (cf. section 2.2), Linked Data (cf. section 2.3), and based on Linked Data the Linked Data Platform (LDP). For distributed software engineering the systems to exchange source code between collaborators are DVCS (cf. section 2.5). In table 3.2 besides the requirements as formulated in section 1.2 the column *datatypes* specifies which kind of artifacts are the subject of collaboration in the respective system: *files* as used in file systems, *articles* as pages describing a certain subject, and the RDF data structures: dataset, resource, and LDP container. *LDP container* is an RDF resource used in a LDP to group resources and manage them with a containment relationship.

Collaborative Document Editor

Collaborative Document Editors support the collaboration on various file types, like text, spreadsheets, or drawings. Collaborators are invited

Approach	Datatype	distributed workspace	dissent	reconcile	asynchrony/synchronize	create and author	publish and explore	provenance
Coll. Document Editor	File	○	suggestions/ discussion	accept	-	●	●/○	edit history
Wiki System	Article	(interlinked)	○/one[b]/ discussion	-/accept	-	●	●	edit history
Semantic Wiki	RDF Resource	(interlinked)	○/discussion	-	-	●	●	edit history
SPARQL	RDF Dataset	(interlinked)	○	-	-	◐	◐	○
Linked Data	RDF Resource	(interlinked)	○	-	-	○	◐	○
Linked Data Platform	LDPR/LDPC[a]	(interlinked)	○/(discussion[c])	-	-	◐	◐	○
DVCS	Source Code Files	●	●	●	●	○	○	●

[a] The LDP specifies Linked Data Platform Resources (LDPR; RDF Resources and non RDF Resources) and Linked Data Platform Containers (LDPC; containers of LDPRs). [b] Some wiki systems provide a feature that requires articles to be reviews before publication, until an article is reviews it remains as the current draft. [c] To implement a discussion system an appropriate vocabulary and protocol is needed, suggestions exist, like LDN and Web Annotations (cf. section 3.1.1). LDN is specified to be used with the LDP.

Table 3.2: Comparison of collaboration systems and approaches regarding their collaborative properties.

by the file owner and can get different levels of access e. g. read only, make suggestions, or full write access. The collaborators are mostly working on a real time synchronized state of the document. This document represents the common consensus of the collaborators or the document owner. Contributors can also propose changes which are reviewed by a user with write access to the document at a later stage. These proposed changes can be accepted and incorporated into the document or rejected. For each document a version history exists that makes it possible to trace back who performed which change and allows to roll back to an old version. Next to the document, collaborators can add comments which can lead to a discussion about parts of a document. Some systems even provide a chat service that is available during an editing process. Enterprises provide SaaS systems, like Google Drive, Apple iWork, or Microsoft Office Online,[1] which support participants to manage the collaborative editing of documents. The infrastructure of such systems is centralized and controlled by the respective providing enterprise. In addition to the systems provided and hosted by an enterprise several systems exist that implement collaboration platforms as known from the respective SaaS providers but with the ability to self-host the service. They mostly achieve or try to achieve the same properties as mentioned before. These are systems like Nextcloud, OwnCloud, Colabora Online, LibreOffice Online, or Etherpad.[2]

Wiki

Currently a widely and well adopted method is the wiki approach with its collaborative and agile principles.[3] For collaborative editing of an interlinked collection of documents often wiki systems are used. Wiki systems can be setup by distributed parties on the Web and can be interlinked. A wiki system consists of many articles which are edited with an integrated editor system. Even though the systems are interlinked, the collaboration happens centrally in one wiki instance for individual subjects. Wiki systems are usually open for contributions by everybody on the Web. Collaborators share a workspace which is thus synchronous between participants to edit articles or other artifacts. Wikis usually do not support real time collaboration. The article represents the result of the collaboration and thus the consensus of the collaborators. At a point in time there is only one current version of an article available. There are some wiki systems that implement a *reviewed article* feature that allows to add an unreviewed, proposed and unpublished version of an article. The consolidation of the unreviewed article into the reviewed article happens by replacing it. A core functionality of a wiki system is versioning that allows to view the linear editing history of an article and revert changes. Discussion in wiki systems happens in a commenting page next to the article page. There are many popular implementations of wikis such as the MediaWiki, XWiki, DokuWiki, and TikiWiki.[4]

Semantic Wiki

Derived from the wiki principles special wiki systems were developed for collaboration on semantic data. With the transfer of the wiki methodology to data, agile data engineering models are fostered. The data expressed in a Semantic Wiki can be accessed in various representations, such as a user readable representation and structured data formats. Collaborative features of wiki systems for ontology authoring where identified in [DGR14] to be: *Multi-mode access to content, Discussion mechanism, Watchlist, Notification mechanism* and *Revision History*. A number of implementations exist such as Semantic Media Wiki [KVV06], Powl [Aue07], OntoWiki [ADR06]; [Fri+15]; [FAM16] and Wikibase.[5]

SPARQL

SPARQL is the standardized read and write interface for RDF data (cf. section 2.2). To collaborate on RDF datasets it is possible to setup a central SPARQL endpoint that is shared by collaborators. The SPARQL endpoint is the shared workspace of the collaborators and changes on the SPARQL endpoint are available to all participants. Similar to a wiki, the data in a store represents the consensus of the collaborators. With the concept of named graphs it is possible to separate portions of data at one endpoint. This concept can be used to organize the collaborative process and suggestions exist to implement functionality that is not provided by the SPARQL standard. Using the named graphs it is possible to implement access control on the data [UFM16]. Further, SPARQL itself does not specify versioning, the access to versioned data, nor rollback operations. To separate versions of the data it is possible to use named graphs or express versions and branches using the general possibilities of RDF by employing an appropriate vocabulary. In section 3.5 we present systems that add versioning functionality on top of a SPARQL endpoint. To enable communication, suggestions and dissent can as well be expressed by using vocabularies and protocols like Web Annotation (cf. Linked Data Platform and section 3.1.1). Each SPARQL endpoint is a centralized workspace while it is possible to interconnect the data accessible at multiple endpoints. To jointly query data spread over multiple endpoints query federation can be employed [PB13]; [Sal+16].

---

[4] See also *Top Ten Wiki Engines*:
[Web:Topa] for a longer list of implementations
[5] *Wikibase*: ht

Linked Data

Linked Data can also be used to collaborate by using the Web's distributed infrastructure. Linked Data on the Web is stored distributed and the data can be interconnected and navigated using links respective hypermedia handles. The individual published items are RDF resources. Data published on the Web is available to all participants and the published data represents the opinion of the publisher. Distributed participants can read the data and only the owner can make changes to the data. In this setup no commonly shared workspace exists. Linked Data highly relies on the HTTP protocol. There is no support to express diverging states of HTTP resources and only one current version is available at a single IRI. To enable linear time travel requests to recover historical states of HTTP resources the memento protocol can be used [VNS13]. Various suggestions exist to enable commenting on Linked Data resources (cf. section 3.1.1). To enable collaborative editing of Linked Data resources an extra protocol, such as Linked Data Platform, needs to be employed.

Linked Data Platform

The Linked Data Platform (LDP) [SAM15] provides a read and write interface on Linked Data. An LDP provides access to Linked Data resources, files, and containers. LDPs can be setup by distributed parties and the data can be interconnected. Users on the Web can access the data to read while the owner can also grant write permission to collaborators on the data. There is always one current version of a resource published under an IRI, but a resource can be replicated, changed and republished under a different IRI. To consolidate diverged versions of a resource there is no specific support other than to overwrite the existing resource. Diverging changes have to be incorporated manually. There is no versioning support for the Linked Data Platform. Discussion can be expressed by distributed comments submitted to the documents inbox using Linked Data Notifications (LDN) [CG17] o r b y u sing the Web Annotations protocol (cf. section 3.1.1). Dokili[6] is an example for an application build on top of the Linked Data Platform. It provides a shared workspace with functionality similar to common collaborative document editors.

Distributed Version Control Systems

In the field of software engineering, D VCS a re u sed t o t rack t he common shared state of the source code files i n t he s oftware development process in distributed teams. Each user can create a copy of the workspace and perform the development tasks locally. To track the progress of the work the user can record versions of the current work at an arbitrary granularity. Different p arallel s tates o f t he w ork c an b e tracked in logically separated branches. These branches can be used to express

---

[6] *dokieli.* clientside editor for decentralised article publishing: [Web:dok]

work in progress and suggestions for changes. Branches can be consolidated by merging them which involves a reconciliation of possible structural conflicts of the source code files. All of these actions can be performed on the local copy of the workspace asynchronously and isolated from the collaborators. To share the state of the work with the collaborators, workspaces can by synchronized by exchanging the recorded versions and branches. Since the local copy of the workspace contains all contributed versions, a user can investigate the provenance of the workspace with the information of who performed which changes at what time. The aspects involved with the software engineering process are further elaborated on in section 3.1.2.

3.1.1 Collaboration in Online Social Networks

Online Social Networks are online platforms for people to build their social networks and communicate with each other. Common features of Online Social Networks are functionalities for sharing text, photos, and videos as well as functionalities to comment shared items. People are able to communicate in Online Social Networks by sharing text and other digital items. Even though this communication can be considered as collaboration in a general sense it is usually not considered as knowledge engineering. From a systems point of view there is not to much difference between sharing text and multimedia documents on the one hand and structured data on the other hand. The possibility to comment on items is a vital aspect to foster discussion in a community. In the following we will look into approaches for commenting systems and Distributed Semantic Social Networks, both with an emphasis on distribution.

Commenting Systems

As soon as data is published on the Web users of the data experience and discover inaccuracies. If users are willing to contribute their experience and suggestions to fix issues back to the publishers, some method is needed to integrate users into the collaborative knowledge engineering process. This method is also called crowdsourcing. There are several possibilities for content providers to gather feedback on published pages. In our case we are interested in possibilities to integrate crowd feedback into a distributed collaboration process. The various systems can be categorized according to the level of distribution as follows:

1. Central to the content provider (simple commenting forms),

2. Integrated into a third party centralized online social network (Commenting Plug-Ins, Social Buttons), and

3. Web wide distributed commenting techniques.

A simple commenting form (1.) is usually provided by weblogging software or Web Content Management Systems (WCMS) such as Wordpress and Typo3.[7] Another option to be included into the website infrastructure of a content provider is Discourse.[8] It provides a commenting form to be integrated into a website, but unlike other third party approaches (cf. 2.) it allows website providers to decide where to host the users comments by also providing the back-end software as Open Source. Those techniques allow users to leave a comment directly on the website of the publisher where the comment is also stored in the domain of the content provider.

The second way of allowing user feedback on a website is the integration of an external web service or online social network (2.). This can happen by integrating social buttons (Google+, Facebook like, Twitter, and Reddit) to encourage users to share the link to a web resource together with a comment on an external online social network. Instead of referring the users to an external website it is possible to directly integrate a commenting form of the external web service through a JavaScript plug-in. A commonly used provider for this possibility is Disqus.[9] Besides the commenting form it provides a central server to host all the user comments and it has Facebook and Twitter integration. Facebook also provides its own Comments Plugin.[10] With this plug-in integrated into a website users are able to leave comments on a website using their Facebook account for authentication and can share the comment on the Facebook online social network as well. All comments are stored in a central location on Facebook's servers. Sidewiki was a project introduced by Google in 2009,[11] it is implemented in the Google Toolbar for Firefox and Internet Explorer, a Plug-In for Chrome, and a Bookmarklet for other browsers but is no longer available.[12] It allowed users to share annotations for web resources with other users of the service. As it seems it relied on a central infrastructure, which was discontinued after just two years in 2011.[13]

Independent of the decision of the website publisher, for users it is always possible to write comments in any place on the Web (3.) such as web forums, personal weblogs, review platforms, or any online social network. This results in a web-wide distributed commenting system. While this is generally out of control for the content provider and it is hard to gather all feedback on a specific resource, it allows the best flexibility for the user. Techniques to target this issue are Trackback and Pingback (cf. [LH02], implemented in Wordpress) which are used among weblogs to create back-links to other posts referring to the own post. Such protocols allow content publishers to get informed about comments which can be distributed on the Web.

The Web Annotation Working Group at the World Wide Web Consortium[14] [San15]; [SCY15] published a protocol, a vocabulary, and a data model for decentralized annotation of web content. The proposed system claims to be comprehensive in targeting the problem of annotations on the Web. The authors state "Web annotation is for all content on all devices."[14] Further the protocol and data model are designed flexible in the scope of supported resource t ypes: " It w ill a llow anyone to annotate anything anywhere, be it a web page, an ebook, a video, an image, an audio stream, or data in raw or visualized form."[14] The protocol highly relies on the Linked Data Platform [SAM15] to store and retrieve annotations (Comment Resources). An annotation builds a relation between a body and target. The target is the annotated Web Resource and the body is the actual Comment Resource. The body can be any kind of resource, e.g. a text, a tag, or a movie but also external resources which could include changesets or patches. The distribution of the protocol and the autonomy of the resource and annotation publishers is a main requirement. "Web annotations can be linked, shared between services, tracked back to their origins, searched and discovered, and stored wherever the author wishes; the vision is for a decentralized and open annotation infrastructure."[14]

Besides the possibility to leave a simple text comment for a publisher revyu.com (cf. [HM07]; [HM08]) is a reviewing and rating web site that allows users to create comments as machine-readable RDF metadata for the Semantic Web. The site is not constrained to a specific set of resources which can be reviewed but allows reviews for any kind of resource. Using RDF as format together with the RDF Review Vocabulary (rev:) enables a flexible e xpression o f r eviews i ncluding ratings, useful votes, and links to external data sources. Additionally, it enables versatile queries via SPARQL. Heath and Motta further discuss the integration of external data sets, the usage of a semantic tagging system, and the general issues of the implementation for the Semantic Web[HM07]; [HM08]. Even though one can argue that revyu.com is just another third-party reviewing system, it was able to improve the situation of commenting and reviewing arbitrary Web Resources by providing a structured user friendly as well as machine readable reviewing system.

Distributed Semantic Social Network

The Distributed Semantic Social Network (DSSN) is an architecture for an open online social network which is distributed across the Web. It is based on Web 2.0 and Semantic Web technologies, such as WebID for authentication, the FOAF vocabulary to describe personal profiles, Semantic Pingback and WebSub (formerly known as PubSubHubbub)

---

[14] *W3C: Web Annotation Working Group:* [Web:W3C]

for active communication [Tra+12], and the Linked Data Platform as distributed read and write data storage. Using the DSSN architecture it is possible to communicate by publishing `sioc:Posts` and activity feeds across server boundaries [AT14]; [Tra+12]. This principle architecture is used as a foundation to allow the distribution and interlinking of online social networking services. The latest development of a DSSN is the Solid platform.

Semantic Pingback[15] (cf. [Tra+10]) is an approach to bring a social dimension to the Linked Data Web by adding semantics to the Web-mention notifications (cf. [Par17]; formerly known as Pingback [LH02]), a technological cornerstone of the blogosphere. By letting services notify each other about relations between RDF resources it "activates" simple RDF relations and makes it possible to implement communication of services by performing actions among edges on the Web of Data. Basically the protocol works as follows: a resource (*source*) with an RDF triple pointing to another resource (*target*) is published on the Web. The Pingback *client* which observes the *source* starts an auto discovery for the Pingback *server* announced by the *target* and sends a Pingback ping to this *server*. The ping contains the URLs of the *source* and *target* as payload. On receiving the ping the *server* verifies it by fetching the *source* and looking for the link to the *target*. If the ping was valid, the *server* can invoke further actions as defined by its implementation.

WebSub is a publish and subscribe protocol for the Web [Gen18]. The basic artifact is a *topic*, which can be any kind of resource on the Web identified by a URL. To allow the distribution of events happening on the *topics* a *hub* operates as dispatcher. A *publisher* of a *topic* notifies the *hub* about updates on the *topics*. The *hub* is responsible to inform the *subscribers* of the *topic* by calling their specified *callback* URLs.

The Linked Data Platform (LDP) defines how to provide a read and write architecture for Linked Data on the Web [SAM15]. The individual operations on the LDP are REST operations which allow to store, retrieve, and manipulate resources and containers of resources. In the regard of storing, retrieving, and manipulating RDF resources the LDP is similar to SPARQL Query and Update (cf. section 2.2). In contrast to SPARQL, with LDP it is not possible to perform complex queries that retrieve data based on query patterns. On the other hand the LDP interface is not limited to RDF resources but is able to store any kind of resource, such as pictures and videos. With the LDP it is possible to build a distributed network of agents to collaborate on RDF data combined with other media objects.

The Solid platform for decentralized social Web applications [Man+16] is the latest advancement of the architecture of a DSSN. In addition to a stack of vocabularies and protocols the Solid platform also specifies the usage of the LDP to store and manage the user's data. A user stores their data in a *personal online datastore* (pod) that is managed

---

[15] *Adding a social dimension to the Linked Data Web:*

by a LDP. Webbrowsers and other clients can connect to the pods to communicate with users or manage the user's data. One protocol that specifies how to interact with a LDP to exchange messages between users is the Linked Data Notifications (LDN) protocol (cf. [CG17]). The basic flow of the LDN protocol is: the *sender* retrieves a *target* resource to discover the *inbox* which can receive notifications for the *sender*. The *inbox* is provided by the *receiver* and follows the LDP specification. The *sender* creates a resource (*notification*) in the *inbox*. If a *consumer* wants to read notifications for a resource (*target*), it discovers the *inbox* in the same way and requests the *notification* from the *inbox*. In contrast to Semantic Pingback a peer that wants to receive LDN notifications (*receiver*) needs to run a LDP and provide storage for incoming messages, while the Semantic Pingback protocol requires the *source* (*sender*) to make the message available to the receiver via HTTP.

3.1.2 Collaboration in Software Engineering

Studer, Benjamins, and Fensel draw a parallel from software engineering to knowledge engineering and point out a need for more methodological approaches [SBF98]. Especially, they point out that the *software crisis* lead to the establishment of engineering processes and methodologies for software. Dijkstra described the situation as follows:

> [...] as long as there were no machines, programming was no problem at all; when we had a few weak computers, programming became a mild problem, and now we have gigantic computers, programming has become an equally gigantic problem.[16]

Consequently, we take a closer look at the methodological approaches in software engineering that helped to overcome the *software crisis* to identify what they can teach us for knowledge engineering with a focus on distributed collaboration on RDF datasets. Ghezzi, Jazayeri, and Mandrioli introduce software engineering as follows:

> Software engineering is the field of computer science that deals with the building of software systems that are so large or so complex that they are built by a team or teams of engineers. Usually, theses systems exist in multiple versions and are in service for many years. During their lifetime, they undergo many changes: to fix defects, to enhance existing features, to add new features, to remove old features, or to be adapted to run in a new environment. [GJM03]

The Software life-cycle or sometimes Software Development life-cycle describes the phases of the development of a software and the related artifacts, e.g. test plan, interface specification, a nd documentation. It comprises the steps: requirements analysis, design, implementation, testing, and operation including maintenance and evolution

---

[16] *The Humble Programmer.* ACM Turing Lecture 1972:

(cf. [GJM03]; [Bal11]; [Som16]). Software process models represent a perspective on the Software life-cycle and define the steps to perform in order to collaboratively develop a software. Various models exist like: the waterfall model, V-shaped model, incremental development, spiral model, and agile development models. Most of the systems include feedback-loops and evolutionary components which should provide room for communication and support the development team to act on failures in previous steps or changing requirements.

The process of creating software could be made more reliable and controllable by introducing software engineering methods like process models. As the software engineering process is a collaborative process, systems are needed to support the collaborative work on the software artifacts. In the 1970s, software configuration management enabled structured collaborative processes where version control is an important aspect for organizing the evolution of software. Early Version Control Systems (VCSs), such as CVS and Subversion, allowed central repositories to be created. The latest version on the repository represents the current state of development and the linear versioning history draws the evolution process of the software. Distributed VCS (DVCS), such as Darcs, Mercurial, and Git, were developed to give every collaborator a complete and independent copy of the source codes repository. These independent copies can be synchronized in a peer-to-peer manner. This setup of distributed repositories allows every member of a distributed team to branch and fork the current state of the programs source code and individually contribute new features or bug-fixes. A fork is an independent copy of the repository. A branch resides in a repository and is a diverged state of the programs source code. Usually one branch is called *master* to denote it as the current stable version of the source code and as the reference branch which concentrates the development activity.

Besides the programming task itself the requirements engineering as subtask of the software engineering process is also a collaboratively performed task [Rie12]. An issue tracker or bug tracker is used to register the requirements and defects of a software in individual entries. Each entry provides, besides its metadata and description, a discussion thread that allows collaborators to discuss the relevance, possibilities to solve, and current status of the issue. The possibility to fork, branch, and merge the source code brought up the concept of *pull-request* (also called *merge-requests*). A *pull-request* notifies a development team about the existence of a changed version of the source code and proposes the changed source code to be incorporated into the *master* branch. A *pull-request* can reference an issue entry to highlight, that the submitted source code contributes to the resolution of an issue. In conjunction with a *pull-request* a discussion thread is opened, similar to an issue entry. This discussion thread allows collaborators to discuss and decide about the acceptance or rejection of the respective contribution. If the *pull-request* is accepted, it can be incorporated into the common development process by merging it into the master branch.

Often attached to the VCS are continuous delivery and continuous integration systems. When a new version of a software component is developed and the changes are submitted to the repository the continuous integration builds the whole system with the new or changed component. Based on this integrated system the defined tests (unit tests) are executed and the system must pass the defined tests (cf. [Som16]). This allows distributed teams to verify that the current shared status of the system is in the specified functional state after committing their contribution. The continuous delivery process comprises the continuous integration process with other automation systems to automatically provide the derived software artifacts. This allows the early and frequent deployment of the software in its intended environment to reduce the risk of misconceptions between development team and stakeholder.

3.1.3 Linked Data Life-Cycle

Around the Linked Data principles and the Semantic Web Stack a knowledge engineering method was developed called Linked Data life-cycle. The Linked Data life-cycle is a life-cycle model that contains phases of transformations performed on RDF datasets. The transformations aim to support the creation and publication of data following the Linked Data principles. These phases can be performed to produce, combine, verify, store, alter, reuse, explore, or organize RDF datasets – in general – to manage RDF datasets. The Linked Data life-cycle [Aue+12]; [ABT14]; [Ngo+14] is depicted in fig. 3.1 and lists the stages *Extraction, Storage, Authoring, Interlinking, Classification, Quality, Evolution/Repair,* and *Search/Browsing/Exploration*. The Linked Data life-cycle is underpinned by implementations of the phases in the LOD2 stack. The LOD2 stack is an integrated distribution of aligned tools which support the whole life-cycle of Linked Data from extraction, authoring/creation via enrichment, interlinking, fusing to maintenance [Aue+12]; [ABT14]. It is built on three pillars, the Debian packaging system as software integration and deployment system, use of a central SPARQL endpoint, and integration of user interfaces based on REST. All tools of the LOD2 stack should support a step in the Linked Data life-cycle.

The individual tasks of the Linked Data life-cycle give an insight to further research areas. The combination of these research areas aims to increase the usefulness of the data and thus the mutual fertilization of the individual tasks. A broad overview on the individual aims, challenges, and existing approaches within the phases of the Linked Data life-cycle is given by Ngonga Ngomo et al. [Ngo+14]. In the following the steps of the life-cycle that are relevant for the Quit methodology are explained.

Storage/Querying The flexible and generic data structure of RDF data causes problems when it comes to its efficient storage and query execution. Even though the data model does not put specific requirements on the format, i.e. how the data has to be represented in a storage

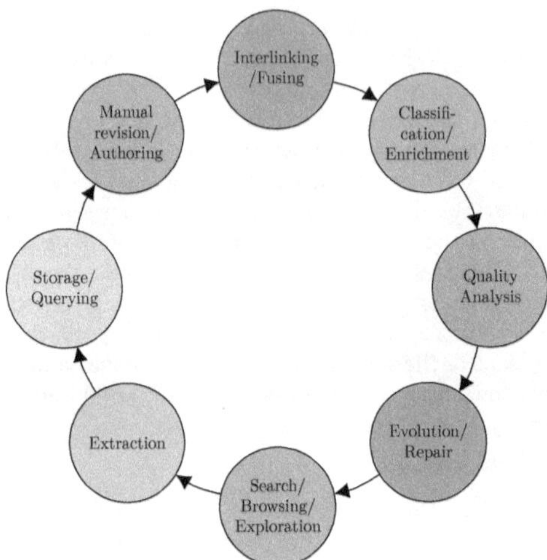

Figure 3.1: The Linked Data life-cycle [Aue+12]; [ABT14]; [Ngo+14] shows phases of transformations performed to manage RDF datasets.

media, it is often stored in so called triple- or quad-stores. Triple- and quad-stores are databases which store the RDF statements as subject, predicate, object, and optionally the graph context. Due to the large amount of interlinks between the statements and their potential combinations, many lookups and efficient indexing techniques are needed to query the data. In contrast to this flexible storage structure less flexible data models exist which can be stored and queried in more efficient ways. Besides the lower flexibility a long tradition and much more mature software and storage architectures helped to improve these systems.

Authoring   Authoring in the Linked Data life-cycle is the process of creating and editing data in an RDF dataset. The authoring process is closely coupled to the process of data curation. "Data curation includes all the processes needed for principled and controlled data creation, maintenance, and management, together with the capacity to add value to data" [Mil14]. Various systems exist to author RDF datasets such as Ontology editors and Semantic Wikis. Ontology editors aim on authoring semantic structures and vocabularies. Semantic Wikis are focused on collaborative authoring of RDF datasets. Due to the generic data modelling system of RDF the user interfaces for authoring systems can provide generic or domain-specific views. In this way the access and exploration interfaces can be adapted to use cases and workflows and ease the application in special domains.

Quality   As Linked Data is integrated from various sources the quality of the data can vary. Data quality is commonly understood as the *fitness for use* for a certain application or use case. The *fitness* *for use* is characterized by the dimensions accuracy, timeliness, completeness, relevancy, objectivity, believability, understandability, consistency, conciseness, availability, and verifiability [Zav+15]; [WS96]. The importance of the individual dimensions differs for different use cases as each use case has its own definition of *use* and *fitness for use*. When dealing with Linked Data on the Web it is important for the use cases to determine the *fitness for use* of certain data. In contrast to the Document Web, on the Semantic Web it is possible to express quality parameters, such as shape and vocabulary constraints, and to provide the necessary meta-information to assess the data's quality along with the data. Important information to assess data quality, especially with respect to verifiability, and thus to build trust are provenance information.

Evolution/Repair   The publication of Linked Data on the Web and the collaborative manner coming along with the distribution and interlinking causes an agile evolution of the data. This agile evolution requires for methods to arrange with the multimodal structure of the process and to overview the evolution. In particular an uncontrolled process can foster creativity of the participants but can also cause failure in the data. These failures can be detected with quality measures and be repaired using collaborative authoring tools which make it easy to correct mistakes rather then make it hard to make mistakes. Collaborative and wiki like authoring methods have proven helpful in this regard. Also the adoption of methods from organizing distributed software engineering processes are promising.

Search/Browsing/Exploration   The highly interlinked nature of Linked Data entails many way to navigate through RDF graphs. These ways for browsing through a graph and exploring its content often provide new insights for users on the data. In combination with taxonomies and other class and property structures it is also possible to provide faceted browsing interfaces and very precise search interfaces. Besides all of these possibilities to navigate to certain resources of an RDF dataset still the data model is often complex and thus cumbersome to understand for users. Especially, if users are not familiar with the RDF data model or the specifically used vocabulary of an RDF dataset they can not easily conceive the data's information and value. To level the hurdles to access the information, user interfaces are needed that are customized and adapted to the respective use case.

3.2 Virtual Organization and Groupware

A Virtual Organization is a corporation consisting of multiple independent and geographically distributed participants who are striving for a common interest or goal and communicate and coordinate their work through information technology [Tra97]; [AC99]. The corporation can be temporary or with a long-term aim. Usually the participants who join in the work for a Virtual Organization are employed at different participating companies. Rohde, Rittenbruch, and Wulf [RRW01] further characterize Virtual Organizations as spatially and temporally distributed; with fluid, informal, and ephemeral organizational boundaries and structures; asynchronous cooperative processes; and an accelerated organizational development. Ahuja and Carley [AC99] transfer the term of Virtual Organizations to a " *Virtual Research Organization,* in which members of various corporate and academic research units voluntarily come together to advance a technology on an ongoing basis."

Collaboration in teams with support of information technology is the subject of research in the field of Computer Supported Cooperative Work.

> Computer Supported Cooperative Work (CSCW) is a generic term that combines the understanding of the way people work in groups with the enabling technologies of computer networking and associated hardware, software, services and techniques. [Wil91]

CSCW is commonly understood as the umbrella term embracing the technologically oriented term of Groupware. The aim of Groupware is to devise technological systems to support business teams in their collaborative work. Johansen [Joh88] introduces Groupware as follows:

> Groupware is a generic term for specialized computer aids that are designed for the use of collaborative work groups. Typically, these groups are small, project-oriented teams that have important tasks and tight deadlines. Groupware can involve software, hardware, services, and/or group process support. [Joh88]

Groupware systems and in general CSCW can be categorized according to the two dimensions *place* i. e. same place vs. different place and *time* i. e. synchronous vs. asynchronous (cf. [SPL07a]; [Joh88]). A number of usage scenarios in the different categories of Groupware are described in [Joh88], such as synchronous face-to-face interaction: group decision support systems and computer-supported face-to-face meetings; asynchronous interaction: presentation support software, project management software, and group memory management; synchronous distributed interaction with: screen-sharing and audio or video teleconferences; asynchronous distributed interaction using: calendar management for groups and group-authoring software. Groupware can perform various tasks while the important relevant concepts of CSCW and Groupware are *awareness, shared artifacts,* and *shared workspace.*

> Awareness refers to the ability of distributed collaborators to keep track of each other's activities and coordinate their work [...]. Shared artifacts (or shared data) collectively refer to software entities on which collaborators perform their

> work. [...] As such, shared artifacts always reflect the current state of collaborative work. [...] In a centralized architecture, shared artifacts are stored and maintained at a single location, and collaborators access and make updates on them. In a replicated architecture, collaborators work on their own copies of shared artifacts and the state is synchronized among the copies synchronously or asynchronously. [...] A shared workspace provides a sense of place where collaboration takes place. It is generally associated with some part of the screen real estate of the user's computer where the user "goes" to work on shared artifacts, discovers work status, and interacts with his/her collaborators. [...] Regardless of how it is provided, the main function of a shared workspace is to provide awareness of work status and activities of individual collaborators on shared artifacts, which, in turn, are essential for coordinating and controlling collaboration and achieving group goals. [SPL07a]

Due to the geographically spread setup of virtual organizations their focus is on distributed systems. The distributed work can be synchronous or asynchronous. In most cases Groupware implements ad hoc synchronization of the shared artifacts and concurrent access by several team members who work on the same task. In cooperative editing systems the intermediate results of other cooperative transactions should be visible to all collaborators. To coordinate the transactions they are bundled in a cooperative transaction group where collaborators read and update uncommitted data from other cooperative transactions. This results in nonserializable synchronization which requires concurrency mechanisms to preserve consistency. (cf. [SPL07b])

Johansen [Joh88] discusses a downside of Groupware that he sees in the notion of "groupthink." On the one hand "groupthink" might be intended but on the downside groups might implicitly discourage dissent and push aside individual viewpoints, even when they are correct. Consecutively this problem has to be kept in mind when designing Groupware.

3.3 Distributed Database Systems

A *database* is an organized collection of data that is stored and retrieved through a *database management system* (DBMS). Some DBMS use a schema to set a formal definition of the database structure while other DBMS refrain from the definition of a schema. *Distributed database*, *distributed DBMS*, and *distributed database system* are defined by Özsu and Valduriez [ÖV11] as follows:

> We define a distributed database as a collection of multiple, *logically interrelated* databases *distributed over a computer network*. A distributed database management system (distributed DBMS[, DDBMS]) is then defined as the software

> system that permits the management of the distributed database and makes the distribution transparent to the users. Sometimes "distributed database system" (DDBS) is used to refer jointly to the distributed database and the distributed DBMS.

When multiple users or systems interact with a DBMS or DDBMS the problems of *concurrency control* and the *recovery problem* arise and were broadly discussed by Bernstein et al. [BG81]; [BHG87].

> Systems that solve the concurrency control and recovery problems allow their users to assume that each of their programs executes atomically – as if no other programs were executed concurrently – and reliably – as if there were no failures.

This abstraction of interaction with a DDBMS is called *transaction* and an algorithm that executes the transactions atomically is called *concurrency control algorithm*. The concurrency control algorithm is implemented by executing concurrent interleaving transactions one after another "to give the illusion that transactions execute serially" [BG81]. Interleaving executions of transactions that have the same effect as serial executions are called *serializable*, which is considered correct because they support the "illusion of transaction atomicity" [BG81]. In addition, for the correctness of a transaction the ACID properties *atomicity, consistency, isolation*, and *durability* are formulated. The properties are defined by Özsu and Valduriez [ÖV11] as follows: *Atomicity* refers to the fact that a transaction is treated as a unit of operation. Therefore, either all the transaction's actions are completed, or none of them are. The *consistency* of a transaction is simply its correctness. In other words, a transaction is a correct program that maps one consistent database state to another. *Isolation* is the property of transactions that requires each transaction to see a consistent database at all times. In other words, an executing transaction cannot reveal its results to other concurrent transactions before its commitment. *Durability* refers to the property of transactions which ensures that once a transaction commits, its results are permanent and cannot be erased from the database.

In subsequent research various concepts for allowing concurrency control were discussed by giving different importance to the ACID properties. Berenson et al. [Ber+95] introduce the *snapshot isolation* type. This isolation type allows reads or writes to be executed on a snapshot which ensures isolation from other transactions but is not serializable. It follows from the isolation guarantee that needs to be provided, that snapshot isolated write operations can only be performed on distinct data items.

The problem to ensure consistency across all replicas of a DDBMS while clients are disconnected from the network was discussed for the *Coda* file system by Satyanarayanan et al. [Sat+90]. If a client is disconnected, be it intentionally or not, the client can still perform local changes in the cached file system. When the client is reconnected a reintegration process starts that tries to execute the cached updates on the file system of all replicas. If conflicts between updates are detected, the conflicting files are temporarily stored in a *covolume* until the conflict is resolved by a user.

Demers et al. [Dem+94] present the *Bayou System*, a client/server platform to replicate databases for the usage on mobile devices like *personal digital assistants*. The system propagates all writes through a peer-to-peer protocol to a *primary* server which accepts writes to be *committed*. All other write operations on *secondary* servers that were not yet committed are *tentative* until they are serialized on the *primary* server and the order of writes propagated to the secondary servers. If conflicts arise, *mergeprocs* are employed that understand the semantics of the data format and domain and can reconcile the conflict.

Another system to reconcile transactions performed on mobile clients is presented by Phatak and Badrinath [PN04]. Similar to the *Bayou System* all transactions need to be transmitted to a server to be globally committed. If a disconnected client performs local transactions, they are tested for serializability when the client is reconnected and are rolled back on conflicts. Further they discuss the weakening of the serializability guarantee which can be enabled by a semantic aware reconciliation and by providing snapshot isolation (cf. [Ber+95]). To implement the multiversion reconciliation the conflict detection and resolution is decoupled, while the server is responsible to detect the conflicts the client provides the conflict resolution function.

Muys [Muy08] provides a discussion about a concurrency control protocol for multiversion RDF data stores. In contrast to relational or object databases in an RDF store the smallest "cell" that can be considered is the entire graph. If multiple graphs are present and can be targeted by an update, the whole RDF dataset needs to be considered as a unit of change. This results in a single global write lock when applying traditional concurrency control protocols on an RDF data store and thus provides very little concurrency. To avoid a single global write lock the usage of predicate locking is proposed with the basic graph pattern (BGP) as predicate that is tested against the update set of a transaction that needs to be serialized. Still the resolution of conflicts is a problem. For this purpose the *single version optimistic concurrency control* protocol is adapted to a multiversion store by specifying the *multiversion optimistic concurrency control* protocol. The multiversion protocol allows to exploit snapshot isolation and thus to execute read-only operations from the validation protocol.

Neumann and Weikum [NW10] are following a similar approach and extend the RDF-3X store to x-RDF-3X. The RDF store provides versioning with the ability for time travelling queries. The store supports snapshot isolation and full serializability with help of predicate locks based on the query BGPs. Due to the snapshot isolation no locks are needed for read operations. To avoid too small locks or unnecessary large locks a lock splitting algorithm is employed. Update operations are performed in a per-transaction workspace that is merged into the differential indexes if a savepoint is issued.

To classify various DDBMS regarding to their architecture Özsu and Valduriez [ÖV11] consider the three aspects *autonomy, distribution,* and *heterogeneity. Autonomy* refers to the distribution of control, not of data and ranges over tight integration (A_0), semi autonomous (A_1), and full autonomy or total isolation (A_2). *Distribution* refers to the distribution of the data and ranges from central (D_0) to client-server distribution (D_1) and peer-to-peer (D_2). The aspect *heterogeneity* covers whether participants in the network can have heterogeneous data models, query languages, and transaction management protocols.

However, in DDBMS it is hard to ensure the ACID properties of transactions while still keeping the availability of a database high at all time. The counterpart of the ACID properties with regard to this problem was formulated as BASE: *Basically Available, Soft state, Eventual consistency.* To describe trade-offs that are necessary between consistency and availability of a DDBMS Brewer [Bre00] formulated the CAP theorem. The CAP theorem says that you can have at most two of the properties *Consistency, Availability,* or *tolerance to network Partitions* for any shared-data system [Bre00]; [GL02]. To deal with this dilemma some federated and peer-to-peer databases support relaxed consistency criteria [Bon+08].

Peer-to-peer Databases

Peer-to-peer (P2P) distributed database systems allow the full distribution of the data in a network of peers. In contrast to the client-server distribution as mostly discussed in this section so far, P2P distribution does not distinguish between a client and a server with different tasks but each peer has full DBMS functionality. The aim of P2P systems is to share computing resources among peers [AS04]; [Bon+08]. The resources of interest in the context of knowledge engineering are storage and content. Some approaches exist to utilize P2P systems to work with RDF data.

EDUTELLA was proposed by Nejdl et al. [Nej+02] as a metadata infrastructure based on RDF on top of the JXTA P2P framework.[17] The system is intended as a network to exchange educational resources. For this purpose the authors describe various services on top of the P2P network, such as a query service, replication service, mapping service, mediation service, and annotation service.

The GridVine system is a P2P network based on a distributed hash table for RDF data (cf. [CAA07]). It follows a three layer architecture to separate the logical layer (semantic mediation layer) from the physical layer. It provides a query service that implements query reformulation based on schema mappings.

Another P2P database system that has gained attention in recent years is Distributed Ledger Technology (DLT) and the construction and

---

[17] *JXTA Community Projects.* Project Homepage (original not available):

maintenance of a Blockchain as shared ledger. Even though a Blockchain establishes a data structure in contrast to other P2P database systems it is not the storage resource that is shared among peers but the computing power. Each peer can add new entries to the Blockchain following specific rules of the network. The shared data structure is replicated to allow its validation by all peers, in this way the data structure allows to represent a shared consensus of the participants in the network. A very big application of DLT and Blockchains nowadays are crypto currencies and their trading. However, also several approaches exist that try to adopt the technology for data management such as the application of a Blockchain to ensure the data integrity in cloud computing [Gae+17], a query language to query a Blockchain [MQN19], and the application of an ontology and its translation to smart contracts for the tracking of provenance [KL18].

3.4 Web Application Engineering

On the Web distributed applications were developed ranging over multiple Web services. The individual services might or might not be under the same administration and their underlying data management system might range from a centralized DBMS over a DDBMS to individual independent distributed storage units. The distributed property of the storage of interrelated data on the Web or in other networks introduces new problems with regard to the data management. Thus, on the Web the problem of consistency cannot be seen in the same way as for tightly coupled database systems. Implementing applications on the Web leads to the problem of managing the state of implemented business processes. In the REST architecture the state is split up into the application state and the resource state. The application state is the path of an application through hypermedia controls while the resource state is the state of a resource stored on a Web Server (cf. [RAR13]).

Ousterhout and Stratmann [OS10] discuss the state problem in Web Applications using asynchronous AJAX requests. They analyze and verify possible solutions for managing states on the client side or on the server side in a Web Application. The authors conclude that both, client side and server side states have drawbacks. Client side state management has "overheads for shipping state between browser and server, and it creates potential security loopholes by allowing sensitive server state to be stored in the browser". Whereas the server-based approach "introduces overheads for saving state as part of sessions, and it has garbage-collection issues that can result in the loss of state". The authors prefer the usage of a server-based state management over that of a browser-based and predict upcoming challenges in state management of Web Applications.

Pardon and Pautasso [PP11] specify a protocol to support atomicity and recovery over distributed REST resources. The authors contribute to the debate in the REST community to whether or not transaction support is needed. The presented approach references and is similar to the position paper by Helland [Hel07]. The need for the protocol is motivated by a business use case on booking two connecting flights from two different a irlines. T he p resented a pproach is b ased on a Try-Cancel/Confirm (TCC) pattern using (a) an initial state, (b) a reserved state and (c) a final s tate. T he r eserved s tate (b) i s c alled *tentative* in [Hel07]. To form a transaction an arbitrary number of REST services are loosely coupled. A transaction is valid if all reserved states (b) are confirmed, a fter t his t he fi nal st ate (c) is en tered fo r ea ch service. Compared to the two-phase commit lock the authors point out, that the TCC approach "offers higher-level semantics and does not hold low-level database locks." The participants "do not block any other work other than the one affected b y t he b usiness r esources t hey reserve." Both approaches [PP11]; [Hel07] mention that an uncertainty is left if one of the loosely coupled systems fails before all systems have reached the final s tate. T he m anagement o f u ncertainty m ust b e implemented in business logic to counter this issue.

Web Applications as well as Semantic Web Applications (SWA) consist of three layers: *Persistence Layer, Data Interchange & Transaction processing*, and *User Interface* [MA10]. Martin and Auer [MA10] present a categorization model for Semantic Web Applications. Following this categorization model our focus is on intrinsic and extrinsic producing SWAs while the level of user involvement, semantic richness, and semantic integration is left open. In an empirical study performed by Heitmann et al. [Hei+12]; [Hei+14] all SWAs have a graph access layer, an increasing amount of SWAs is concerned with data creation, and some applications even provide structured data authoring interfaces. The data flow t o a llow c ollaborative k nowledge a cquisition, visualization, and creation requires for a management of concurrent and possibly conflicting o perations. T he a bove p resented r esearch o n non-semantic Web Applications is mostly concerned with distributed state management. Methods like Flux[18] can be used in client applications to bundle the data flow t owards t he b ack-end w ithin an a pplication. A store object ensures that all view component's requests to the back-end system are executed and controlled in a single place which can represent a client side state. The issue of communicating the global state of the store between back-end and client application is underrepresented in research. A reason for a lack of research in this area by the Ajax/REST community might be the fact, that Ajax/REST applications usually encode parts of the business logic in the back-end. In contrast to that, SWAs are able to encode semantics in the data store and thus are able to directly communicate with the RDF store as persistence layer.

Pardon, Pautasso, and Zimmermann [PPZ18] discuss the problem of organizing backups in a microservice system. Microservices are independent services that are loosely coupled to implement an application. Relations between entities in microservices can be implemented using hypermedia controls [PPZ18]. While there is no guaranty "[...]

---

[18] *Flux: Application Architecture for Building User Interfaces.* In Depth Overview:

a basic notion of consistency can be introduced for the microservice-based application, requiring that such reference can always be resolved, thus avoiding broken links" [PPZ18]. Inspired by the CAP theorem (cf. [Bre00]), the authors introduce the BAC theorem that states that it is not possible to have both availability and consistency when backing up an entire microservice architecture. Due to the independence of the microservices each stateful service relies on its own storage. The problem of inconsistency manifests after the recovery from backup as *missing state*. The missing state can be broken links, when references from one service to another cannot be followed anymore, or orphan state, when a resource is not referenced anymore. To the contrary, a consistent backup can only be achieved by violating the independence of the microservices by coordinating the backups. To overcome the problem it is either necessary to deal with the inconsistency or to adapt the architecture in a way that fits the desired business case.

3.5 Versioning of RDF Datasets

Versioning of changes on a dataset allows to analyze and organize its evolution. The analysis covers actions like to backtrace the origin of changes, to analyze the evolution of the data, or to travel in time on the dataset. To organize the evolution a versioning log allows to revert unwanted changes and to synchronize datasets at different states of the development. Various systems to version and archive RDF datasets or to describe and support the versioning process were proposed in the past.

In the following we look into existing approaches that target problems related to the versioning of RDF datasets. First, we consider abstract models, vocabularies, and methods to express changes and evolution of RDF datasets in section 3.5.1. Second, we look at possibilities to express provenance information on RDF data in section 3.5.2. Then we provide an overview on systems for calculating the difference on RDF data in section 3.5.3. We examine and characterize implementations dealing with versioning and archiving of RDF data in section 3.5.4. Finally, applications built on top of RDF versioning systems are presented in section 3.5.5.

3.5.1 Abstract Models and Vocabularies

Berners-Lee and Connolly [BC01] give a general overview on the problem of synchronization and how to calculate the difference of RDF graphs. The authors identify the generation of differences generally as a graph isomorphism problem, while a well labeled graph is needed. This work considers the transfer of changes to datasets by applying patches. As a result, the authors introduce a conceptual ontology that describes patches in *a way to uniquely identify what is changing* and *to distinguish between the pieces added and those subtracted.*

Haase and Stojanovic [HS05] introduce their concept of ontology evolution as follows:

> Ontology evolution can be defined as the timely adaptation of an ontology to the arisen changes and the consistent management of these changes. [...] An important aspect in the evolution process is to guarantee the consistency of the ontology when changes occur, considering the semantics of the ontology change.

The work of Haase and Stojanovic focuses on the linear evolution process of an individual dataset. To deal with inconsistency respective consistency three levels are defined: *s tructural, l ogical, a* nd *user-defined* consistency. In the remainder of the paper the authors mainly focus on the implications of the evolution with respect to OWL (DL) rather than a generic approach based on the abstract syntax of RDF.

Auer and Herre [AH06] propose a generic framework to support the versioning and evolution of RDF graphs. The authors introduce the concept of *atomic graphs*, which provides a practical approach to deal with blank nodes in changesets. The concept of atomic graphs can be compared to the concept of RDF Molecules by Ding et al. [Din+05] while the definition o f A uer a nd H erre [AH06] i s m ore c oncise. Tummarello et al. [Tum+07] provide a recursive definition f or t he concept under the name *Minimum Self-Contained Graph*. Additionally Auer and Herre [AH06] introduce a formal hierarchical system to structure a set of changes and evolution patterns that lead to the changes of a knowledge base.

3.5.2 Expressing Provenance Information

Currently, various vocabularies exist that allow the description of provenance. As a *World Wide Web Consortium* (W3C) Recommendation, the PROV ontology (PROV-O) [Leb+13] is the de-facto standard for the representation and exchange of domain-independent provenance. The *Open Provenance Model* [Mor+11] predates the PROV-O, but both use very similar approaches as their core components. Both vocabularies enable the description of provenance data as relations between *agents*, *entities*, and *activities* or their respective equivalent.

Another popular standard for general-purpose metadata is *Dublin Core* respective the *Dublin Core Metadata Terms* [DCM12]. The main difference t o t he p rior o ntologies i s i n t heir p erspective o n expressing provenance. While the PROV-O is more focused on activities that lead to a specific entity, D ublin C ore focuses on t he r esulting e ntities. Both vocabularies provide means to express provenance metadata.

An advantage of using a domain-independent vocabulary is its generic applicability. The domain-independent design also allows the reuse of analysis tools across domains. PROV-O-Viz[19] is an example of a visualization tool working with the data expressed according to the PROV ontology that can be used across domains.

---

[19] *PROV-O-Viz:*

3.5.3 Comparing Ontologies and RDF Knowledge Bases

There are important approaches to support the distributed ontology engineering process using description logic expressed with OWL [W3C12]. Zaikin and Tuzovsky [ZT13] describe two tools[20] they have developed to target this problem. The first tool *owl2diff* detects changes between different versions of OWL ontologies and the second tool *owl2merge* helps to resolve conflicts and perform a Three-Way-Merge. Both tools can be integrated to be used with the *Git* version control system. The focus of this system is to compare ontologies based on the direct semantics of OWL considering entities and axioms. This focus on OWL makes the tool not usable in a generic way to support collaboration based on the abstract syntax of RDF.

Various tools to compare RDF graphs or datasets are further listed in the Semantic Web Activity Wiki.[21] The *SemDiff*[22] web service can compare individual Linked Data resources and output the result in an RDF file containing either all added or deleted statements, or summarized as RSS or RDF, while the changed statements are encoded in comments in a custom string format. *rdf-utils*[23] similarly outputs the result in two ZIP compressed RDF files containing all added respective deleted statements. *rdfdiff* from the redland raptor[24] software toolbox produces a human readable list of added and deleted triples. The *TopBraid Composer*[25] in the payed version expresses patches using the `diff:` ontology while it also provides a graphical user interface for exploring the changes. The *GUO Graph Diff* web service is no longer functionally available[26] but it provided a custom RDF format for differences as well. The RDFLib Python API provides a module called *rdflib.compare*[27] which allows to calculate the differences between two models. A generally feasible option is to serialize the files in a canonical form to compare the serialized representation by using a line-based diff tool. This has the drawback of loosing support for blank nodes. Thus many systems exist to compare RDF graphs but with some drawbacks. None of the listed tools provides comparison of RDF datasets respective multiple RDF models at once. The support for blank nodes is limited and the output formats are very diverse and often not integrable with standard RDF interfaces.

3.5.4 Practical Knowledge Base Versioning Systems

Approach	Archiving Policy	Quad Support	Standard RDF Interface	Random Access	Branches/ Merge	Synchronize (Push/Pull)
Frommhold et al. [Fro+16b]	CB	●	●	○	○	○
stardog	IC	●	●	○	○	○
Meinhardt, Knuth, and Sack [MKS15]	hybrid (IC and CB)	○[a]	○[d]	●	○	○[l]
Cassidy and Ballantine [CB07]	CB	○	○[e]	○	○/◖[h]	◖[m]
Völkel and Groza [VG06]	IC	●	○[f]	●	●/●	○
Sande et al. [San+13]	TB	○[b]	●	●	●/○[i]	○
Graube, Hensel, and Urbas [GHU16]	CB	●[b,c]	○[g]	●	●/(●)[k]	○
dat	FB (*chunks*)	n/a	○	●	○	●

[a] The granularity of versioning are repositories; [b] The context is used to encode revisions; [c] Graphs are separately put under version control; [d] HTTP Push API; [e] Redland API; [f] Java API; [g] Extension of SPARQL 1.1 but incompatible with SPARQL 1.1; [h] Only linear change tracking is supported; if subsequent patches of a duplicated workspace can be applied to the original copy this is called merge in this system; [i] Merge mentioned but not implemented; [k] A merge interface exists, but could not be tested; [l] Only one way history replication via memento API; [m] Synchronization happens by exchanging patches, no full history replication

Table 3.3: Comparison of the (D)VCS systems for RDF data. Custom implementations exist for all of these systems and they are not re-using existing VCSs. At the level of abstraction all of these systems can be located on the *data interchange* layer.

Table 3.3 provides an overview of the related work and compares the approaches presented with regard to different aspects. One aspect to categorize versioning systems is its archiving policy. Fernández et al. [FPU15] define three archiving policies. IC - *Independent Copies*, where each version is stored and managed as a different, isolated dataset. CB - *Change-based* (delta), where differences between versions are computed and stored based on a *basic language of changes* describing the change operations. TB - *Timestamp-based* where each statement is annotated with its temporal validity. These three archiving policies do not cover the full range of possible archiving systems and thus additionally we need to define the archiving policy FB - *Fragment-based*. This policy stores snapshots of each changed fragment of an archive. Depending on the requirements fragments can be defined at any level of granularity (e.g. resources, subgraphs, or individual graphs in a dataset). An index is maintained that references the fragments belonging to a version of the dataset. This approach abandons the necessity of fully repeating all triples across versions when following the IC policy. In contrast to CB it is not necessary to reconstruct individual versions by applying the change operations to restore or query a version.

Besides the used archiving policy, we compare the systems with regard to the aspects *quad support, standard RDF interface, random access, branches/merge,* and *synchronization.* The aspect *quad support* tells whether a system can track versions of multiple RDF graphs and thus allow the collaboration on and archiving of complete RDF datasets. This ensures that users are able to organize the stored knowledge in individual organizational units as it is required by the use case or application. A standardized RDF data access interface is important to allow existing system such as arbitrary RDF editors to read data from and write data to the versioning system. *Random access* on versions is the ability to retrieve or query any version of the data in the archive without the need to restore the respective state. The aspect *branches* specifies i f t he s ystem i s a ble t o s upport t he d ivergence of the versioning log, the aspect *merge* is concerned with the possibility to *reconcile diverged states* into a common versioning log. In a distributed setup the aspect *Synchronize* is important to let instances of the system participating in a common network exchange recorded versions e.g. by using push and pull mechanisms. The aspects *branches* and *merge* implement the requirements *dissent and reconciliation* according to definition 3 . T he p ossibility t o *s ynchronize* o n d emand is necessary to fulfill t he r equirements *a synchrony a nd synchronization* according to definition 4 w hich i n t urn i s a p rerequisite t o p rovide a *distributed workspace* according to definition 2.

TailR as presented by Meinhardt, Knuth, and Sack [MKS15] is a system to preserve the history of arbitrary RDF datasets on the Web. It follows a combined delta and snapshot storage approach. The system is comparable to the approach presented by Frommhold et al. [Fro+16b], as both systems are linear change tracking systems. None of the systems provides support for branches to allow independent evolution of RDF graphs.

Another approach is implemented by *stardog*,[28] a triple store with integrated version control capabilities. The versioning module provides functionality to tag and calculate the difference b etween revisions.[29] Snapshots contain all named graphs from the time the snapshot was taken. RDF data and snapshots are stored in a relational database. The current state of the database can be queried via a SPARQL interface. While older states of the database can be restored, to our knowledge, random access to the revisions is not possible. An additional graph containing the version history is provided.

Cassidy and Ballantine [CB07] present a version control system for RDF graphs based on the model of *Darcs.* Their approach covers the versioning operations *commute, revert,* and *merge.* Even though *Darcs* is considered a DVCS in contrast to other DVCS the presented approach only supports linear version tracking. Further, the merge operation is

---

[28] *Stardog:*
[29] *Stardog 5, The Manual: Versioning:*

implemented using patch commutation which requires history rewriting and thus loses the context of the original changes.

Graube, Hensel, and Urbas [GHU16] propose the R43ples approach that uses named graphs to store revisions as deltas. To express the provenance information it uses the RMO vocabulary,[30] which is an extended and more domain-specific version of the PROV-O. To query and update the triple store the SPARQL language is extended with keywords for the version selection. As the SPARQL language is extended by this implementation it is no longer compatible with the SPARQL 1.1 standard, thus the store can not be queried with standard SPARQL requests.

Völkel and Groza [VG06] propose the SemVersion system which was developed as part of the Knowledge Web project [Völ06]. The versioning system is inspired by the Concurrent Versions System (CVS) system. It stores full snapshots of the graph for each version. To query the graph a Java API can be employed. The system provides support for branching and merging. The merge operation is quite equal to the Three-Way-Merge but slightly different: to merge C into D with the common merge base B the $diff(B, D)$ is applied to C (cf. section 4.2.3). Also a conflict detection is discussed with the conclusion that conflicts can not arise between RDF models but only on the ontological layer (cf. section 5.3). To improve the support for blank nodes, SemVersion attaches a custom property as inverse functional property to ground each blank node.

R&Wbase by Sande et al. [San+13] is a tool for versioning an RDF graph. It tracks changes that are stored in individual named graphs that are combined on query time. Because the named graph context is used to represent the version-context of a statement the system can not be used to manage RDF datasets with multiple named graphs. Further, the system implements an understanding of coexisting branches within a versioning graph. This concept is very close to the concept of Git branches. A merge strategy is mentioned but not implemented.

In the dat[31] project a tool to distribute and synchronize files in a distributed setup is developed. The aim is to synchronize any file type peer to peer. We can see this as a collection of files which are logically related but the data is not necessarily structured and accessed through a common interface. According to Özsu and Valduriez [ÖV11] dat can be considered as a general distributed data management system. Also it has no support to manage branches, merge diverged versions, and is not focusing on RDF data.

Looking at the above knowledge base versioning systems as listed in table 3.3, it is clear that three of them can fulfill the requirement to express *dissent* by providing a branching model, namely SemVersion [VG06], R&Wbase [San+13] and R43ples [GHU16]. SemVersion comes with proper support for merge operations, while the other two currently only have very limited support to fulfill the requirement *rec-*

---

[30] *Revision Management Ontology*. The r43ples Revision Management Ontology:

onciliation (cf. definition 3). None of these three system provides support for *asynchrony and synchronization*. Moving on to the support for the requirement for *synchronization* we see TailR [MKS15], the approach by Cassidy and Ballantine [CB07], and *dat*. Given the limited support for RDF, we can ignore *dat*. TailR and the approach by Cassidy and Ballantine do not bring support for a branching system and thus cannot fulfill the requirement for *dissent and reconciliation*. The patch-based synchronization by Cassidy and Ballantine as well as the memento replication in TailR can not handle intended asynchrony of the workspaces to later synchronize them (cf. definition 4). None of the presented systems provides support for a *distributed workspace* according to definition 2.

3.5.5 Applications to Exploit Knowledge Versioning

The Git4Voc system, as proposed by Halilaj et al. [Hal+16a] is a methodology and collection of best practices for collaborative creation of RDF vocabularies using Git repositories. To support vocabulary authors to create RDF and OWL vocabularies Git4Voc is implemented using pre- and post-commit hooks to validate the vocabulary and generate documentation. To validate the vocabulary specification a combination of local and online tools is used. In preparation of the presented Git4Voc system, Halilaj et al. have formulated important requirements for collaboration on RDF data. Based on Git4Voc Halilaj et al. have created the VoCol [Hal+16a] system as an IDE for vocabularies. For VoCol the three core activities *modeling*, *population*, and *testing* are formulated. VoCol as well as Git4Voc are not focused on providing a versioning system for RDF data in general but rather tools built on top of a versioning system to specifically support the development of vocabularies.

The Git2PROV[32] tool [De +13] allows to generate a provenance document using the PROV ontology for any public Git repository. It can be used as a web service or can be executed locally. Since our aim is to provide provenance for RDF data on graph- and triple-level Git2PROV is not suited as a component since it is only able to handle provenance on a per-file-level.

3.6 Conclusion

The related work examined comprises systems in related and overlapping fields. In section 3.1 methodologies were examined for collaboration on the Web, with a focus on knowledge engineering. We could identify three categories of systems: shared workspaces, i.e., collaborative document editors, wikis, ans semantic wikis; Semantic Web protocols, i.e., SPARQL, Linked Data, and LDP; and DVCS. In their support for the requirements formulated in section 1.2 they are complementary, while the shared workspaces put a focus on the collaboration features,

---

[32] *git 2 prov.* (original not available): [

the Semantic Web protocols provide support for working on knowledge bases, and DVCS support distributed workspaces, asynchrony, synchronization, dissent, reconciliation, and provenance.

We can see that collaboration is organized in different ways on different types of artifacts. While the collaboration on text is in realtime on a shared workspaces, that collaboration in the engineering task i.e. on source code is organized asynchronously. For RDF data wiki approaches and shared storage infrastructure can be established while they are not prepared for asynchronous collaboration and to express dissent and appropriate means for reconciliation. Combining the conclusions from online social networking and software engineering we learn that communication of distributed parties is important, that commenting systems are helpful to highlight and discuss issues, and mechanisms like pull-requests can be used to exchange and discuss contributions in their original format. Furthermore, DVCS can allow the application of continuous delivery and continuous integration systems on data to verify the adherence to defined specifications. Using companying methods in addition to the DVCS such as an issue tracker and pull-requests can allow to structure and formalize the process for building a consensus about contributions to a knowledge base. Various proposals for commenting systems and social interaction implemented on the Semantic Web exist already. The Linked Data life-cycle highlights the tasks to be supported in the life-cycle of a knowledge engineering process on Linked Data.

From the field of CSCW we have taken a closer look at collaboration with Groupware and in Virtual Organizations in section 3.2. This helps to position the research in this book in the overall context of collaboration in groups on a common subject with the support of digital technology. The shared artifacts are mainly RDF knowledge bases and we want to establish individual workspaces connected to a common distributed workspace for collaboration. Awareness among the collaborators has to be established to discuss issues and pull-requests and further means e.g. by using distributed social networking systems.

As the presented system is concerned with storing data and managing it in a distributed system it has to be positioned in relation to Distributed Database Systems (DDBMS; cf. section 3.3). The system might not generally be considered as a DDBMS. According to the aspects introduced by Özsu and Valduriez [ÖV11] it provides full autonomy for the local systems and is peer-to-peer distributed while it is difficult to position the system regarding its heterogeneity as the provided criteria do not fully apply. When multiple users or systems interact with a DBMS or DDBMS the problems of *concurrency control* and the *recovery problem* arise and were broadly discussed by Bernstein et al. [BG81]; [BHG87]. These two problems are also relevant for the system presented in this book, while transactions are understood similar to commits, as they are used in DVCS. In contrast to DDBMS, we have a different notion of consistency where serializability is not always important.

In contrast to organized environments as for DDBMS in Web Application Engineering multiple distributed autonomous environments have to be managed to organize state (cf. section 3.4). Web Applications are organized in three layers: *Persistence Layer, Data Interchange & Transaction processing*, and *User Interface* [MA10]. Ousterhout and Stratmann [OS10] come to the conclusion, that preferably the state should best be managed on the server-side i.e. the persistence layer, which corresponds to the Abstract Language and Repository layers of the Semantic Web Layer Cake. Thus, the state should be manage in the data model and persisted and exchanged through the repository. According to Pardon, Pautasso, and Zimmermann [PPZ18] the BAC theorem has to be kept in mind when designing a microservice architecture to avoid missing state or to deal with it.

In section 3.5 the state of the art in RDF versioning is examined. The state of the art RDF versioning systems, similar to wiki systems, only provide one synchronously available version of the dataset which necessarily has to maintain some kind of consensus. It should be noted, that Cassidy and Ballantine [CB07] has support for linearization of diverged versioning logs based on the distribution of patches. This allows, beyond the other state of the art RDF versioning systems, to have limited support for asynchronous work and reconciliation. However, there is no RDF versioning system with full support to work with branches and independent workspaces in a distributed setup. As an overall conclusion, there is no sate of the art system that provides support for distributed collaboration on versioned decentralized RDF knowledge bases according to the requirements in section 1.2.

4 The Quit Methodology

This chapter provides an overview on the Quit methodology for distributed collaborative knowledge engineering. The aim of the Quit methodology is to improve the flexibility and the communication flow within knowledge engineering projects by adapting processes and models from the field of software engineering. In their respective work on agile knowledge engineering methodologies, XP.K by Knublauch [Knu02] and on RapidOWL by Auer [Aue07] both authors adopt the view of Cockburn [Coc99]; [Coc00] who defines a methodology as follows.

> A methodology is an agreement of how multiple people will work together. It spells out what roles they play, what decisions they must reach, how and what they will communicate. A person working alone may still choose to follow a full methodology, and will then play the various roles in turn.

Figure 4.1 provides an overview on the aspects involved in the Quit methodology. People play the central role of each methodology, they follow certain paradigms that come with involved processes and models. Tools support the people in following the models and performing the processes.

The results presented in this chapter were first published in Arndt, Radtke, and Martin: "Distributed Collaboration on RDF Datasets Using Git: Towards the Quit Store" [ARM16]; Arndt and Radtke: "Quit Diff: Calculating the Delta Between RDF Datasets und Version Control" [AR16]; Arndt, Naumann, and Marx: "Exploring the Evolution and Provenance of Git Versioned RDF Data" [ANM17]; Arndt and Martin: "Decentralized Evolution and Consolidation of RDF Graphs" [AM17]; Arndt et al.: "Decentrali Collaborative Knowledge Management using Git" [Arn+19a]; and Arndt and Radtke: "Conflict Detection, Avoidance, and Resolution in a Non-Linear RDF Version Control System: The Quit Editor Interface Concurrency Contro [AR19].

Figure 4.1: The aspects volved in the Quit methodology according to Alista Cockburn and visualized parallel to the work of A [Aue07].

The Quit methodology aims to improve knowledge engineering in the area of the Semantic Web by adopting and adapting concepts from the field of software engineering. The respective paradigms, Semantic Web and software engineering, are depicted in the upper part of fig. 4.1. Derived from the paradigms the relevant models in the right part of the figure, i.e. languages, standards, and technologies are RDF, SPARQL, and Git as already introduced in chapter 2. RDF is the basic concept of data representation used on the Semantic Web in combination with its standardized query language SPARQL. Git in turn is a DVCS that has been successfully used to coordinate distributed software engineering processes. The people, depicted in the middle of fig. 4.1, participating in a methodology play various roles, which should respect their own skills. Roles can be fulfilled by many people but also can one person be assigned with various roles at the same time. For the Quit methodology we have identified the three roles user, engineer, and maintainer that are known from software engineering. The knowledge user is working with the knowledge base and derived artifacts, applies it to new contexts and might report back experiences and failures. The knowledge engineer accumulates knowledge and enters it into the knowledge base, it should be a domain expert. The knowledge maintainer incorporates knowledge contributed by knowledge engineers into a shared version of the knowledge base, organizes the structure of the repository, and is responsible for keeping the knowledge base in a consistent state. The principles of the Quit methodology are depicted in the left part of fig. 4.1. The knowledge engineering and especially the Quit methodology is highly collaborative. Collaboration nowadays happens distributed on the Web. In both fields, on the Semantic Web and in software engineering, collaboration is important to achieve a common understanding of a certain domain and of the way to encode the gained knowledge. To enable the collaboration throughout the methodology the knowledge has to be shared as often as possible. New knowledge that is submitted to the shared knowledge base has to pass a review process. Subsequently, the submission can be incorporated or rejected, in which case it can be resubmitted after it was "repaired." This sharing process implies that contradicting versions of the knowledge base might exist, as participants have different background knowledge and opinions. An aspect of the Quit methodology is to support dissent throughout the sharing process. On the shared versions of the knowledge base the participants can discuss to reach an agreement. In order to support the participants in the Quit methodology to perform the involved processes and follow the models a set of tools was developed. The core part of the tools is the Quit Store (cf. fig. 4.2). It provides a repository that allows to store RDF knowledge bases and query them via SPARQL. The synchronization among distributed collaborators is supported using the Git protocol. Throughout the collaboration process the Quit Store tracks the provenance information and makes it available via SPARQL. To provide the support for dissent multiple versions of the knowledge base can be stored in parallel in so called branches. In order to incorporate new knowledge into the shared version the branches can be merged by the knowledge maintainer. To support knowledge engineers in adding new knowledge to the store authoring interfaces can be provided by utilizing the SPARQL protocol. These authoring interface allow to guide the knowledge engineer in the process of encoding knowledge using the shared vocabulary. The result of the knowledge engineering process can be presented to the knowledge user through an exploration interface.

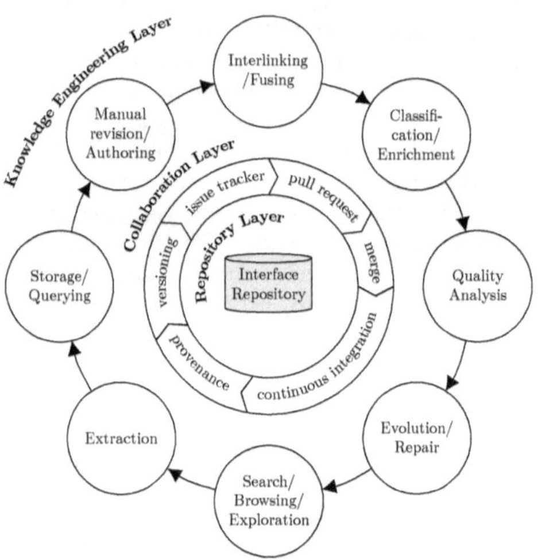

Figure 4.2: The three layered evolutionary collaborative knowledge engineering process of the Quit methodology. The knowledge engineering process as described by the Linked Data life-cycle (cf. section 3.1.3) is supported by collaboration methods from software engineering and stored in an interface repository for distribution.

The Quit methodology is a combination of the knowledge engineering process that is supported by methods from the field of software engineering. It can be seen as a cyclic layer model as it is depicted in fig. 4.2. The *knowledge engineering layer* is the overall process of the knowledge engineering as it is described by the Linked Data lifecycle model (cf. section 3.1.3). To perform this process collaboratively in the Quit methodology a set of techniques from the field of software engineering is employed as can be seen in the *collaboration layer*. The *versioning* allows to track all steps in the evolutionary process and is a foundation for the synchronization of the changes with the collaborators, while the *provenance* allows to reproduce the evolution. The *versioning* and *provenance* especially support the *manual revision/authoring*, the *evolution/repair*, and also the *quality analysis* steps. An *issue tracker* can be used to coordinate the overall collaborative process. The concept of *pull requests* support the submission of distributed contributions and their discussion by the community, it can also be used by *extraction* processes to deliver the extraction result to the collaborative process. The *merge* allows to integrate the contributions into a consolidated work state and can support processes like *fusing* and *enrichment*. *Continuous integration* is a practice used for software engineering that allows to automatically perform quality assessment steps on every contribution. The evolutionary steps recorded with the versioning are stored in the *repository*. In a distributed collaboration process this repository as abstract storage of all relevant data is synchronized between collaborating parties and serves as common *interface repository* for the distributed collaboration.

In the following, we derive requirements that are relevant for the conceptual versioning model of the Quit methodology from the abstract requirements introduced in section 1.2. These abstract requirements are: support for a distributed workspace (a), to support dissent (b), support for asynchrony (c), to synchronize asynchronous states (d), and to reconcile diverged states (e). Also the tracking of the provenance (h) during the process of changing data is a basic requirement for any version control system.[1]

Distributed Workspace The Web is a global communication system based on the exchange of data. It consists of servers and clients that are distributed and embedded in various organizational units. Also the collaborators are contributing from various locations and organizations and it might not be possible to find a central server that is able to serve all collaborators. This requires for a system where each collaborator can autonomously take part in the collaboration process. Thus, the collaboration happens on a distributed workspace.

Support Dissent In collaborative scenarios contributors may differ in their motivation to contribute, for example because of their organizational role, may differ in their opinion to the subject of collaboration, or may provide contradicting contributions in any other way. Thus the existence of multiple different versions of the dataset is preferable, for instance to express dissent, disagreement, or situations in which a consensus was not yet reached. Especially in distributed collaborative setups it can happen, that collaborating parties are not always sharing a common understanding of a certain topic. But also because of organizational structures the evolution of a dataset is not necessarily happening in a linear manner, for instance if partial subjects are discussed in sub-working groups. Thus the system needs to be able to handle diverging states of a dataset.

Support Asynchrony As the workspaces are distributed on the Web and autonomously managed a constant connection to the network can not be ensured. Further the organizational distribution can lead to a temporal shift to transmit changes. Also use cases in mobile scenarios or in general with limited connectivity are relevant. This leads to the requirement for a version tracking system that supports asynchronous versioning logs as distributed parties.

Synchronize Collaborating on a single centralized copy of a dataset causes much coordination difficulties. For instance if a simultaneous access to the central dataset is not possible for all participants (e.g. from mobile devices). Thus we focus on a distributed setup of collaboration

---

[1] The requirements *create and author* (f) and *publish and explore* (g) data are covered in chapters 6 and 7

systems. To support the collaboration of multiple distributed parties across system boundaries it is necessary to exchange data between systems. The system should support the synchronization of their available states of the dataset with the available states of remote setups. This is also important to keep up a collaborative process if participating systems fail. This synchronization process can happen in real-time or asynchronously.

Reconcile Diverged States The aim of collaboration is to eventually contribute to a common subject. To combine the contributions in diverged states of a dataset to a common dataset a possibility to conflate and reconcile the diverged states is needed. Because diverged states can encode dissent it is necessary to identify possible conflicts before actually combining the states of the datasets. The definition of conflict depends on the semantics of the data and the application domain, thus different strategies are needed to identify conflicts. When possibly identifying conflicts, the system needs to offer workflows to resolve identified conflicts and contradictions.

Track and Store Provenance of Contributions The Web is organized in a distributed manner and provides manifold possibilities to interchange data. In such a collaborative agile data engineering environment often small changes to the data are performed by different parties. For people and systems it is necessary to get hold of information on which it is possible to decide which data can be trusted or not [Car+05]. An important concept to build trust is *data provenance* which includes information about entities, activities, and people involved in the creation of data [Mor+13b]. According to the Oxford online dictionary, *provenance* has to be with the *origin or earliest known history of something.*[2] Tracking provenance during the process of changing data is a basic requirement for any version control system. It is therefore important to record the provenance of data at any step of a process, that involves possible changes of a dataset (e. g., creation, curation, and linking). To support developers of provenance systems Groth et al. [Gro+12] provide general aspects that should be considered by any system that deals with provenance information. The aspects are categorized as follows [Gro+12]:

- *Content* describes what should be contained in provenance data, whereas entities, contributing sources, processes generating artifacts, versioning, justification, and entailment are relevant dimensions.

- *Management* refers to concerns about how provenance should be captured and maintained, including publication and access, dissemination, and how a system scales.

- *Use* is about how user specific problems can be solved using recorded provenance. Mentioned are understanding, interoperability, comparison, accountability, trust, imperfections, and debugging.

The versioning system needs to track the result of update operations in individual versions. To maintain the origin of the changes the system needs to track the predecessor relations for an updated dataset. During the execution of update operations on a dataset also the association to the contributing user (author information) needs to be tracked along with the additional metadata. The additional metadata include the change reason and date of change, while the system has to be extensible to include custom information depending on the use case. The tracked information needs to be stored in a way that it can be associated with the contribution. For the automated interaction with the system executed operations have to be documented, e. g. the update operation or data source.

Access to Provenance Information To be able to assess trust on the data appropriate means to access the recorded provenance information is needed. Also, the access to the data's provenance all the way down to the atomic level (insertions and deletions) can be very useful to backtrack the data transformation process and spotlight possible errors on different levels during the data life-cycle as well as in the data itself. Therefore, the provenance can be explored to improve data management and engineering processes. To utilize the provenance information that are recorded during the evolution of a dataset, they need to be represented in a queryable graph. Access to this graph has to be provided through a query interface. The interface has to return a structured representation of metadata recorded for the selected versions of a dataset. This is necessary as a prerequisite of the aspects publication and access, as well as dissemination and use of the provenance information (cf. [Gro+12]; [Hal+16a])

Random Access to any Version For a collaboration system it should be possible to randomly access any version of the dataset without the need for a rollback of the latest versions resp. resetting the storage system. For instance, when collaborators are working on different versions of the data at the same time. This allows queries across versions and it can support the debugging process.

Deltas Among Versions It is required to calculate the difference between versions generated by contributions of collaborators. The difference should express the actual changes on the dataset rather than changes to the serialization of the data in the repository. This is necessary when reviewing contributions to a dataset, e. g. by external contributors or in peer reviewing processes. The calculated difference should be expressed in a machine readable format.

The remainder of this chapter is structured as follows. We provide the basic definitions for a formal versioning model in section 4.1. Followed by a specification of the operations in section 4.2 which are performed within the Quit Model. In section 4.3 a system is presented which is able to automatically track the provenance information which accrues during the use of the Quit system. The collected information on the authors of changes and their reasons for a change lead to an often complex nexus of provenance information. With our provenance access interface this nexus can be queries in a structured way. To debug the evolution of provenance of a graph the comparison of versions is often necessary. The Quit Diff system is presented in section 4.4, it provides various structured formats to express, export, and transmit differences between versions of a dataset. Finally, we will draw our conclusions from this chapter in section 4.5.

4.1 Definitions

In this section we introduce a formalization to express changes to RDF graphs based on additions and deletions of atomic subgraphs. This foundational formal model is used to describe the more complex operations in sections 4.2 and 5.3. As it is commonly used in RDF and as we have defined it in section 2.1 we define a *graph* as a set of RDF triples and a *dataset* as a collection of graphs. We also consider isomorphic sub-graphs as identical and de-duplicate these sub-graphs during our operations.

According to Auer and Herre [AH06] an *Atomic Graph* is defined as follows:

Definition 6 (Atomic Graph) *A graph is called atomic if it can not be split into two nonempty graphs whose respective sets of blank nodes are disjoint.*

This implies that all graphs containing exactly one statement are atomic. Furthermore a graph is atomic if it contains a statement with at least on blank node and each pair of occurring blank nodes is connected by a sequence of statements where subject and object are blank nodes. If one of these statements additionally contains a second blank node, the same takes effect for this blank node recursively. A recursive definition of *Atomic Graphs* is given under the term *Minimum Self-Contained Graph* (MSG) by Tummarello et al. [Tum+07].

Let $\mathbb{A}$ be the set of all *Atomic Graphs* and let $\approx$ be the equivalence relation such that $G \approx H$ holds for any $G, H \in \mathbb{A}$ iff G and H are isomorphic as defined for RDF graphs in [CWL14]. Essentially two graphs are isomorphic in this sense if a bijection between these graphs exists that is the identity mapping for non-blank nodes and predicates and a bijection between blank-nodes. By $\mathcal{P} := \mathbb{A}/\approx$ we denote the quotient set of $\mathbb{A}$ by $\approx$. We assume a canonical labeling for blank nodes for any graph. The existence of such a labeling has been shown by Hogan [Hog15]. Thus a system of representatives of $\mathcal{P}$ is given by the set $\mathbb{P} \subset \mathbb{A}$ of all canonically labeled atomic graphs.

Based on this we now define the *Canonical Atomic Partition* of a graph as follows:

Definition 7 (Canonical Atomic Partition) *Given an RDF graph G, let $P_G \subset \mathbb{A}$ denote the partition of G into atomic graphs. We define a mapping $r : P_G \to \mathbb{P}$, such that $r(a) = p$, where p is the canonically labeled representative of a.*

The Canonical Atomic Partition *of the graph G is defined as*

$$\mathcal{P}(G) := \{r(x) | x \in P_G\}$$

$\mathcal{P}(G) \subset \mathbb{P}$ *and especially* $\mathcal{P}(G) \subset \mathbb{A}$.

Each of the contained sets consists of exactly one statement for all statements without blank nodes. For statements with blank nodes, it consists of the whole subgraph connected to a blank node and all neighboring blank nodes. This especially means that all sets in the *Atomic Partition* are disjoint regarding the contained blank nodes (cf. [AH06]; [Tum+07]). Further they are disjoint regarding the contained triples (because it is a partition).

Since $\mathcal{P}(G)$ is a set of atomic graphs, the union of its elements is a graph again and it is isomorphic to G,

$$\bigcup \mathcal{P}(G) \approx G.$$

Because we build a system for distributed collaboration on datasets, we need to find a way to express the changes that lead from one dataset to another. To express these changes we start by comparing two graphs by calculating the *difference*.

Definition 8 (Difference) *Let G and G' be two graphs, and $\mathcal{P}(G)$ resp. $\mathcal{P}(G')$ the* Canonical Atomic Partitions.

$$
\begin{aligned}
C^+ &:= \bigcup \left(\mathcal{P}(G') \setminus \mathcal{P}(G) \right) \\
C^- &:= \bigcup \left(\mathcal{P}(G) \setminus \mathcal{P}(G') \right) \\
\Delta(G, G') &:= (C^+, C^-)
\end{aligned}
$$

Looking at the resulting tuple (C^+, C^-) we can also say that the inverse of $\Delta(G, G')$ is $\Delta^{-1}(G, G') = \Delta(G', G)$ by swapping the positive and negative sets.

We now have the tuple of additions and deletions that describes the difference between two graphs. Thus we can say that applying the changes in this tuple to the initial graph G, leads to G'. Furthermore we can define a *Changeset* that can be applied on a graph G as follows:

Definition 9 (Changeset) *Given an RDF graph G, a changeset is a tuple of two graphs (C_G^+, C_G^-) in relation to G, with*

$$
\begin{aligned}
\mathcal{P}(C_G^+) &\cap \mathcal{P}(G) = \emptyset \\
\mathcal{P}(C_G^-) &\subset \mathcal{P}(G) \\
\mathcal{P}(C_G^+) &\cap \mathcal{P}(C_G^-) = \emptyset \\
\mathcal{P}(C_G^+) &\cup \mathcal{P}(C_G^-) \neq \emptyset
\end{aligned}
$$

Since blank nodes cannot be identified across graphs, there cannot
be any additions of properties to a blank node, nor can properties be
removed from a blank node. If a change to a statement involving a
blank node takes place, this operation is transformed into the removal
of one atomic graph and the addition of another atomic graph. Thus
$\mathcal{P}(C_G^+)$ and $\mathcal{P}(G)$ have to be disjoint. This means an addition cannot
introduce just new statements to an existing blank node. Parallel to the
addition, a blank node can only be removed if it is completely removed
with all its statements. This is ensured by $\mathcal{P}(C_G^-)$ being a subset of
$\mathcal{P}(G)$. Simple statements without blank nodes can be simply added
and removed. Further, since $\mathcal{P}(C_G^+)$ and $\mathcal{P}(C_G^-)$ are disjoint we avoid
the removal of atomic graphs that are added in the same changeset and
vice versa. Since at least one of $\mathcal{P}(C_G^+)$ or $\mathcal{P}(C_G^-)$ cannot be empty we
avoid changes with no effect. We define the *Application of a Change* as
follows:

Definition 10 (Application of a Change) *Given an RDF graph G, let $C_G =$*
(C_G^+, C_G^-) be a changeset on G. The function Apl is defined for the
arguments G, C_G respective $G, (C_G^+, C_G^-)$ and is determined by

$$Apl\left(G, (C_G^+, C_G^-)\right) := \bigcup \left((\mathcal{P}(G) \setminus \mathcal{P}(C_G^-)) \cup \mathcal{P}(C_G^+)\right)$$

We say that C_G is applied to G with the result G'.

4.2 Operations

Based on the formal model to express changes on RDF graphs, we can
now introduce our model to represent versioning operations. Collaborative editing of a common knowledge base is an evolutionary process
of creating new versions of the knowledge base. In order to manage
collaboration on Linked Data we face the problem of distributed authoring, distributed versioning, and parallel access to the knowledge
base. Evolution of data and contributions by distributed parties introduce the problem of overlapping update operations. The problem
was extensively studied as the problems of concurrency control and recovery in the context of conventional databases and collaborative file
exchange systems (cf. section 3.3). But these approaches treat changes
or transformations of the dataset as transactions which are executed
serially to support the illusion of transaction atomicity, which is considered correct [BHG87]. As we build a method to support people in
collaboration by expressing dissent we introduce a concept of diverging
version logs that does not require or enforce serializability. Moreover,
the diverged versioning log even allows to postpone the reconciliation
of diverged versions. This divergence does also help to express asynchrony of the knowledge base in a distributed workspace. Our version
tracking operations bring in support for non-linear versioning. The presented operations are *commit* to record changes in section 4.2.1, *branch*
to support divergence in section 4.2.2, *merge* in section 4.2.3, and *revert* to undo changes in section 4.2.4. Each version is related to the

respective RDF dataset and thus the versioning operations are related to the respective transformations of the RDF dataset.

4.2.1 Commit

Figure 4.3 depicts an initial commit $\mathcal{A}$ without any ancestor resp. parent commit and a commit $\mathcal{B}$ referring to its parent $\mathcal{A}$.

Figure 4.3: Two commits with an ancestor reference.

$$\mathcal{A}\left(\{G^0\}\right) \xleftarrow{(C^+_{G^0}, C^-_{G^0})} \mathcal{B}_{\{\mathcal{A}\}}\left(\{G\}\right)$$

Let G^0 be a graph under version control. $\mathcal{A}(\{G^0\})$ is a commit containing the graph G^0. G will be the new version of G^0 after a change $(C^+_{G^0}, C^-_{G^0})$ was applied on G^0; $Apl(G^0, (C^+_{G^0}, C^-_{G^0})) = G$. Now we create a new commit that contains G and refers to its ancestor commit, from which it was derived: $\mathcal{B}_{\{\mathcal{A}\}}(\{G\})$. Another change applied on G would result in G' and thus a new commit $\mathcal{C}_{\{\mathcal{B}_{\{\mathcal{A}\}}\}}(\{G'\})$ is created. In the further writing, the indices and arguments of commits are sometimes omitted for better readability, while clarity should still be maintained by using distinct letters. Further also the changeset on top of the arrow is omitted if it is obvious.

The evolution of a *graph* is the process of subsequently applying changes to the graph using the *Apl* function as defined in definition 10. Each commit expresses the complete evolution process of a set of graphs, since it refers to its ancestor, which in turn refers to its ancestor as well. Initial commits holding the initial version of the graph are not referring to any ancestor.

The entities involved in the commit operation are depicted in fig. 4.4. A commit, also called version, refers to its parent commit. One commit is created to describe the RDF dataset at this state of its evolution. As an RDF dataset can be in the same state at different points of its evolution (e. g. after a revert operation, cf. section 4.2.4), the same dataset can be contained in multiples commits. One RDF dataset consists of multiple graphs.

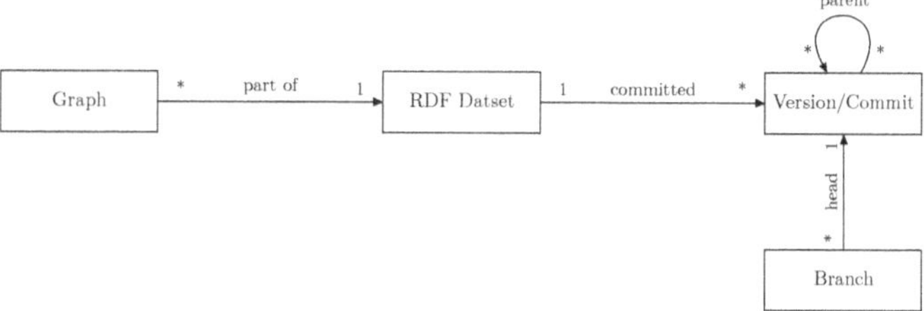

Figure 4.4: The conceptual model of Git as it is used by Quit. Inspired by the depiction by De Rosso and Jackson [DJ13].

4.2.2 Branch

Since a commit refers to its ancestor and not vice versa, nothing hinders us to create another commit $\mathcal{D}_{\{\mathcal{B}_{\{\mathcal{A}\}}\}}(\{G''\})$. Taking the commits $\mathcal{A}$, $\mathcal{B}_{\{\mathcal{A}\}}$, $\mathcal{C}_{\{\mathcal{B}\}}$, and $\mathcal{D}_{\{\mathcal{B}\}}$ results in a directed rooted in-tree, as depicted in fig. 4.5. The commit $\mathcal{D}$ is now a new *branch* or *fork* based on $\mathcal{B}$, which is diverged from $\mathcal{C}$. We know that $G \not\approx G'$ and $G \not\approx G''$, while we do not know about the relation between G' and G''.

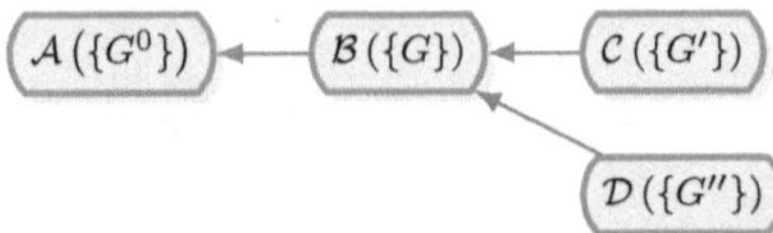

Figure 4.5: Two branches evolved from a common commit.

Because we do not know anything about the relation between G' and G'' we can consider them as independent. From now on the graph G is *independently* evolving in two branches, while *independent* means possibly independent, this means two contributors performing a change do not have to know of each other or do not need a direct communication channel. The contributors could actually communicate, but communication is not required for those actions. Thus by branching a dataset's evolution the contributors can be working from distributed places and no central instance for synchronization is required. We thus define the *branch* operation as follows:

Definition 11 (Branching) *Branching is the (independent) evolution of a graph G with two graphs G_1 and G_2 as result, where $Apl(G, C_1) = G_1$ and $Apl(G, C_2) = G_2$. The changes C_1 and C_2 might be unequal, but can be the same. The same applies for G_1 and G_2, they can be different after the independent evolution, but can be similar as well.*

To refer to a new branch we reference to the latest commit in this branch, called *HEAD*. In fig. 4.4 this is depicted by the entity *branch* that points to a commit as its HEAD. Multiple branches can refer to the same HEAD version, while each branch has exactly one HEAD version.

4.2.3 Merge Different Branches

After creating a second branch, the tree of commits is diverged, as shown in the example of fig. 4.5. We now want to merge the branches, in order to get a version of the graph, containing changes made in those different branches or at least take all of these changes into account. The notation of the merge is defined as follows:

Definition 12 (Merge of two Evolved Graphs) *Given are two commits $\mathcal{C}_{\{\beta\}}(\{G'\})$ and $\mathcal{D}_{\{\gamma\}}(\{G''\})$. Merging the two graphs G' and G'' with respect to the change history expressed by the commits $\mathcal{C}$ and $\mathcal{D}$ is a function*

$$Merge(\mathcal{C}(\{G'\}), \mathcal{D}(\{G''\})) = \mathcal{M}_{\{\mathcal{C}, \mathcal{D}\}}(\{G^\mu\})$$

The *Merge* function takes two commits as arguments and creates a new commit dependent on the input commits, this new commit is called *merge commit*. The graph G^μ is the *merged graph* resulting from G' and G''. The merge commit resulting from the merge operation has two ancestor commits that it refers to. If we take our running example, the merge commit is $\mathcal{M}_{\{\mathcal{C}_{\{\mathcal{B}\}}, \mathcal{D}_{\{\mathcal{B}\}}\}}(\{G^m\})$. Taking the commits $\mathcal{A}$, $\mathcal{B}_{\{\mathcal{A}\}}$, $\mathcal{C}_{\{\mathcal{B}\}}$, $\mathcal{D}_{\{\mathcal{B}\}}$, and $\mathcal{M}_{\{\mathcal{C}, \mathcal{D}\}}$, we get an acyclic directed graph, as it is depicted in fig. 4.6.

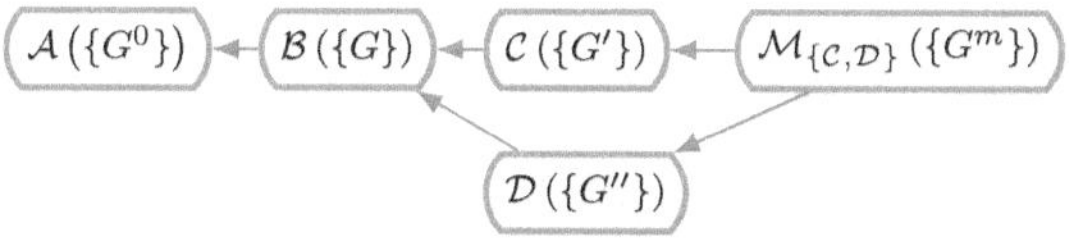

$$\mathcal{A}(\{G^0\}) \leftarrow \mathcal{B}(\{G\}) \leftarrow \mathcal{C}(\{G'\}) \leftarrow \mathcal{M}_{\{\mathcal{C},\mathcal{D}\}}(\{G^m\})$$
$$\mathcal{D}(\{G''\})$$

Figure 4.6: Merging commits from two branches into a common version of the graph

Note that the definition does not make any assumptions about the ancestors of the two input commits. It depends on the actual implementation of the *Merge* function whether it is required that both commits have any common ancestors. Furthermore different merge strategies can produce different results, thus it is possible to have multiple merge commits with different resulting graphs but with the same ancestors. Possible merge strategies are presented in section 5.3.

4.2.4 Revert a Commit

Reverting the commit $\mathcal{B}_{\{\mathcal{A}\}}(\{G\})$ is done by creating an inverse commit $\mathcal{B}^{-1}_{\{\mathcal{B}\}}(\{\tilde{G}^0\})$ (while the commit $\mathcal{A}$ is specified as $\mathcal{A}(\{G^0\})$). This inverse commit is then directly applied to $\mathcal{B}$. The resulting graph $\tilde{G}^0$ is calculated by taking the inverse difference $\Delta^{-1}(G^0, G) = \Delta(G, G^0)$ and applying the resulting change to G. After this operation $\tilde{G}^0 = G^0$.

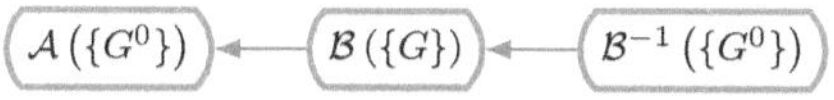

$$\mathcal{A}(\{G^0\}) \longleftarrow \mathcal{B}(\{G\}) \longleftarrow \mathcal{B}^{-1}(\{G^0\})$$

Figure 4.7: A commit reverting the previous commit

A versioning log containing three commits is shown in fig. 4.7. The last commit reverts its parent and thus the graph in $\mathcal{B}^{-1}$ is again equal or at least equivalent to the graph in the first commit ($\mathcal{A}$). While it is obvious how to revert the previous commits, it might be a problem if other commits exist between the commit to be reverted and the current top of the versioning log. In this case a merge is applied (cf. section 5.3). For this merge, the merge *base* is the commit to be reverted, branch $\mathcal{A}$ is the parent commit of the commit that is to be reverted, and branch $\mathcal{B}$ the current latest commit. Arising conflicts when reverting a commit can be resolved in the same way, as for merge commits.

4.3 Provenance

Our system is built as a tool stack on top of Git to extend it with semantic capabilities. We focus on a generic solution to present provenance information that can be applied to arbitrary domains. Since our approach gains all of its versioning and storage capabilities from the underlying Git repository, most of the metadata is already captured and maintained (cf. *Use* and *Management*, [Gro+12]). With respect to the *Quit Stack* the two main concerns are, (1) to make the already existing provenance information from Git semantically available and (2) check how and to which extend additional and domain-specific metadata can be stored in the version control structure.

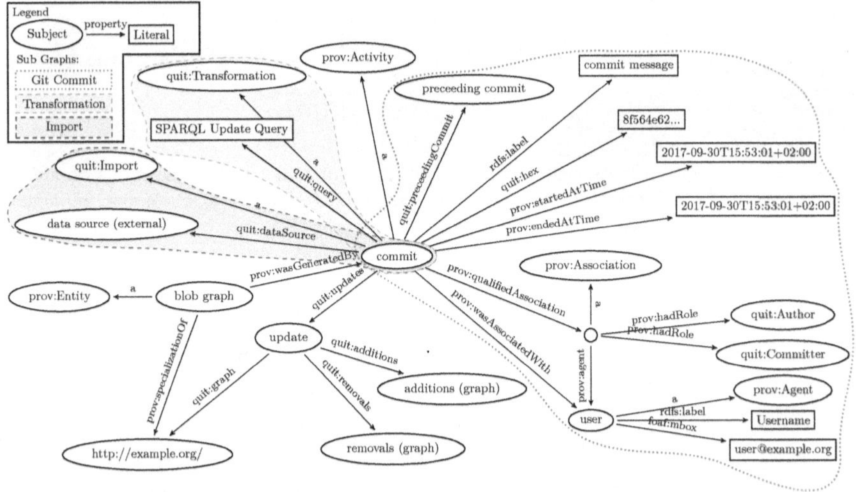

Figure 4.8: The provenance graph of a commit

Our effort is to transform the metadata, stored in the data model of Git (cf. section 2.5) to RDF making use of PROV-O. Figure 4.8 provides an overview of provenance data that we provide for a commit. The *Git Commit*-sub-graph shows the information that could be extracted from the metadata associated with a commit in Git. Commits in Git can be mapped to instances of the class `prov:Activity` associated with their author and committer. We follow the idea of De Nies et al. [De +13] and represent the start and end time of the activity with the author and commit date of Git, which can be interpreted as the time till a change was accepted. PROV-O has no concept for commenting on activities, therefore we follow the suggestion of PROV-O and use `rdfs:comment` for commit messages. Git users are instances of `prov:Agent`, stored with their provided name and email. We represent Git names as `rdfs:label` since they do not necessarily contain a full name nor necessarily a nick name. Additionally the role of the user is provided through a `prov:Association`. To represent the roles used by Git we provide `quit:author` and `quit:Committer`. Further we store the commit ID using the custom property `quit:hex`.

In addition to the information that we can extract from the Git data model, we enrich the commits stored in Git with additional metadata. The two additional provenance operations that we support are *Import* and *Transformation*, which are shown on the left side in fig. 4.8. For an import we store `quit:Import`, a subclass of `prov:Activity`, together with a `quit:dataSource` property. The *Import* sub-graph contains the source specification of a dataset by recording its original URL on the Web. The *Transformation* sub-graph describes a change on the dataset that is represented as a `quit:Transformation` activity and a `quit:query` property to record the SPARQL Update Query, which was executed and resulted in the new commit. To enable the highest portability of this additional provenance data we want to persist it alongside Git's commit data structure. The main problem here is that Git itself offers no built-in feature to store any user-defined metadata for commits or files. What Git offers instead is a functionality called `git notes`, which is a commentary function on commits. Hereby, Git creates a private branch where text files, named after the commit they comment on, resides. The problem with this functionality is, that notes are not integrated into the commit storage. These notes are not included in the calculation of the object hash resp. commit ID and thus they are not protected against unperceived changes. Because we want to rely on all provenance information equally our decision is to provide and obtain additional metadata as part of the commit message as shown in listing 4.1. Commit messages are unstructured data, meaning it will not break the commit when additional structured data is provided at the start or end of a message. More specific key words to identify provenance operations other than *Source* and *Update* can be added as needed.

```
tree 31159f4524edf41e306c3c5148ed7734db1e777d
parent 3fe8fd20a44b1737e18872ba8a049641f52fb9ef
author pnaumann <patrick.naumann@stud.htwk-leipzig.de> 1487675007 +0100
committer pnaumann <patrick.naumann@stud.htwk-leipzig.de> 1487675007 +0100

Source: http://dbpedia.org/data/Leipzig.n3

Example Import
```

Listing 4.1: Git commit with additional data.

Additionally to the metadata that we can extract from a Git commit or that we encode in the commit message we have extended the graph with more information on the content of the dataset. In this case we store every named graph contained in a file as an instance of `prov:Entity`. We link the `prov:Entity` with the respective commit via `prov:wasGeneratedBy`. Each entity is attributed to the general graph URI using the `prov:specializationOf` property. The general graph is the URI of the graph under version control. Optionally we can also extend the provenance graph with the complete update information. For this purpose the `quit:update` property is used to reference the update node.

The update node is linked to the original graph and the two named-graphs containing the added and deleted statements.

Accessing Provenance Information To access the provenance information we follow the recommendation of the *PROV-AQ: Provenance Access and Query* [Mor+13a]. We provide two kinds of SPARQL interfaces, one service for the provenance graph and one individual interface for each state in the history of the dataset (cf. section 5.1). The provenance graph is built from the metadata provided by Git and combined with the additional metadata stored in the commit messages.

By employing a standard SPARQL interface to access and query the provenance information it is possible to analyze the information with specified tools. In fig. 4.9 a merge activity performed using the Quit Store is visualized from the provenance graph using the PROV-O-Viz tool [HG14]. The figure shows which activities were influences by which other activities and which artifacts were generated or taken into account by the respective activities.

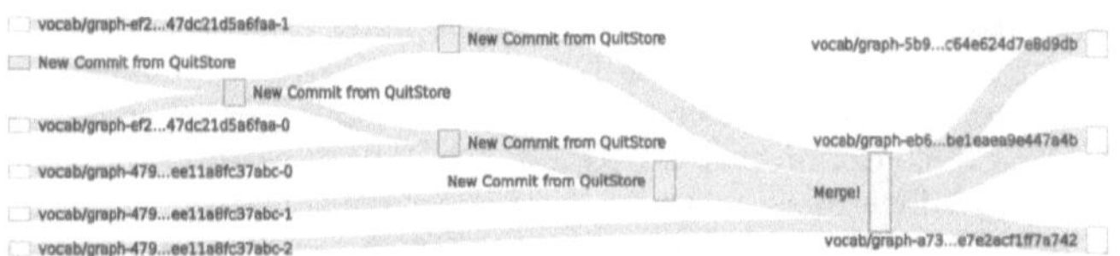

Figure 4.9: The PROV-O-Viz tool visualizing a merge activity on the provenance graph retrieved through the provenance SPARQL endpoint.

Quit Blame As an example for the usage of the provenance feature we built a blame method for graphs. The blame method retrieves for the current version of a dataset the origin of each individual statement and associates it with its entry in the provenance graph. This feature is similar to the functionality of `git blame` for source code. This is especially relevant for debugging work on the data and to trace the accountability for contributed changes to the data. The example in fig. 4.10 shows three versions of a dataset and on the right side the "blame." For each statement the version when it was inserted is identified, in the figure this is highlighted using colors. By attaching this information to each statement it is possible to identify the respective authors and time of insertion. To implement this behavior on our provenance graph we utilize the SPARQL query as depicted in listing 4.2. As an input to the query we list all statements for which we want to identify the origin with subject `?s`, predicate `?p`, object `?o`, and named-graph `?context` in listing 4.2, line 13. For the execution of the query we loop through the list of commits starting at the current commit that is bound to the variable `?commit`. The query is then executed on the provenance graph until for all statements an originating commit was found.

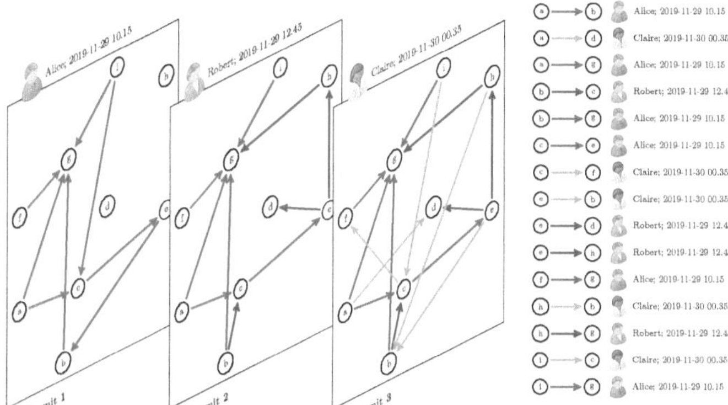

Figure 4.10: Analysis of the provenance of statements in a graph that evolved over three commits using Quit blame.

```
1  SELECT ?s ?p ?o ?context ?commit ?name ?email ?date
2  WHERE {
3    ?commit prov:endedAtTime ?date ;
4            prov:wasAssociatedWith ?user ;
5            quit:updates ?update .
6    ?user   foaf:mbox ?email ;
7            rdfs:label ?name .
8    ?update quit:graph ?context ;
9            quit:additions ?additions .
10   GRAPH ?additions {
11     ?s ?p ?o
12   }
13   VALUES (?s ?p ?o ?context) {
14     ...
15   }
16 }
```

Listing 4.2: Query for git blame implementation.

4.4 Quit Diff

Distributed actors working on a common RDF dataset regularly encounter the issue to compare the status of one graph with another or generally to synchronize copies of a dataset. A versioning system helps to synchronize the copies of a dataset, combined with a difference calculation system it is also possible to compare versions in a versioning log and to determine in which version a certain statement was introduced or removed. In this section we present *Quit Diff*,[3] a tool to compare versions of an RDF dataset. It is especially targeted at Git versioned quad store like the Quit Store but is also applicable to individual unversioned RDF datasets. It can be integrated into an existing Git system as *difftool* to compare different versions of an RDF dataset and allows the exploration of the versioning log. iWe are following an approach to abstract from differences on a syntactical level to differences on the level of the RDF data model while we leave further semantic interpretation on the schema and instance level to specialized applications. In contrast to the syntactical changes, printed by `git diff`, *Quit Diff* is able to calculate the actual differences of the RDF data model and in turn displays them in various RDF formats and as SPARQL Update queries. For expressing differences between RDF datasets multiple formats exist, such as the changeset vocabulary (`cs:`), the `eccrev:` vocabulary or TopBraid's `diff:` vocabulary. But also SPARQL 1.1 Update [GPP13] queries can be used to specify a set of added and deleted triples. These diff-formats can help to transmit and apply only the changes of datasets as patches instead of copying the complete store. *Quit Diff* can generate patches in various output formats and can be integrated into the DVCS of the *Quit Store* which provides a foundation for a comprehensive co-evolution work flow on RDF datasets.

4.4.1 The Problem of Difference Calculation

A diff utility on file systems is used to show the differences between two files in a line-based approach. Typically but not necessarily these are two different versions that originate from the same original file. The diff tool shipped with Unix in the early 1970s was described by their programmers Hunt and McIlroy [HM76] as follows: *The program* diff *reports differences between two files, expressed as a minimal list of line changes to bring either file into agreement with the other.* The produced output is called *diff* or *patch*. Those changes may be deletions or insertions of lines, a changed line is expressed as a combination of deletion and insertion. The file which is given at the first position is interpreted as the old version of the file while the second file is the new version. A common usage of the diff tool is to compare two versions of a program code file in order to determine the actual changes or to

---

[3] *QuitDiff*. The QuitDiff Repository at GitHub: `https://github.com/AKSW/Quit Diff` [Web:Qui18a]

generate a patch.[4] Transferring and applying this patch to an existing source code repository is easier and more flexible then reinitializing a complete new file structure.

By using textual representations of RDF data with any line-based serialization format the syntactical diffs are sufficient to reconstruct a version of an RDF file by applying a patch. But to generate an expressive diff between the files that can be used to identify which information in terms of RDF statements was added or removed the syntactical diff is not appropriate. Since for RDF several serialization formats are available it is not possible to to compare the same RDF datasets expressed in different serializations. The syntactical approach would not always include all necessary information for a statement e.g. for formats like RDF-XML or Turtle. For example with Turtle the diff includes only a predicate-object pair or a single object, if abbreviations are used. Further blank nodes introduce the problem of switching between scopes when comparing two files or applying a patch. Canonical representations of the data can be used to allow a stable comparison. A suitable representation can be a canonical skolemized RDF serialization format [CWL14] with N-Triples or N-Quads. This can produce line-based diffs which are equivalent to the triple-based changes of the serialized RDF graphs. But using a canonical representation would introduce the complexity of temporary canonicalization of the graph representations for the purpose of the comparison. The resulting line-based difference then still needs to be parsed with a special parser that understands the semantics of the diff/patch format.

When comparing RDF datasets consisting of multiple graphs it is further relevant to find the correct graphs to compare. If both, the remote file and the local file, are RDF datasets, it is straight forward to compare each contained graph with the graph identified by the same IRI respectively. While if one compares an RDF Graph serialization with an RDF dataset file, the RDF graph can only be compared with the default graph of the RDF dataset.

4.4.2 The Quit Diff Approach

In order to generate patches between different versions of RDF data, we decided to take an approach to generate logical diffs. The *Quit Diff* tool can calculate the difference between RDF datasets independent of the used serialization formats. For example *Quit Diff* is able to compare a Turtle serialized RDF graph with an RDF/XML serialized RDF graph or multiple RDF graphs in different files with a quad serialized RDF dataset. The delta between the individual graphs is then determined in two sets each, added and removed triples per graph. For the output multiple formats are supported, three changeset ontologies and SPARQL 1.1 Update queries.

The diff tool expects two parameters, *left* and *right*, that may be a path of a file or a path of a directory. In our example let there

---

[4] This can be achieved with `diff -Naur old new > changes.patch` which can then be
applied with the `patch` utility

```
<http://aksw.org/NatanaelArndt>
    ↪ <http://www.w3.org/1999/02/22-rdf-syntax-ns#type>
    ↪ <http://xmlns.com/foaf/0.1/Person> <http://aksw.org/> .
<http://aksw.org/NatanaelArndt> <http://xmlns.com/foaf/0.1/mbox>
    ↪ <mailto:arndt@informatik.uni-leipzig.de> <http://aksw.org/> .


aksw:NormanRadtke a foaf:Person ;
    foaf:mbox <mailto:radtke@informatik.uni-leipzig.de> .
```

Listing 4.3: A N-Quads file (in revision A) describing Natanael Arndt.

Listing 4.4: A Turtle file (in revision A) describing Norman Radtke.

be a directory *profiles* containing two files, *arndt.nq* (listing 4.3) and *radtke.ttl* (listing 4.4). In case of a directory the Diff Tool will analyze all containing files and distinguish between RDF serialized files and the rest. RDF serialized files will be detected by their suffix and will be loaded in a separate ad hoc in-memory quad store for each *left* and *right*. After the loading procedure is completed the two resulting stores are canonicalized using the `IsomorphicGraph()` class from the `rdflib.compare`[5] package. The algorithm is based on the work of Sayers and Karp [SK04]. To get two comparable canonicalized graphs the triples of each named graph and of the default graph (if no named graph is given e.g. for triple serializations) are collected for each directory *left* and *right*.

```
<urn:changeset:453a9f60> a cs:ChangeSet ;
    cs:addition [ a rdf:Statement ;
            rdf:object aksw:NatanaelArndt ;
            rdf:predicate foaf:knows ;
            rdf:subject aksw:NormanRadtke ] .


<urn:changeset:453a9f61> a cs:ChangeSet ;
    cs:addition [ a rdf:Statement ;
            rdf:object aksw:NormanRadtke ;
            rdf:predicate foaf:knows ;
            rdf:subject aksw:NatanaelArndt ] ;
    cs:subjectOfChange <http://aksw.org/> .
```

Listing 4.5: A diff between revision A and B serialized as a patch, expressed using the changeset ontology.

To create a new revision B on top of A which we can use for the comparison we add a `foaf:knows` statement between the two persons respectively. If we run *Quit Diff* to create a patch between these two revisions, a possible result is shown in listing 4.5. Going on from revision B to revision C we add a triple to the N-Quads file *arndt.nq* containing the phone number. We add the same information to the Turtle file *radtke.ttl* resulting in the files shown in listings 4.6 and 4.7. When we now calculate the difference between revision A and C we receive the patch expressed as a SPARQL 1.1 Update query is given in listing 4.8.

Since *Quit Diff* should allow its users to further exploit the information gained from a diff operation it offers multiple output formats. The following ways of expressing patches or changes between

---

[5] *RDFLib compare.py*. The Graph comparison module of the RDFLib at GitHub:

```
<http://aksw.org/NatanaelArndt>
    ↪ <http://www.w3.org/1999/02/22-rdf-syntax-ns#type>
    ↪ <http://xmlns.com/foaf/0.1/Person> <http://aksw.org/> .
<http://aksw.org/NatanaelArndt> <http://xmlns.com/foaf/0.1/knows>
    ↪ <http://aksw.org/NormanRadtke> <http://aksw.org/> .
<http://aksw.org/NatanaelArndt> <http://xmlns.com/foaf/0.1/mbox>
    ↪ <mailto:arndt@informatik.uni-leipzig.de> <http://aksw.org/> .
<http://aksw.org/NatanaelArndt> <http://xmlns.com/foaf/0.1/phone>
    ↪ <tel:+49-341-9732323> .
```

Listing 4.6: A N-Quads file (in revision C) describing Natanael Arndt.

```
aksw:NormanRadtke a foaf:Person ;
    foaf:knows aksw:NatanaelArndt ;
    foaf:phone <tel:+49-341-9732323> ;
    foaf:mbox <mailto:radtke@informatik.uni-leipzig.de> .
```

Listing 4.7: A Turtle file (in revision C) describing Norman Radtke.

two RDF datasets are supported so far: SPARQL 1.1 Update (cf. listing 4.8), Changeset Ontology (cf. listing 4.5), Topbraid and Eccenca Revision. The most straight forward format to apply a patch might be the SPARQL 1.1 Update under the condition that a SPARQL endpoint with update functionality is available. The other formats need an implementation to apply the patches and they would allow querying and reasoning on the RDF model.

4.4.3 Integration of RDF Difference Calculation

The *Quit Diff* tool is designed as a stand-alone difftool for RDF datasets as well as drop-in replacement for `git diff` respective for usage with `git difftool` in Git repositories containing RDF datasets. Due to the implementation as command line tool it could also be integrated as back-end for compare operations in graphical RDF editing tools such as protégé[6] or OntoWiki[Fri+15]; [FAM16]. The main features of *Quit Diff* are not only to compare triples contained in individual RDF graphs but also RDF datasets in quad serialization formats as well as directories of multiple RDF graph files. It brings an integration for Git and support for three RDF vocabularies to express patches and for SPARQL Update operations.

Quit Diff is designed to be integrated in Git as a socalled *difftool*. This enables the user to call it by executing the command `git difftool`

---

[6] *protégé Ontology Editor.*

```
insert data {
    aksw:NormanRadtke foaf:phone <tel:+49-341-9732323> .
    aksw:NormanRadtke foaf:knows aksw:NatanaelArndt .
    aksw:NatanaelArndt foaf:phone <tel:+49-341-9732323> .

    graph <http://aksw.org/> {
        aksw:NatanaelArndt foaf:knows aksw:NormanRadtke .
    }
}
```

Listing 4.8: A diff generated as SPARQL Update.

or `git diff`. The differences between these two approaches and the advantages to couple *Quit Diff* with Git is to directly navigate on the complete Git versioning graph and comparing arbitrary commits. Further the `--dir-diff` option for `difftool` allows us to compare complete directories as RDF datasets with quad serialization formats.

```
[diff "quitdiff"]
    command = quitdiff.py

[difftool "quitdiff"]
    cmd = quitdiff.py --diffFormat sparql --local=\"$LOCAL\"
        ↪ --remote=\"$REMOTE\" --merged=\"$MERGES\" --base=\"$BASE\"
```

Listing 4.9: The ~/.gitconfig configuration file for Git to use *Quit Diff* as comparison tool. Git understands two kinds of comparison commands with a different syntax, diff and difftool, where the later can also perform three-way-comparison. Quit Diff supports command syntax formats.

```
*.nq diff=quitdiff
```

Listing 4.10: The .gitattributes configuration file to configure an individual Git repository to use the difftool as previously configured to compare N-Quads files.

Listing 4.9 shows a section of the `~/.gitconfig` file to integrate *Quit Diff* with G it. In order to set the configured difftool as default comparison method for a file type in the repository the `.gitattributes` configuration file needs to be created and customized.[7] To set the difftool as configured in listing 4.9 as default for N-Quads files the `.gitattributes` file just needs to contain the line as shown in listing 4.10.

4.5 Conclusion

In this chapter the Quit methodology was introduced. The methodology combines concepts from the knowledge engineering in particular the Semantic Web and the Software engineering. Based on the abstract requirements (a-f, h) a set of concrete requirements to be fulfilled by the methodology are defined. To be able to work with the combined concepts from Semantic Web and Software engineering four models were defined to fulfill the re quirements: the formalized model of change and graph calculations in section 4.1, the non-linear versioning model in section 4.2, the provenance model in section 4.3, and the quit diff model to calculate changes in section 4.4.

With the Atomic Graphs we are able to identify the smallest possible unit of change that can be exchanged while still maintaining the context of blank nodes. Based on the Canonical Atomic Partition of a graph we are able to perform difference calculation on a graph with respect to blank nodes. With this difference operation to express the change of a

---

[7] *Git: Git Attributes*:

graph we can express a changeset and the application of the changeset to a graph. With this application of a changeset we are able to express the evolution of a graph.

Based on the graph calculations we build a versioning system of datasets and define the versioning operations *commit, branch, merge* and *revert*. The *commit* operation is the fundamental operation of creating a new state of a dataset derived from an ancestor state. The *branch* operation allows to create a new diverging versioning log that can be reconciled using the *merge* operation. With the *revert* operation changes performed in the versioning log can be undone in a later stage. With this non-linear versioning model we are not constrained to reach serializability of all performed operations. Instead, we could provide a model to express multiple diverging versioning logs to express dissent and asynchrony. The dissent and asynchrony can also be reconciled to build a new common versioning log. This conceptual model is the foundation for the subsequent chapters.

We provided a model for storing and accessing provenance information which are created during the collaboration process for the distributed evolution of a knowledge graph. We are able to track the provenance information on any update operation on the dataset. The combination of all provenance information is stored in an RDF provenance graph. This includes the complete branched and merged version history expressed following the standardized PROV-O model extended with some custom properties. With this graph we are able to explore the recorded data using a standard SPARQL interface. Due to the atomic level of provenance tracking the provenance information can be derived in two dimensions. From changes to individual atomic graphs we can directly conclude to a resource, graph, and dataset. In this way statements like *The dataset was changed by X on date Y* and also *The resource Z was changed by X on date Y* are possible. Also on the granularity level of the executed operations we make information available on the level of the individual addition or deletion of an atomic graph respective statement. But also the combination of changes bundled in one commit is stored alongside with the executed query that lead to the change. Thus the provenance information is available on all levels of both dimensions *data-granularity* and *granularity of the change operation*. Using `quit blame` we are able to track down the origin of any individual statement in a dataset. The *Quit Diff* method allows to perform further *debugging* tasks on the data by comparing arbitrary versions of the dataset. It can be integrated into the DVCS Git to explore changes of RDF datasets under version control. In contrast to the diff tool provided by most operating systems and the tool shipped with Git the *Quit Diff* tool interprets the RDF datasets and calculates the actual changes according to the RDF data model. The tool supports multiple output formats which allow the transmission and application of patches to various system. Especially the SPARQL Update output allows the application of patches to any system that provides a standard SPARQL 1.1 Update interface.

5 The Quit Stack

Tools to create and edit RDF knowledge bases exist but often lack support for collaborative scenarios. It involves a high complexity to extend existing single place editing and exploration systems with collaboration functionality. We introduce the *Quit Stack* as a layered approach that defines appropriate interfaces. It provides an integration layer to make the collaborative features of the abstract Quit methodology accessible to applications operating on RDF datasets.

As introduced in section 1.2 and already discussed in chapter 4 the relevant requirements to the implementation of the Quit Stack are to provide a *distributed workspace* (a) with support for *dissent* (b) and *asynchrony* (c) as well as the possibility to *synchronize* (d) asynchronous workspaces and to *reconcile* (e) dissent knowledge bases. Further, it is also relevant for this section to consider to track and publish *provenance information* (h). With the implementation of the Quit Stack we build on the conceptualized abstract versioning system as specified in section 4.2. The Git system (cf. section 2.5) is employed to implement the distributed workspace, branching, merging, and synchronization. It stores the version history of the data together with the RDF provenance metadata (cf. section 4.3). To query and update the knowledge base the standardized SPARQL 1.1 Query and Update Language is used (cf. section 2.2). Also the associated provenance graph is accessed using the SPARQL 1.1 Query Language. Each HTTP request containing SPARQL Update requests effecting the knowledge base is executed and committed to the underlying repository. The repository interface allows to perform branching operations to express dissent with different versions of a knowledge base and it allows to perform merge operations to reconcile knowledge bases. As the versioning model of the Quit Stack is stored in a Git repository it is possible to synchronize asynchronous repositories using the Git protocol. In addition to the fundamental requirements for a distributed collaboration system we formulate two more requirements that are relevant for the collaboration on RDF knowledge bases.

Support of RDF Data Sets and Modularization of Graphs   The system should be able to handle multiple RDF graphs (i. e. RDF datasets) in a repository. This allows users respective collaborators to organize the stored knowledge in individual structural units as it is required by their application. This requirement is also necessary to support the vocabulary authoring process to create modular vocabularies to reduce complexity and support ownership, customization, and reuse of individual components [Hal+16a]. Modularization of RDF datasets into individual graphs is important on different levels of granularity and to support various func-

The results presented in this chapter were first published in Arndt, Radtke, and Martin: "Distributed Collaboration on RDF Datasets Using Git: Towards the Quit Store" [ARM16]; Arndt and Martin: "Decentralized Evolution and Consolidation of RDF Graphs" [AM17]; Arndt, Naumann, and Marx: "Exploring the Evolution and Provenance of Git Versioned RDF Data" [ANM17]; Arndt et al.: "Decentralized Collaborative Knowledge Management using Git" [Arn+19a and Arndt and Radtke: "Conflict Detection, Avoidance, and Resolution in a Non-Linear RDF Version Control System: The Quit Editor Interface Concurrency Control" [AR19].

tionality. Such functionality that requires modularized datasets are for instance access control, separation of concerns, replication of graphs,[1] application specific provenance tracking, and application specific versioning (e. g. when working on data of historic periods of time). This is of interest when the system is integrated with existing systems.

Standard Data Access Interface Different implementations of collaborative user interfaces can access a common repository and enable collaboration on it. Collaborators are used to different RDF editors to contribute to the repository. The possibility to attach single place systems to a collaboration infrastructure by using well defined interfaces allows the creation of collaborative setups without the need of creating new tools. An architecture that includes well established tools for special tasks and employs standardized interfaces to integrate these tools is called a microservice and follows and supports the single responsibility principle as formulated in the context of the *UNIX philosophy* as "make each program do one thing well" [Gan95]; [Gan03]. Users can thus continue using their existing tools, daily workflows, and familiar interfaces. To some extent the methodology should even be robust to manual editing of RDF files contained in the repository. In contrast to the requirement *Editor agnostic (R8)* as formulated in [Hal+16a], we do not require the syntax independence on the repository and understand the editor agnosticism as transparency of the provided application interface. Besides the adherence to the RDF data format the system also has to provide a data access and update interface following the SPARQL 1.1 standard (cf. section 2.2).

In the remainder of this chapter we will first specify the interfaces provided by the Quit Stack in section 5.1. We discuss and introduce the canonical representation of the dataset that is used throughout the Quit Stack in section 5.2. Several implementations of the merge operation with different properties are presented in section 5.3. Finally, we conclude the chapter in section 5.4.

5.1 Quit Interface

> *Interface:* A common boundary between two systems, devices, or programs. [...] Specification of the communication between two program units.
> (*A Dictionary of Computer Science*, [BNK16])

An interface is a boundary as well as a shared medium following a specification to enable communication. The communication follows a common language of concepts to interact between two levels of abstraction. This allows to make different parts of a system transparent to an application and even its users. With the *Quit Application Programming*

---

[1] *Managing RDF Using Named Graphs:* h

Interface (Quit API) we provide an interface to communicate with each component of the *Quit Stack*. An overview of the individual components of the Quit Stack with the defined interfaces is given in fig. 5.1. The Quit Stack consists of three subsystems: the *Repository Interface*, the *Query & Update Interface*, and the *Provenance Interface*. Both, the *Query & Update Interface* and the *Provenance Interface* provide query and update interfaces following the Semantic Web standards SPARQL 1.1 Query & Update to retrieve RDF data. In addition the *Query & Update Interface* allows to retrieve a dump of the RDF dataset. The *Blame* and *Commits* interfaces allow to retrieve metadata describing the RDF dataset. The *Repository Interface* is a management interfaces to control the versioning logs and to exchange them with remote workspaces.

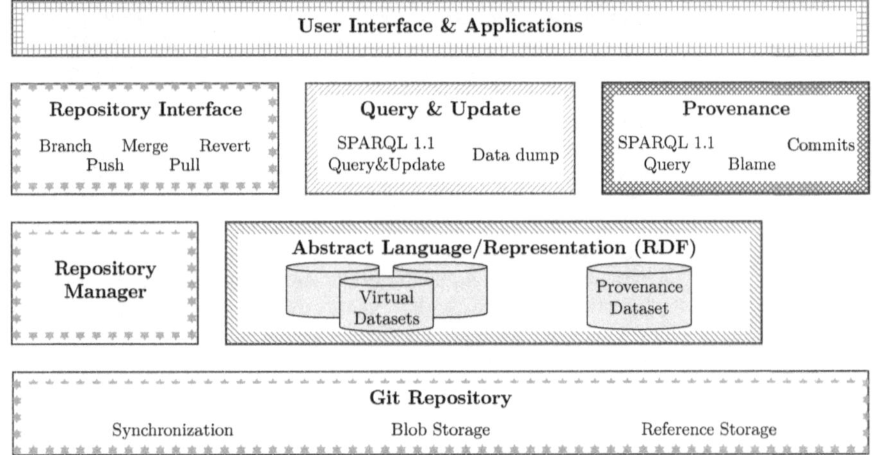

underlying storage of the RDF dataset is implemented by an in-memory quad store as provided by the RDFlib and a local Git repository that is kept in sync with the corresponding named graphs in the store. Every graph is stored in a canonicalized N-Quads serialization (cf. section 5.2).

Dataset Access   To provide access to the versioned RDF dataset a number of standard SPARQL 1.1 Query & Update endpoints are provided. The default endpoint provides access to the current latest version of the dataset (cf. listing 5.1, line 1). For each branch (cf. listing 5.1, line 2) and for each version in the history respective commit in the repository (cf. listing 5.1, line 3) of the dataset an additional endpoint is provided. All of these endpoints execute the SPARQL requests on a number of *virtual graphs* (cf. fig. 5.1). The virtual graphs are instantiated on request from the Git data structure (cf. fig. 5.2 and section 5.2) and stored in the internal quad store. The graphs are combined to a virtual dataset, the Query or Update request is evaluated on the dataset, and the result is returned to the user. For Update requests effective changes on the dataset are applied to the Git storage structure and a new commit is created. For better response times the latest version of the dataset as well as the most recently used graphs are cached (cf. fig. 5.2) in the quad store.

In a distributed collaborative system with write access also the concurrency problem has to be considered. The SPARQL 1.1 standard does not provide measures to deal with concurrent access. We have extended the SPARQL 1.1 protocol in a fully backward compatible manner to support concurrency with the Quit Editor Interface Concurrency Control which is further described in section 6.2.

For the provenance data we provide a dedicated SPARQL 1.1 Query endpoint (cf. listing 5.1, line 4). The provenance data is stored in a data set consisting of the provenance graph which is available through the default graph. The additional named graphs contain changesets of statements added and deleted for the creation of the commits. The provenance graph is built from the metadata provided by Git and combined with the additional metadata stored in the commit messages. The metadata is extracted from the Git data structure and transformed to an RDF graph. The Git commit history of each branch is traversed from the latest to the oldest commit. The depth of this traversal as well as the selection of the relevant branches are configurable according to the user's needs. Therefore the size of the provenance graph can be reduced for devices with low storage capacities at the cost of time to construct the graph on request.

Listing 5.1: Dataset endpoint URLs.

Git Interface   The major operations on a versioning system are *commit* to create a new version in the version log as well as *merge*, and *revert* as operations on the version log. The commit operation is implemented by Update-Queries though the dataset access interface. To also allow the execution of *branch, merge,* and *revert* we make the operations provided by Git available through a web interface (cf. listing 5.2).

```
1 http://quit.local...
2   /branch/<oldbranch>:<newbranch>
3   /merge/<branch>:<target>?method=<strategy>
4   /revert/<target>?commit=<commitId>
```

Listing 5.2: Merge and Revert Interfaces.

Synchronization Between Instances   So far all operations were executed on a local versioning graph that can diverge and be merged, but still, no collaboration with remote participants is possible. To allow collaboration on the World Wide Web, the versioning graph can be published (*push*) to a remote repository, from where other collaborators can copy (*clone*) the whole graph. If a collaborator already has cloned a previous version of the versioning graph, they can update their local graph by executing a *pull*. The default Git operations *pull* and *push* are also available via the Quit Store HTTP interface as shown in listing 5.3. They allow the user to synchronize with remote repositories.

```
1 http://quit.local/push/<remote name>/<local>:<remote branch>
2 http://quit.local/fetch/<remote name>/<remote branch>
3 http://quit.local/pull/<remote name>/<remote branch>:<local>
```

Listing 5.3: Push and Pul Interfaces.

5.2 Dataset Storage and Canonical Representation

To store the versioned RDF dataset we build on the basic concepts of Git (cf. section 2.5). Each versioned object in Git (i.e. files, directory trees, as well as commits) is stored as a binary large object (blob) and can be retrieved using a hash that is calculated based on the content. Each Git blob can be retrieved randomly on average in linear time. When a new commit is prepared new blobs containing snapshots of the changed files and directory trees are created. Unchanged files already exist in the blob storage as the blobs were created for a previous commit. To construct the new commit in Git a new commit object is created that references all contained newly created and preexisting blobs. Due to this concept as many objects as possible are reused for a new revision. In the case of an RDF dataset new Git blobs are created only for the modified RDF graphs. Each version of the dataset can be reconstructed by combining the respective graph snapshots. Figure 5.2 depicts the reuse of snapshots between versions in the repository. To reconstruct the dataset from a certain commit the respective graph blobs have to be loaded into the virtual graphs that constitute the dataset. The setup of the repository corresponds to the archiving policy *fragment based* (FB) as defined in section 3.5.4. To further reduce the storage consumption for the dataset fragments a delta-compression is employed. This delta compression is called as garbage collection[6] from time to time. It removes orphan objects and combines multiple Git blobs in a pack that reduces redundancy within the data. The garbage collection feature is enables on startup of the store using the -gc command line argument.

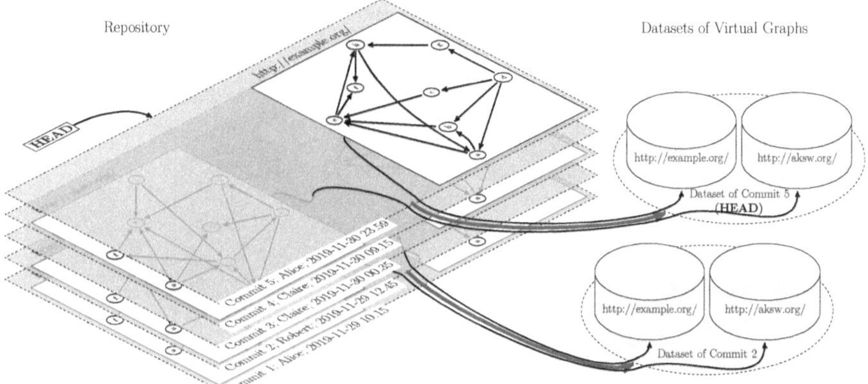

Figure 5.2: Creating a dataset from all available revisions of named graphs.

RDF graphs and RDF datasets can be serialized in different formats and thus the same RDF statements can result in completely different textual representations. Even the same graph or dataset serialized twice in the same serialization format can be textually different. The standardized serialization formats are RDF/XML, Turtle, TriG, RDFa, N-Triples, N-Quads, and JSON-LD (cf. section 2.1.3). As we want to store the RDF dataset decomposed in individual RDF graphs we do not need one of the Quad serialization formats, TriG or N-Quads. The RDFa format is designed to be embedded in HTML documents and thus does not fit our n eeds. The formats RDF/XML, Turtle, and JSON-LD, in contrast to N-Triples do not store one statement per line. Also due to additional syntax features besides the pure RDF data, like prefixes and the abbreviation features of Turtle (using ; or , as delimiter) as well as multi line literals, automatic line merges can destroy the syntax. Similar problems would occur with the other serialization formats listed above. To allow a good readability, exploitation of the storage capabilities, and processability of the differences b etween t wo versions in the VCS, we have to find an easy t o c ompare c anonical serialization format.

For our approach we have decided to use the N-Triples serialization [CS14a] in Git repositories. N-Triples is a line-based plain text format

---

that represents one statement per line. Since many Git tools also treat lines as atoms statements in N-Triples are automatically treated as atomic units. The serialization of N-Triples follows the *canonical form of N-Triples* that includes the canonical representation of IRIs, blank nodes, and Literals [CS14a]. To further ensure stability and comparability of the files we maintain a sorted list of statements during the serialization.

The Quit Stack is designed to enable the collaboration on RDF Datasets. This requires the system to manage multiple RDF Graphs that can be identified using IRIs. To include the graphs IRI into our repository layout we attach IRIs to the graph files stored in the repository. We follow the method used by the *Open Link Virtuoso* bulk loading process.[7] This method involves an additional file next to each graph serialization with the same filename and the additional file extension `.graph` that contains the graph IRI. For example, to load the file `example.nt` into the graph `http://example.org/` the additional file `example.nt.graph` is created and only contains the string of the IRI.

5.3 Merge Strategies

Since we are not only interested in the abstract branching and merging model of the commits, we want to know what a merge operation means for the created graph in the commit. In the following we present some possible implementations of the merge operations. Note, that *merging* in this context is not – generally – to be understood as in the *RDF 1.1 Semantics Recommendation* [HP14] as the union of two graphs.

5.3.1 Union Merge

Merging two *graphs* G' and G'' could be considered trivially as the union operation for the two graphs: $G' \cup G'' = G'''$. This merge, as it is mentioned above, is well defined in the *RDF 1.1 Semantics Recommendation* [HP14] in section "4.1 Shared blank nodes, unions and merges." But this operation does not take into account the actual change operations leading to the versions of the graphs. Furthermore, the union merge does not allow the implementation of conflict detection or resolution operations. The union merge is intended in situations, where data is only added from different locations.

5.3.2 All Ours/All Theirs

Two other merge strategies that do not produce merge conflicts are *ours* and *theirs*. These merge strategies just take the whole graph $G' =: G'''$ or $G'' =: G'''$ as new version, while they are ignoring the other graph respectively. This strategy can be chosen to completely discard changes from a certain branch.

---

[7] *Virtuoso Open Source Bulk loading process:*

| A | B | base | result | $\Delta(G, G')$ | | $\Delta(G, G'')$ | | |
G'	G''	G	G^m	C_A^+	C_A^-	C_B^+	C_B^-	
○	○	○	○	○	○	○	○	Non existing statements
●	●	●	●	○	○	○	○	Atomic graph existent in all graphs will also be in the result
●	○	○	●	●	○	○	○	An atomic graph added to G' is also added to the result
○	●	○	●	○	○	●	○	An atomic graph added to G'' is also added to the result
○	●	●	○	○	●	○	○	An atomic graph removed from G' is also not added to the result
●	○	●	○	○	○	○	●	An atomic graph removed from G'' is also not added to the result
●	●	○	●	●	○	●	○	An atomic graph added to both branches is also added to the result
○	○	●	○	○	●	○	●	An atomic graph removed from both branches is also not added to the result

Table 5.1: Decision table for the different situations on a Three-Way-Merge. ● = atomic graph exists, ○ = atomic graph does not exist.

5.3.3 Three-Way-Merge: An Unsupervised Approach to Merge Branched Knowledge Bases

A methodology used in DVCS for software source code files, such as Git and Mercurial, is the Three-Way-Merge.[8] The merge consists of three phases: (1) finding a common *merge base* for the two commits to merge, (2) comparing the files between the *merge base* and the individual branches and inferring which lines where added and removed, and (3) creating a merged version by *combining* the changes made in the two branches.

Implementing this function for *combining* the changes is the actual problem and task of the selected merge algorithm. A merge algorithm can take several aspects into account when deciding whether to include a line into the merged version or not. If the algorithm cannot decide on a certain line, it produces a merge conflict. For source code files in Git this is the case if two close-by lines where changed in different branches. Since the order of source code lines is crucial, a merge conflict is produced.

We transform this situation to RDF datasets. We take into account the versions of the graphs in the two commits to be merged $C_{\{B\}}(\{G'\})$, $D_{\{B\}}(\{G''\})$. To find the merge base (1) this strategy relies on the existence of a common ancestor δ, such that for C and D there must exist an ancestor path $C_{\left\{\cdot\raise1pt\hbox{$\cdot$}_{\{\delta,\dots\}}\right\}}$ resp. $D_{\left\{\cdot\raise1pt\hbox{$\cdot$}_{\{\delta,\dots\}}\right\}}$ to δ. In our case we find the most recent common ancestor $\delta := B(\{G\})$. Now we have to compare (2) the graphs between the *merge base* and the individual branches and calculate their difference:

$$(C_C^+, C_C^-) \;=\; \Delta(G, G')$$
$$(C_D^+, C_D^-) \;=\; \Delta(G, G'')$$

In contrast to source code files in the RDF data model order is not relevant. Thus we can just take the resulting sets of the comparison and merge them into a new version (3) as follows:

$$G''' = \bigcup \left((\mathcal{P}(G') \cap \mathcal{P}(G'')) \cup \mathcal{P}(C_C^+) \cup \mathcal{P}(C_D^+) \right)$$

The Three-Way-Merge can also be depicted as $Apl(G', (C_D^+, C_D^-)) = G'''$ [VG06]. A more visual representation of the Three-Way-Merge is given as decision matrix in table 5.1. The table shows in the first three columns, all combinations of whether a statement is included in one of the two branches and their *merge base*. The fourth column shows whether a statement is present in the merge result as defined for the Three-Way-Merge. The other four columns visualize the presence of a statement in the deltas between the two branches and the *merge base* respectively.

This merge strategy purely takes the integrity of the RDF data model into account. This especially means, that semantic contradictions have to be dealt with in other ways. One possibility to highlight possible contradictions as merge conflicts is the Context Merge strategy (cf. section 5.3.4). But also beyond a merge operation, semantic contradictions within the resulting RDF graph can be handled using continuous integration tools, as pointed out in chapter 9.

5.3.4 Context Merge: A Supervised Approach to Identify Conflicts

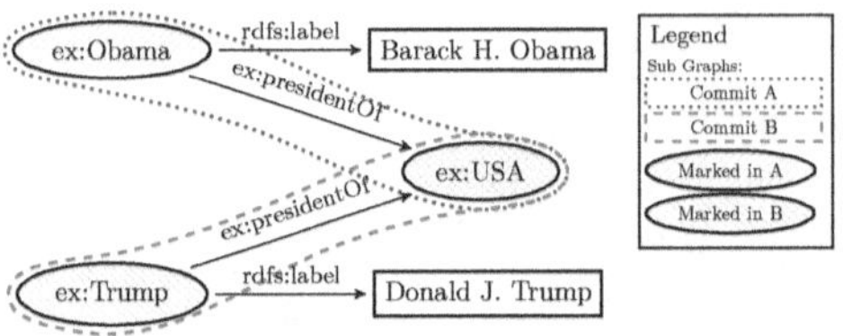

Figure 5.3: An example for a conflict using the C text Merge

Since the Three-Way-Merge does not produce any merge conflicts, it can happen, that during a merge semantic conflicts are introduced. Even though the result is a valid RDF graph two statements could contradict each other. Looking at fig. 5.3 we see, that in commit A the statement *Obama is president of the USA* was introduced, while in commit B the statement *Trump is president of the USA* is added. The result of the Three-Way-Merge would be the whole graph as shown in fig. 5.3.

Since we do not want to apply any specially encoded semantic rules to identify conflicts we have to rely on the pure RDF data model.

Thus we can take into account the semantics of nodes and edges and the semantics of additions and deletions as we have seen them in the Three-Way-Merge. Let us transfer the principle of producing conflicts in a Three-Way-Merge as implemented in Git from source code files to graphs. In case of source code files a conflict is produced as soon as the merge strategy cannot decide on two lines coming from two different commits in which order they should be stored. The lines thus are overlapping. The Context Merge for RDF is based on the Three-Way-Merge in a way, that it performs the merge by taking into account the two commits and their *merge base*. In contrast to the merge as defined in section 5.3.3 it produces *merge conflicts*, as soon as the changes of both merged commits overlap at a node. If an atomic graph is added resp. removed in both commits, there is obviously no contradiction and hence no conflict. The merge process marks each subject and object of an added or removed atomic graph. Along with the mark it stores the information about the originating commit of the atomic graph (cf. fig. 5.3, Sub Graphs). As soon as a node is marked for both commits, this node is added to the list of conflicting nodes. The user is presented with all atomic graphs of both changesets that contain nodes that are listed as conflicting nodes.

The possible changes in question to be marked as a conflict are those statements[9] that where added or removed in one of the merged branches. Looking at table 5.1 we see, that both branches agree on the last two lines, while they do not agree on lines 3 to 6.

To perform a Context Merge we first need to calculate the changesets:

$$
\begin{aligned}
(C_{\mathcal{C}}^{+}, C_{\mathcal{C}}^{-}) &= \Delta(G, G') \\
(C_{\mathcal{B}}^{+}, C_{\mathcal{B}}^{-}) &= \Delta(G, G'')
\end{aligned}
$$

As a precondition to identify the conflicts we thus only need these statements for which two branches do not agree. We denote the set of statements present respective absent in $\mathcal{C}$, where $\mathcal{C}$ and $\mathcal{B}$ disagree as follows (disagreed statements):

$$
\begin{aligned}
\tilde{C}_{\mathcal{C}\backslash\mathcal{B}}^{+} &= C_{\mathcal{C}}^{+} \setminus C_{\mathcal{B}}^{+} \\
\tilde{C}_{\mathcal{C}\backslash\mathcal{B}}^{-} &= C_{\mathcal{C}}^{-} \setminus C_{\mathcal{B}}^{-}
\end{aligned}
$$

Also to identify the nodes of a statement, the set of all subject nodes and object nodes of G is defined as:

$$
N(G) := \{x \mid \exists p, o : (x, p, o) \in G \vee \exists s, p : (s, p, x) \in G\}
$$

The set of potentially conflicting nodes is the intersection of the nodes of the disagreed statements:

$$
I_N = N\left(\tilde{C}_{\mathcal{C}\backslash\mathcal{B}}^{+} \cup \tilde{C}_{\mathcal{C}\backslash\mathcal{B}}^{-}\right) \cap N\left(\tilde{C}_{\mathcal{B}\backslash\mathcal{C}}^{+} \cup \tilde{C}_{\mathcal{B}\backslash\mathcal{C}}^{-}\right)
$$

---

[9] For simplicity, we deal with statements in the following definitions and formulas rather then atomic graphs. To transfer the method to atomic graphs, a slightly changed definition of $N(G)$ and $f_I(G)$ with respect to atomic graphs is needed.

Now we have to find the respective statements that have to be marked as conflicts, thus the set of all statements in G which contain a node in I is defined on G and I as:

$$\notin_I(G) := \{(s,p,o) \in G \mid s \in I \vee o \in I\}$$

Thus we have the following sets of potentially conflicting statements:

$$\notin_{I_N}\left(\tilde{C}^+_{C\backslash B}\right), \notin_{I_N}\left(\tilde{C}^-_{C\backslash B}\right), \notin_{I_N}\left(\tilde{C}^+_{B\backslash C}\right), \notin_{I_N}\left(\tilde{C}^-_{B\backslash C}\right)$$

While the set of statements that will be contained in the result without question is:

$$(\mathcal{P}(G') \cap \mathcal{P}(G''))$$
$$\cup \left(C^+_A \backslash \notin_{I_N}\left(\tilde{C}^+_{C\backslash B}\right)\right) \cup \left(C^+_B \backslash \notin_{I_N}\left(\tilde{C}^+_{B\backslash C}\right)\right)$$

Assuming a function R that gives us the conflict resolution after a user interaction, we end up with a merge method as follows:

$$G''' = \bigcup\Bigg((\mathcal{P}(G') \cap \mathcal{P}(G''))$$
$$\cup \left(C^+_A \backslash \notin_{I_N}\left(\tilde{C}^+_{C\backslash B}\right)\right) \cup \left(C^+_B \backslash \notin_{I_N}\left(\tilde{C}^+_{B\backslash C}\right)\right)$$
$$\cup R\Big(\notin_{I_N}\left(\tilde{C}^+_{C\backslash B}\right), \notin_{I_N}\left(\tilde{C}^-_{C\backslash B}\right),$$
$$\notin_{I_N}\left(\tilde{C}^+_{B\backslash C}\right), \notin_{I_N}\left(\tilde{C}^-_{B\backslash C}\right)\Big)\Bigg)$$

This merge strategy relies on the local context in graphs by interpreting subjects and objects of statements as nodes, while predicates are seen as edges. In a context where a different treatment of predicates is needed, the method can be extended to also mark statements that identify overlapping usage of predicates as well.

Following the foundational work of the last chapters in this chapter we describe the architecture of our system.

5.4 Conclusion

In this chapter we have introduced methods and algorithms to implement the abstract operations of the Quit Model as defined in section 4.2 as well as the access to the provenance subsystem as specified in section 4.3. Additionally, we built an interface to allow to integrate the Quit Stack into collaboration scenarios. This interface comprises methods to read and update the RDF dataset, to manage the branching model of the versioning logs for collaboration, and to access the provenance meta data.

We have implemented the conceptual Quit Model to target the requirements as formulated in section 1.2 (a-e). Building on the Git

DVCS we are not constrained to reach serializability of all performed operations. Instead, our store maintains multiple diverged version logs (branches) to express *dissent* (b) while each branch can represent a different state and latest version of the database. The branched versioning logs allow us to postpone the serialization of operations (*reconciliation*, e) and incorporate it into the data engineering process while it is still possible to strive for an eventually conflated and serialized versioning log. To actually perform the abstract merge operation as presented in section 4.2.3 we have introduced several algorithms for implementing the merge strategy. The merge strategies comprise naive implementations like *Union, All Ours*, and *All Theirs*. To allow more complex merges we have transferred the Three-Way-Merge, as it is used in Git, to the application on atomic graphs to use it on RDF datasets. For allowing more manual control over the merge process also the Context Merge was introduced that is able to identify merge conflicts. The distribution of the Git commits using the Git protocol allows us to build a *distributed workspace* (a) with support for *asynchrony* (c) that can be *synchronize* (d) by exchanging the complete versioning graph between individual workspaces. In addition it is possible to assess the provenance of the data using the provenance interface (h). By exploiting the commit system we can providing virtual endpoints for each version in the version log and allow random access to arbitrary versions of the Quit Store.

6 Data Creation and Authoring

The process to create data and update existing data is called the data authoring process. It is a creative process that is one of the two, besides the consumption of the data, main processes of the human interaction with data. The authoring process constitutes the integration of human knowledge into the data engineering process. In the Linked Data lifecycle (cf. section 3.1.3) the authoring process is depicted as a dedicated step *Manual revision/Authoring*. In section 1.2 we have formulated the requirement for the Quit methodology to support to *create and author* (f) data. The authoring process is closely coupled with the data exploration and publication which is subject to chapter 7.

The results presented in this chapter were first published in Arndt et al.: "Structured Feedback: A Distributed Protocol for Feedback and Patches on the Web of Data" [Arn+16 Arndt et al.: "Decentralize Collaborative Knowledge Management using Git" [Arn+19a]; and Arndt and Radtke: "Conflict Detection, Avoidance, and Resolution in a Non-Linear RDF Version Control System: The Quit Editor Interface Concurrency Control" [AR19].

The distributed data creation process is collaborative and can involve various roles. Embedded in the knowledge engineering processes this can be a team of knowledge engineers and knowledge maintainers, such as information professionals or domain experts, and knowledge users, such as citizen scientists or the crowd. The possible organization of such a collaborative and distributed setup is depicted in fig. 6.1 as two prototypical use cases. Both use cases (a and b) depict a research workflow of gathering and authoring data that is partially published as open data. In the use case (a) *unstructured feedback* a distributed team of knowledge engineers collaborates in a distributed workspace and exchanges the shared dataset (1). A subset of the shared artifacts is periodically published as open data on the Web (2). Knowledge users (e. g. citizen scientists) explore the data that is published on the Web (👁). During the exploration of the data they identify errors or know about additions to the data that they report to a knowledge engineer (✉). The second use case (b) *structured feedback* integrates the feedback of the knowledge users into the knowledge engineering workflow. To report errors or additions a data editing interface is used. This data editing interface, which is integrated into the public exploration interface, allows knowledge users to propose changes or additions on the dataset (✎). All changes made by the knowledge users are stored in the collaboration repository (💾) that is synchronized with the repositories of the team of knowledge engineers (3). Now, each member of the team can review the proposed changes (as knowledge maintainer) and incorporate them into the shared dataset.

The abstract requirement *create and author* (f) from section 1.2 can now be specified. From the use case as described above we derive relevant user requirements. In the following we present the requirements for a distributed collaboration system with respect to data authoring and an open federated system to gather feedback on the Web. The requirements target the data creation process on top of the distributed collaboration process described in the previous chapters.

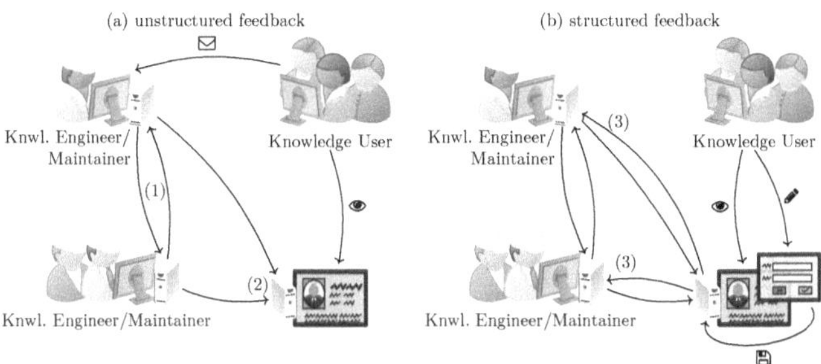

Figure 6.1: Integration of a crowdsourcing process into a collaborative uration process. Use case (a) depicts the unstructured flow of crowdsourcing feedback, while use case (b) integrates it into the distributed knowledge engineering workflow.

Decentralized Storage of Comment Resources The Web is organized in a distributed manner. External collaborators, such as citizen scientists, might want to be autonomous in deciding where to store their contribution but still want to be able to suggest changes to a dataset. *Comment Resources* can be stored in any location on the Web. The location has to be publicly available and has to be identifiable and locatable by a URL. The location of a *Comment Resource* should be selected by its author.

Structured Feedback for Web Resources Besides the classic way of giving feedback for a Web Resource by adding a simple full text comment it should be possible to give a more precise structured comment to a resource. This enables users to directly fix the mistake and provide the resource publisher with a patch to apply to the Web Resource, instead of verbally describing the position of a mistake in a document. This behavior is comparable to the concept of source code patches or pull-requests in software engineering e. g. on Git-based collaboration platforms.

Comment Container for a Web Resource All comments related to a specific Web Resource have to be aggregated in a single place, which can be referenced from this Web Resource. This aggregated resource has to contain references to the original comments. The Comment Container can be an RDF resource or an RSS web feed (cf. [RSS09]).

Active Updating of the Comment Container with new Comment Resources and Notification of Subscribers The Comment Container has to be updated if new Comment Resources for the respective Web Resource are created. This is needed to have an up-to-date resource available to the content publisher to get informed about new comments and to be able to integrate structured patches into their data set. Web users which are interested in a specific Web Resource should be able to subscribe to a Comment Container related to the Web Resource of interest. This Comment Container should be kept up to date regarding new comments. Subscribers have to be actively informed of updates on Comment Containers they are subscribed to.

Detect and Resolve Overlapping Edit Operations   During the collaboration of *domain experts* on the same workspace it can happen that the dataset was updated by two collaborators at the same time. When one collaborator reads the data in the datasets and prepares an update operation, another collaborator might update the dataset in the meantime. These overlapping update operations can lead to an uncontrolled state of the dataset that was not intended by any of the collaborators. This problem is called concurrency. To avoid this problem a system is needed to detect overlapping edit operations and resolve such a situation.

The Semantic Web is about collaboration and exchange of information. In the following two methods are presented to support the distributed authoring process. The *Structured Feedback* approach provides a system to incorporate external contributors into a distributed collaboration process, it is introduced in section 6.1. The concepts presented with the *Structured Feedback* system are comparable with bug reports and pull-requests in software engineering. While the data on the Semantic Web is constantly evolving and meant to be collaboratively edited there is no practical transactional concept or method to control concurrent writes to a dataset and avoid conflicts. The *QuitEditor Interface* allows the integration of domain adapted application specific editing interfaces through the SPARQL 1.1 Update interface of the *QuitStore* section 6.2. In addition to the standard update interface it exploits the concepts of the underlying DVCS to identify, avoid, and resolve conflicts during concurrent interactions.

6.1 Structured Feedback

For content providers and publishers of open data it is often important to gather feedback from their users or to allow a discussion among the users about the presented topic and resources. The proposed architecture and protocol is based on several existing technologies and protocols used on the Web of Data. From a general perspective it is based on HTTP. Specifically it is relying on and following the widely used Linked Data principles which are slightly extended to support our needs (cf. section 2.3). Since this proposal is overlapping with research in the area of online social networks it comprises the two main protocols from the Distributed Semantic Social Netwok (DSSN, cf. section 3.1.1), which are Semantic Pingback and WebSub.

In respect of these three categories the proposed Structured Feedback protocol is a crossover approach. It allows the integration of an Annotation Client directly into the website of the publisher to encourage users to leave comments. Also the website publisher keeps track of the comments in a Comment Container stored at a location of their choice. Users still have the choice whether to use the integrated client or any external commenting platform or even a stand-alone client. By following the proposed protocol, Comment Resources can be stored in any place of the Web, while its still possible to inform the content publisher via Semantic Pingback. Interested third parties can subscribe to the comments on a resource using WebSub.

The Structured Feedback protocol relies on the Linked Data rules (cf. section 2.3), by assuming that all resources are identified using an HTTP URI and it is possible to query the URI of a Web Resource, Comment Resource and Comment Container. When one of these resources is requested it assumes to receive RDF data either directly or by content-negotiation using HTTP Accept-Headers. Further links are used to connect the resources and services, and all resources are published according to these rules. One issue we were facing with Linked Data was that the specification is vague about retrieving named graphs. According to the RDF Recommendation [CWL14]: *[...] it is sometimes desirable to work with multiple RDF graphs while keeping their contents separate.* The recommendation document further describes the concepts of RDF datasets and RDF graphs as follows:

> An RDF dataset is a collection of RDF graphs. All but one of these graphs have an associated IRI or blank node. They are called named graphs, and the IRI or blank node is called the graph name. The remaining graph does not have an associated IRI, and is called the default graph of the RDF dataset. [CWL14]

In our protocol we implement the Comment Container using named graphs to represent a feed as a collection of Comment Resources related to a Web Resource. In order to be able to serve those datasets as Linked Data, without the need of a querying service, we decided to extend the interpretation of the Linked Data rules to support named graphs. The retrieval of statements is discussed in the section *Browsable graphs* in [Ber09]. Especially *describing a node* is defined as:

1. Returning all statements where the node is a subject or object; and

2. Describing all blank nodes attached to the node by one arc.

When applying those rules to an RDF dataset, we have interpreted these two rules to be executed on the default graph,[1] while we have extended these two rules by the following two rules to target the other named graphs of an RDF dataset:

3. If a named graph with the same URI, as the node, as graph name is defined and accessible, returning all quad-statements of the identified named graph; and

4. All quad-statements of a named graphs with a blank node as graph name, where the blank node is contained in the set of blank nodes following the second rule, are returned.

---

[1] This interpretation should be inline with the non-normative section *Content Negotiation of RDF Datasets* of the RDF Recommendation [CWL14]

The suggested additional rules, are interpreted in a fully backward compatible way, which means only if a serialization format with RDF dataset support is accepted by the requesting client the additional quad-statements are returned.

The Internet and the World Wide Web (WWW) in particular provide an infrastructure for retrieving information through web resources. With the advent of discussion forums, blogs, short message services like Twitter and online social networks like Facebook, the web evolved towards the Web 2.0. With the Semantic Web resp. Web of Data, the web is now evolving towards a Web 3.0 consisting of structured and linked data resources (Linked Data, cf. [Ber09]). Even though Web 2.0 services can be transformed to provide Linked Data [Fer08], there is a need for services to collaboratively interact with meaningful data and enable (Linked) Data Services to be integrated into the existing social web stack. Currently the Distributed Semantic Social Network (DSSN, section 3.1.1 and [Tra+12]) is available as a framework respectively platform to build social services based on the Web of Data. In addition to providing static RDF datasets, which can be queried as Linked Data or via a SPARQL service, it enables active communication along edges of the Giant Global Graph[2] and a *follow*-function for resources.

Building on the existing stack, we propose an open protocol on the Web of Data, which is distributed across multiple services, to integrate a collaborative feedback mechanism on structured and unstructured web resources. The protocol integrates elements of the architecture for a Distributed Semantic Social Network (cf. [Tra+12]), in particular the Semantic Pingback protocol (cf. [Tra+10]) and can be extended by a publish-subscribe system using WebSub (cf. [Gen18]).

Current mechanisms to provide feedback on web resources are, but are not limited to, leaving a comment through (1) a form provided by a publisher of a web page, (2) publishing a comment along with a link to the web resource on an online social network or doing so on a personal weblog. The problems with this kind of commenting are: either it is hard for the publisher of the web resource to get an overview of the available feedback to their content (in case of 2), or the user who leaves the comment is limited to the possibilities provided by the publisher to express the feedback and is not able to select the location of the comment and maybe specify the audience on their own (in case of 1). In contrast to this situation, we are proposing a crossover approach, which serves the upsides of the current situation to both parties, commenters and publishers. It gives commenters the possibility to publish comment resources at their leisure in an arbitrary location on the Web. It is integrated in the DSSN and has the possibility to be integrated in further online social networks. Publishers are actively informed about distributed comments on the Web. In addition, it provides better possibilities to express the user's feedback by creating structured patches

---

[2] *Giant Global Graph.* Description of the paradigm of the Giant Global Graph

(original not available):

to be sent to the publisher, which in turn are easier to apply than a verbal description about a mistake.

Nevertheless, the social network is just a part of the Web and the Linked Open Data Cloud[3] [SBP14]. Nowadays the Web of Data is a big worldwide database of structured data in a varying quality, which is constantly growing by human as well as machine generated data. This global graph covers a huge amount of topics, disciplines, and areas and is highly interlinked [SBP14]. But this graph is mainly static and there are no commonly established practices for the crowd to contribute to the data quality or content of the data sets in an ad hoc way, as it is possible for Wiki systems (like the Wikipedia) or in online social networks. With the ability of our approach to provide structured patches to web resources, crowd-based quality assessment and web data cleansing processes become feasible.

In the remainder of this section we first introduce the architecture and protocol of the Structured Feedback system in section 6.1.1. Then, we describe the design decisions and considerations we made during the implementation in section 6.1.2. The section is concluded by a brief demonstration of the system in section 6.1.3.

6.1.1 The Structured Feedback Architecture and Protocol

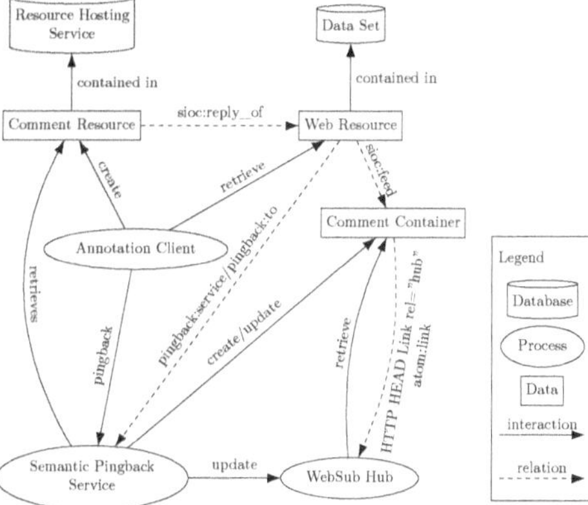

Figure 6.2: An architectural overview of the Structured Feedback protocol, participating components, their interaction, and references

The proposed approach, Structured Feedback, is an open protocol, distributed across multiple communicating components. It is based on several Semantic Web and DSSN protocols. Especially it follows the Linked Data paradigm (cf. section 2.3) and applies the Semantic Pingback and WebSub (cf. section 3.1.1) protocols. All components that interact through the protocol are depicted in fig. 6.2.

Web Resource   Any resource published on the WWW. It can be represented in any format, but has to be identifiable and retrievable by a URL. It is encouraged to use resources in an RDF format, but baseline functionality is possible for other types as well. The Web Resource has to announce a Semantic Pingback Service and a Comment Container as shown in listing 6.1, or using the according header link relations `rel="pingback"` and `rel="alternate"`.

```
dbpedia:Leipzig
  pingback:to <https://pingback.feedback.aksw.org/> ;
  sioc:feed fb-feed:dbpedia-Leipzig .
```

Listing 6.1: A minimal example of the necessary triples of a Web Resource to announce a Semantic Pingback Service and a Comment Container.

Comment Resource   An RDF Resource of the type `sioc:Item` representing any kind of comment or feedback related to a Web Resource. The Comment Resource is linked to the commented resource using a `sioc:reply_of` relation. It is possible to create Comment Resources for different kinds of feedback:

- a simple plain text contribution to a discussion using the type `sioct:Comment` as shown in listing 6.2,

- a structured patch as proposal to improve the quality of the Web Resource, e.g. by creating an instance of `cs:ChangeSet` as shown in listing 6.3, or

- any other resource type, which can be interpreted by the publisher of the Web Resource, e.g. using the RDF Review Vocabulary (`rev:`) from revyu.com.

```
fd-res:4ez-comment a sioct:Comment ;
  sioc:reply_of dbpedia:Leipzig ;
  foaf:maker <http://aksw.org/NatanaelArndt> ;
  sioc:created_at "2016-01-19T09:55:25.470Z"^^xsd:dateTime ;
  sioc:content "I'd␣like␣to␣ask␣..." .
```

Listing 6.2: A Comment Resource containing a simple text contribution (`sioc:content`) for a Web Resource.

Annotation Client   An application providing an interface for a user to create a Comment Resource related to a given Web Resource and store it in a Resource Hosting Service. The Annotation Client can be shipped together with the Web Resource, e.g. as a JavaScript Application, a third party Web Service, or a stand-alone client application. Depending on the implementation, the Annotation Client is also responsible of acting as a Pingback Client and triggering a Semantic Pingback ping to the Semantic Pingback Service, advertised by the commented Web Resource.

```
fb-res:2ug-patch a sioc:Item, cs:ChangeSet ;
  sioc:reply_of dbpedia:Leipzig ;
  cs:subjectOfChange dbpedia:Leipzig ;
  foaf:maker <http://aksw.org/NatanaelArndt> ;
  cs:creatorName "Natanael Arndt" ;
  sioc:created_at "2016-01-22T09:55:25.470Z"^^xsd:dateTime ;
  cs:createdDate "2016-01-22T09:55:25.470Z"^^xsd:dateTime ;
  cs:changeReason "Revised Triple ..." ;
  cs:addition [ a rdf:Statement ;
    rdf:subject dbpedia:Leipzig ;
    rdf:predicate ex:propA ;
    rdf:object "Hello" ;
  ] ;
  cs:removal [ a rdf:Statement ;
    rdf:subject dbpedia:Leipzig ;
    rdf:predicate ex:propA ;
    rdf:object "Hey There" ;
  ] .
```

Listing 6.3: A Comment Resource containing a commit and a revision proposed as a patch for a Web Resource.

Semantic Pingback Service The Semantic Pingback Service implements the Semantic Pingback protocol to accept ping requests and the Web-Sub protocol to publish the activity feed (cf. section 3.1.1). On arrival of a valid ping it is responsible for arranging an update of the Comment Container. This service further implements the publisher role of the WebSub protocol. If updates are available on the container it sends an update notification to the hub. The roles of the Semantic Pingback Service might as well be split into separate controllers responsible for receiving the Semantic Pingback ping, updating the Comment Container and notifying the hub. This would result in a high flexibility for distribution, but would highly depend on the implementation and is out of scope for specification of this protocol.

Comment Container To be able to keep all comments on one Web Resource in a single container the Comment Container was added. It is comparable to the roll of an RSS-Feed (cf. [RSS09]), especially to a comment feed, as it is published by some weblogs. The Comment Container is the item which is published to the hub. Users can subscribe to the container if they want to follow the comments on a Web Resource. Listing 6.4 shows an example of a Comment Container.

WebSub Hub The hub is an implementation of the hub role of the Web-Sub protocol (cf. section 3.1.1). It manages subscriptions from agents interested in notifications upon updates of the Comment Container.

Procedure of the Structured Feedback Protocol

A sequential overview of the protocol is given in figs. 6.3 and 6.4. The protocol is initiated by the Annotation Client in fig. 6.3, which provides a means for a user to create a comment for any Web Resource. The

```
fb-feed:dbpedia-Leipzig a sioc:Container ;
  atom:link <http://hub.feedback.aksw.org/> ;
  sioc:container_of fb-res:4ez-comment , fb-res:2ug-patch .

fb-feed:dbpedia-Leipzig {
  fb-res:4ez-comment a sioct:Comment;
    sioc:reply_of dbpedia:Leipzig ;
    foaf:maker <http://aksw.org/NatanaelArndt> ;
    sioc:created_at
      "2016-01-19T09:55:25.470Z"^^xsd:dateTime ;
    sioc:content "I'd␣like␣to␣ask␣..." .

  fb-res:2ug-patch a sioc:Item, cs:ChangeSet ;
    sioc:reply_of dbpedia:Leipzig ;
    cs:subjectOfChange dbpedia:Leipzig ;
    foaf:maker <http://aksw.org/NatanaelArndt> ;
    cs:creatorName "Natanael␣Arndt" ;
    sioc:created_at
      "2016-01-22T09:55:25.470Z"^^xsd:dateTime ;
    cs:createdDate
      "2016-01-22T09:55:25.470Z"^^xsd:dateTime ;
    cs:changeReason "Revised␣Triple␣..." ;
    cs:addition [ a rdf:Statement ;
      rdf:subject dbpedia:Leipzig ;
      rdf:predicate ex:propA ;
      rdf:object "Hello" ;
    ] ;
    cs:removal [ a rdf:Statement ;
      rdf:subject dbpedia:Leipzig ;
      rdf:predicate ex:propA ;
      rdf:object "Hey␣There" ;
    ] .
}
```

Listing 6.4: A Comment
Container containing two
Comment Resources, whi
are partially mirrored in
named graph.

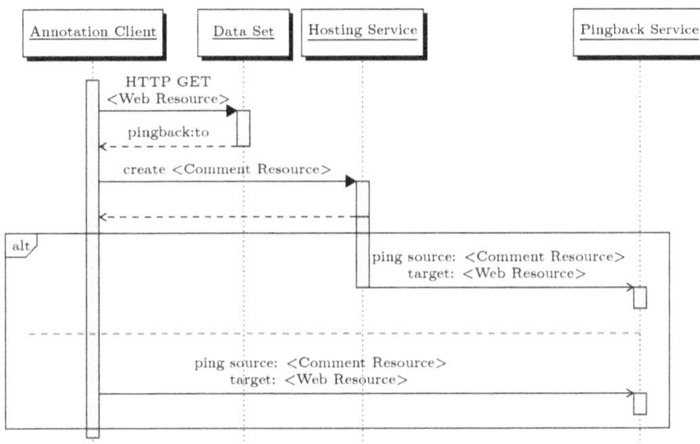

Figure 6.3: Sequence diagram of the initiation of the protocol and the creation of a Comment Resource by an Annotation Client

Annotation Client retrieves the Web Resource from its Data Set and looks for a `pingback:to`[4] or `pingback:service` relation to the Semantic Pingback Service in charge of the requested resource. The user creates a Comment Resource using the Annotation Client, which has to contain a `sioc:reply_of` relation to the commented Web Resource. The Annotation Client then takes care of storing the Comment Resource in a Resource Hosting Service from where it is available as Linked Data. A Resource Hosting Service can be any SPARQL service or even a publicly available static web page hoster, which is writable by the Annotation Client, e. g. through access delegation. After the Comment Resource was published the Annotation Client notifies the Semantic Pingback Service by sending a pingback request with the Comment Resource as source and the commented Web Resource as target. Depending on the implementation this task can also be completed by the Hosting Service, but to keep the selection of a Hosting Service as flexible as possible it is a good idea to hand over this task to the Annotation Client. When the pingback request was received by the Pingback Service it retrieves the Comment Resource from the Hosting Service for verification of the ping, as depicted in fig. 6.4. When the Comment Resource was verified by the Semantic Pingback Service it updates the corresponding Comment Container of the Web Resource. After the Comment Container was updated the Semantic Pingback Service (Publisher) notifies the hub of the update, which in turn retrieves the updated Comment Container (Topic) and informs its subscribers about the update.

---

[4] It is recommended to us the simple Semantic Pingback protocol instead of the protocol based on XML/RPC.

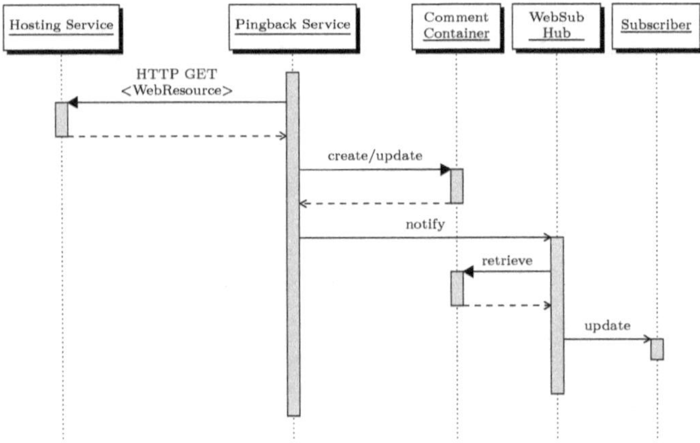

Figure 6.4: Sequence diagram of the delivery of the Comment Resource by the Pingback Service and WebSub Controller

6.1.2 Implementation

We have built a reference implementation in order to validate the interoperability of the components and verify the viability of the protocol. In the following section we discuss some design decisions and problems, which occurred during the implementation.

Annotation Client

The Annotation Client is a piece of software that enables a user to create comments or structured patches on Web Resources. The actual implementation of the Annotation Client is a JavaScript website extension. It identifies the resource URI of the current HTML representation by looking for the relation links `foaf:primaryTopic`, `alternate` and `describedby` in the header. Then it requests the respective RDF resource as RDF/JSON[5] (cf. [DSH13]) formatted structured data. Additionally the URI of the Semantic Pingback Service is retrieved, the URL of the Resource Hosting Service is pre-configured in the Annotation Client, but should be configured by the user in the future.

The Annotation Client presents two dialogs (cf. section 6.1.3). At invocation it prompts a simple form for plain comments. To identify the author of the feedback, a URI to the WebID or any other personal web resource is requested. In this implementation the URI needs to be entered by the user themself using the respective input in the front-end. For future implementations the user identity could be obtained using OAuth or could be provided by the including platform, on which the extension is running. A second dialog, invocable by the user provides an editable list of all properties of the currently selected resource to

---

[5] RDF/JSON was preferred over JSON-LD because it has one straight forward way of data representation, which has no need for an extra parser to work with the data.

the user. It provides basic property editing, deletion and insertion operations. In this dialog, the user as well has to provide an identifying URI and additionally a commit message.

The Annotation Client generates upon changes, deletions and insertions done by the user, changesets according to the changeset vocabulary [TD09], to generate a patch resource (cf. listing 6.3). The presented patch structure in [TD09] is expressed using reification, where added statements are expressed as instances of `rdf:Statement` and attached to the changeset using the property `cs:addition` (deletions are handled accordingly). Additionally a reference to the commented Web Resource is provided using a `sioc:reply_of` relation, together with some metadata such as date and author. Due to a lag of reliable parser and serializer libraries capable of processing RDF datasets, the implementation sends string concatenated N-Quads as serialization format.

After the resource was successfully written to the Resource Hosting Service the Annotation Client directly sends the pingback request to the Semantic Pingback Service. This behavior is in contrast to the specification in [Tra+10], where the pingback request would be sent by the Resource Hosting Service. We have decided to implement it in this way to keep the requirements towards a Hosting Service as minimal as possible and increase the selection for a service as flexible as possible, to allow a more decentralized infrastructure in the end. The source code for the Annotation Client is available on GitHub.[6]

Resource Hosting Service

For the reference implementation of the architecture we have created a simple read/write hosting platform for RDF resources and RDF graphs in Python, inspired by the Linked Data Platform [SAM15]. To demonstrate the simplicity we have implemented a REST interface which understands HTTP `GET`, `POST` and `PUT` requests. It is designed around our extended interpretation of the Linked Data paradigm (cf. section 2.3). To conform to the protocol, a `GET` request on a resource URI results in an RDF description of the requested resource coming from the default graph and if available the named graph with this URI.

Before a resource is sent to the Resource Hosting Service, the client executes a `GET` request to the service's base URL to request an available URI. This request was introduced to avoid collisions of resources on the Resource Hosting Service as well as to have some kind of guaranty from the service, that the URI will be publicly routable on the Internet. A free resource URI is generated using a random hash and a subsequent SPARQL-ASK query to the internal store. The actual write operations are implemented as `POST` and `PUT` requests directly on the resource URI. This again makes sure that the resource will be available as Linked Data. The body of these requests has to contain the same data, which should be returned on a GET request to the same URI. The source code for the Resource Hosting Service is available on GitHub.[7]

Semantic Pingback Service and Publish Subscribe System

The Semantic Pingback Service was implemented in PHP based on the existing generic Semantic Pingback reference implementation.[8] This implementation stores received pings in a MySQL database. The Semantic Pingback Service also comes with a web-form to manually send pingbacks to the service, this can help "self-publishers" of Comment Resources to also integrate their resources in the protocol flow. When a valid pingback was received, the controller for the management of the Comment Container is invoked by a callback function.

The retrieved Comment Resource is stored internally in a Saft respective EasyRdf[9] triple store with a MySQL back-end. Due to the lack of widely available PHP implementations of serializers for RDF formats with support for RDF datasets, the generation of the Comment Container resources and graphs was mainly done using basic string operations. To enable a flexible usage of one instance of the service for multiple data sets by providing feeds for any resource in the data set, the generation of the URI for the Comment Containers was implemented dynamically. Following to the host name and base path of the instance the feed URI is generated based on the according Web Resource. For example the feed URI for the resource http://aksw.org/Groups/ES is https ://feed.feedback.aksw.org/aksw.org/Groups/ES. The WebSub publication part is done using the php-publisher implementation provided by the pubsubhubbub project.[10]

As WebSub hub we are using Google's PubSubHubbub instance.[11] To increase the independence from central infrastructure further hub implementations can be used as listed in the WebSub implementation report.[12] The source code for the Semantic Pingback Service is available on GitHub.[13]

6.1.3 Demonstration

Based on our reference implementation of the relevant services in the protocol we have built a test setup.[14] It comprises a Resource Hosting Service to store Comment Resources[15] (cf. section 6.1.2) and a Semantic Pingback Service[16] (cf. section 6.1.2), which receives pingbacks, manages the Comment Containers and updates the WebSub hub. The Annotation Client (cf. section 6.1.2) is deployed for the mmoon project (cf. section 8.1).

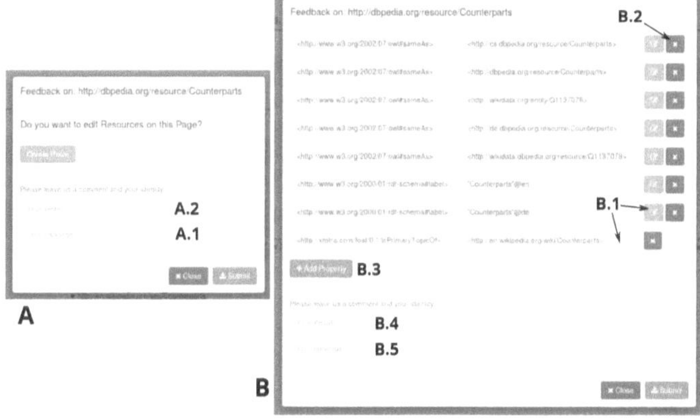

Figure 6.5: Screenshot of the Annotation Client. A: The Annotation Client showing the generic form for simple text comments. B: The Annotation Client showing the statement editor form for generating a structured commit resource to propose a patch for a Web Resource.

Using the user scripts browser extension Greasemonkey[17] for Mozilla Firefox we could also load the Annotation Client on other data sets, e. g. DBpedia,[18] and include them in tests of the infrastructure as well. Figure 6.5 shows screenshots of the Annotation Client loaded on the DBpedia Web Resource `dbpedia:Counterparts`. Figure 6.5 (A) shows the dialog for entering a simple text comment to a resource (A.1), the URL entered in the top input is used to identify the author (A.2). The generated Comment Resource is stored as `sioct:Comment` on the Resource Hosting Service. In fig. 6.5 (B) the resource editor is displayed. It provides basic functionality to edit existing properties (B.1), to delete (B.2) and to add new properties (B.3). Similar to the simple text comment form, the user should provide a URL for identification (B.4) and additionally a commit message to describe the change (B.5).

6.2 Quit Editor Interface

Collaboration and exchange of information is deep-seated in our culture. Collaborative editing of a common knowledge base is an evolutionary process of creating new versions of the knowledge base. In order to manage collaboration on Linked Data we face the problem of distributed authoring, distributed versioning, and parallel access to the knowledge base. Evolution of data and contributions by distributed parties introduce the problem of overlapping update operations, called concurrency. The problem of concurrency control was extensively studied in the context of conventional databases and collaborative file exchange systems [Ber+95]; [BHG87]; [Dem+94]; [PN04]; [Sat+90]. But the architecture of Semantic Web Applications is mostly Web oriented and similar to the architecture of Ajax/REST Web Applications. Web Applications as well as Semantic Web Applications consist of three layers: *persistence layer, data interchange & transaction processing*, and *user interface* [MA10]. The problem of distributed consistency is studied with regard to the transfer of distributed states in Web Applications [PP11]; [Hel07]; [OS10].

However, the role of the persistence layer and thus the data interchange in Semantic Web Applications is different to the architecture of conventional applications. The informal Semantic Web Layer Cake is a layer model to express several tasks in Semantic Web Applications and among Semantic Web Applications to be performed on Linked Data and the interfaces between the tasks (cf. section 2.4). This model accords with the three layers described in [MA10]. The bottom layers cover the abstract representation to encode data as triples of IRIs, Literals, and Blank Nodes and their serialization (cf. *persistence layer* [MA10]). To query the data model the SPARQL 1.1 Query and Update Language is standardized [GPP13]; [HS13] (cf. *data interchange & transaction processing*). The top most layer represents *User Interface & Applications* that are used to read and change the data. Read and update operations are affecting all of the layers, from the state of the user interface and the interaction to initiate the operation, through the execution on the query and update layer, to the persistence and consistency on the abstract representation layer. Only little research is performed with regard to the management of concurrent updates on RDF data. For SPARQL 1.1 (cf. [The13]) there is no standardized transaction interface available even though several approaches[19] exist. The performed research mainly tries to adapt the protocols from conventional databases [Muy08]; [NW10]. Innovative concepts that take into account the possibilities of distributed versioning systems and the abstract concept of RDF knowledge bases are missing.

In this section we present the Quit Editor Interface Concurrency Control (QEICC), a method to handle conflicting write operations on a SPARQL 1.1 Update interface of a distributed multiversion RDF quad

---

[19] *Apache Jena - Jena Transactions:*

store. It is able to detect, avoid, and resolve conflicts of update operations based on snapshot identification in a non-linear version control system. Building on the Quit version control system for RDF knowledge bases (cf. sections 4.1 and 4.2), we are not constrained to reach serializability of all performed operations. Instead, our store maintains multiple *diverged* version logs (*branches*) while each branch can represent a different state and latest version of the database. The branched versioning logs allow us to postpone the serialization of operations (*reconciliation*) and incorporate it into the data engineering process while it is still possible to strive for an eventually conflated and serialized versioning log. In addition we exploit the commit system and the random access to arbitrary versions of the Quit Store to provide snapshot isolation for the operations. To give full control to editing interfaces we provide three optimistic strategies which differ in their conflict handling and support for data-centric reconciliation.

The remainder of this section is structured as follows. We provide a problem description in section 6.2.1. Then we present the Quit Editor Interface in section 6.2.2 with the three conflict resolution strategies *reject*, *branch*, and *merge*.

6.2.1 Problem Description

In user facing applications, in particular in Web Applications, the user interface is constructed of many components. Each of the user interface components might send read request to the back-end system. When the user performs any action that induces an update operation the user might take into account any information displayed in the user interface for their update decision. These requests are sent by the individual components or can be coordinated using a method like Flux. In many traditional systems the back-end system implements parts of the business logic and can thus manage the state of the front-end in interaction with the store object. For a Semantic Web Application the data store can directly serve as back-end and be accessed using the SPARQL 1.1 Protocol [Fei+13].

In fig. 6.6 an example of two conflicting operations based on updating data through a form is depicted. We assume the content of the SPARQL Store are the statements shown in listing 6.5. Both clients retrieve the data from the store with a SPARQL Query and receive the respective result set containing the task to do. While user A changes the task description with the update operations in listing 6.6, user B has already performed the task and changed it to "completed" with the update operation in listing 6.7. In the final state of the store the changed task will be marked as completed even though this is not correct.

Listing 6.5: Initial
data in the triple store.

```
@prefix ex: <http://example.org/> .
ex:garbage a ex:Todo;
    ex:task "Take out the organic waste" .
```

For SPARQL 1.1 no transactional concept is standardized. The SPARQL 1.1 Update language allows to build update operation of the

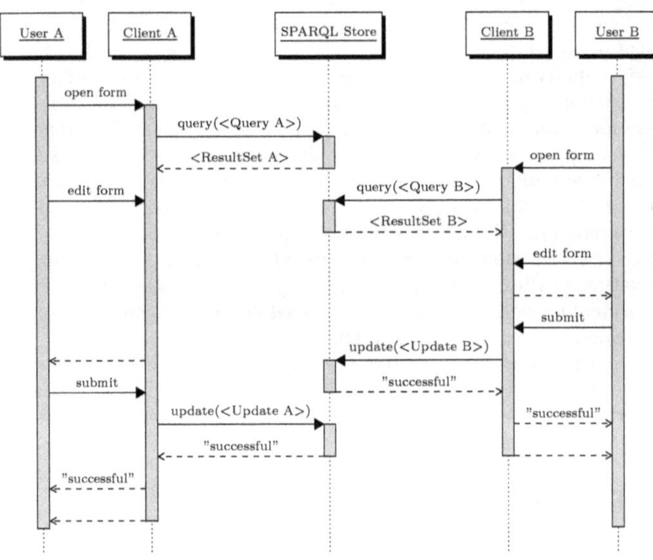

Figure 6.6: Sequence diagram of two overlapping update operations which result in an uncontrolled state of the shared data store.

```
PREFIX ex: <http://example.org/>
DELETE { ?todo ex:task ?task }
INSERT {
  ?todo ex:task "Take␣out␣the␣organic␣waste␣and␣the␣residual␣waste"
}
WHERE {
  BIND (
    "Take␣out␣the␣organic␣waste" as ?task)
  ?todo ex:task ?task
}
```

Listing 6.6: SPARQL Update operation <Update A>.

```
PREFIX ex: <http://example.org/>
INSERT DATA {
  ex:garbage ex:status ex:completed
}
```

Listing 6.7: SPARQL Update operation <Update B>.

form `DELETE {} INSERT {} WHERE {}` [GPP13]. The `WHERE` part can be used to encode preconditions for the update operations and bind variables used in the update operations, as shown in listing 6.6. But enclosing all preconditions inferred from all read operations that were used to compose the user interface is not a practical way to ensure that it is not conflicting with other operations. Furthermore, write operations in SPARQL 1.1 can also be performed without any precondition (`INSERT DATA, DELETE DATA`). The question is: how to ensure a controlled state of the SPARQL Store when performing non transactional write operations?

6.2.2 The Quit Editor Interface

In the following we present the Quit Editor Interface Concurrency Control (QEICC), a method to handle concurrency of write operations in a distributed multiversion RDF quad store. QEICC is built on top of the Quit Store. We first introduce the essential preliminaries of the Quit concept. Then, a fully backward compatible[20] protocol to control concurrency on top of the SPARQL 1.1 Protocol [Fei+13] is presented. Based on this protocol the three conflict resolution strategies *reject*, *branch*, and *merge* are presented.

The QEICC builds on the Quit methodology to support DVCS for RDF knowledge bases. The underlying DVCS allows not only linear versioning logs but also non linear *diverged* versioning logs represented by an acyclic directed graph of multiple *branches*. Because of the non linear versioning log we are not constrained to reach serializability of all performed operations. Instead, the store maintains multiple branched versioning logs while each branch can represent a different state and latest version of the database. Each version in the versioning log is identified by a unique hashed *commit id*, further each version references its predecessor as parent commit. A *branch* is identified by its name and is a pointer to the currently latest commit id in its versioning log. The store allows random access to arbitrary versions in the versioning log for query and update operations. Thus it is possible to start a new diverged versioning log at any existing version in the log. The latest version (*HEAD*) of each version log respective branch can also be queried and updated through virtual SPARQL Endpoints.

The QEICC method exploits the commit system and the random access feature of the underlying DVCS to provide a state identification of the data store to the client. As shown in fig. 6.7 the state is transferred on query and update operations. A query operation is sent to the store following the standard SPARQL 1.1 Protocol [Fei+13]. The result set for the query is returned along with the additional two HTTP-Headers `X-CurrentBranch` and `X-CurrentCommit`. The `X-CurrentBranch` header field contains the name of the branch that was requested. The `X-CurrentCommit` header field contains the commit id of the current HEAD of the selected branch in the store. With these two header

---

[20] The protocol still allows standard SPARQL 1.1 Query and Update operations, which of course will not benefit from the concurrency control features.

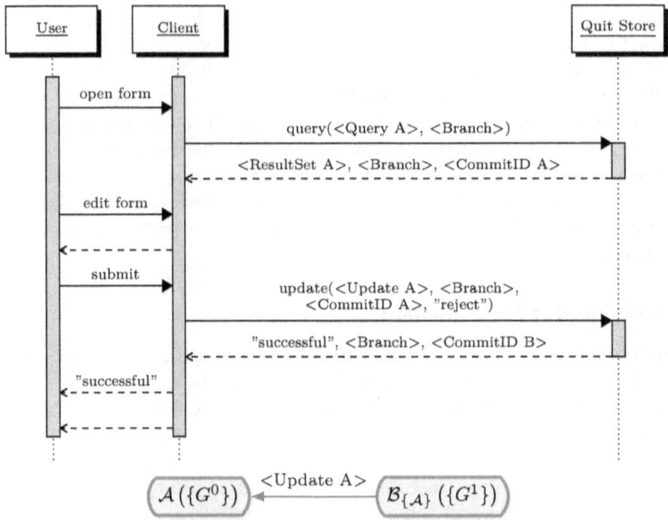

Figure 6.7: Sequence diagram showing the execution of an update operation with the parameters specified by the Quit Editor Interface. In the lower part, the commit graph is depicted which exists at the Quit Store after the update operation.

fields the store encodes the current snapshot state of the store at the time of the execution of the query.

When the client sends an update operation to the store, the same encoded state is transferred in HTTP form-encoded or query string request parameters along with the update operation to the store. This transfer of the state allows the client to express towards the store, which state it assumes to be the most recent, respective which is the currently most recent commit on a branch. The request fields added to transfer the state from the client to the store are `parent_commit_id` and `resolution_method`. The value of `parent_commit_id` is the commit id which the client has received with the last query operation on the same branch. The `resolution_method` is one of the values `reject`, `branch`, or `merge`. This specifies the strategy which the Quit Store should follow when a conflict is detected. On an update operation the store identifies the current selected branch based on the chosen virtual endpoint. Then the store compares the commit id of the HEAD with the value of `parent_commit_id` which is sent along with the update request.

If no overlapping update operation was performed in the meantime, both commit ids will be equal. In this case the store commits the update operation and returns the commit id of the new HEAD of the selected branch. The now updated commit graph is depicted in the lower part of fig. 6.7. The state before the update is encoded in commit $\mathcal{A}$ with graph G^0, the update is performed using the update operation <Update A> which leads to the new state $\mathcal{B}_{\{\mathcal{A}\}}$ which was derived from $\mathcal{A}$ and points to its predecessor (cf. section 4.2).

If the commit ids are different, a conflict is detected. This case is depicted in fig. 6.8. The conflict is handled according to the specified value for the `resolution_method`. To give full control to editing interfaces we provide three optimistic strategies which differ in their conflict handling. The preconditions and the conflicting update operation are enclosed in the *Overlapping Edit* block. This block is referenced in the later figures, figs. 6.9 to 6.11.

Reject

If a conflict is detected on the server side, choosing the *reject* strategy will abort the execution of the operation and will leave the store unchanged. This allows to perform update operations in a try-catch or trial-and-error manner. Figure 6.8 shows a rejected update operation performed by the client. The commit log in the lower part of fig. 6.8 shows the state of the store after the successful commit of the update operation from the other client. After the rejected operation, it is up to the client's implementation how to proceed.

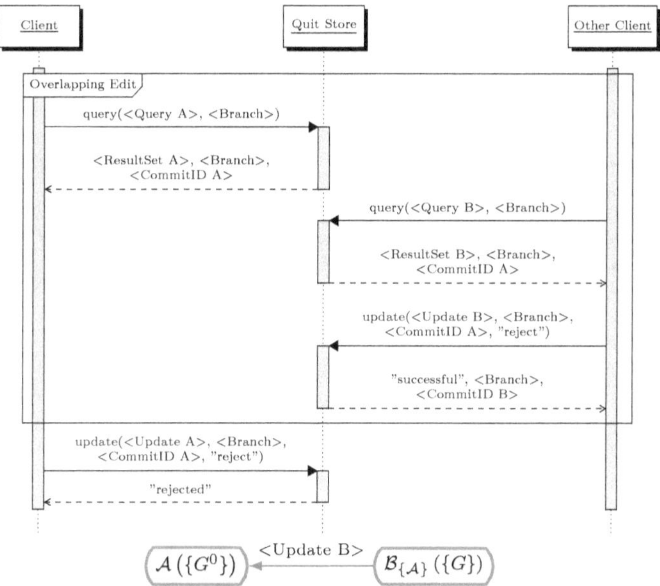

Figure 6.8: Sequence diagram showing two overlapping update operations, where the first operation is committed, while the second operation is aborted according to the selected strategy *reject*. The commit graph shows the state of the store after the successful update operation was committed.

One possibility to resolve the conflict on the client side is depicted in fig. 6.9. The *Overlapping Edit* block is reused by reference from fig. 6.8. To resolve the conflict this method involves anew retrieval of the data that is been edited on the client side. Just after the update operation was rejected the query operation is performed again and returns now an up-to-date result set *ResultSet A'*. This result set is compared to the original result set in two alternative blocks. By comparing the result sets we can ensure that the operation with which we are conflicting did not change the part of the graph (subgraph) that was queried with our query operation. This involves the assumption that the update operation was constructed based on the result set retrieved by the query operation *Query A* (cf. fig. 6.8). The top block is for the case that the result set of the query operation did not change, the bottom part for if the result set changed. If the result set is the same as the original result set, the update operation is resent with the updated commit id as parameter. If the update affected the subgraph of our interest, the client needs to resolve the conflict locally. This resolution can happen by informing the user about the changes and let the user review its input under the new circumstances and resubmit the form. After the conflict was resolved on the client side the adapted update operation can be submitted to the store along with the new commit id. The bottom part of fig. 6.9 shows the version log with the update operation by the other client (as shown in fig. 6.8) and the adapted update operation after the client side conflict resolution and the new commit $\mathcal{C}$.

Branch

The *branch* strategy actually exploits the possibilities of our non-linear version log system. Figure 6.10 shows the execution of an update operation that conflicts and is resolved with the branch strategy. The update operation is committed to a new branch that can be use to postpone the resolution. In contrast to the other two strategies the branch strategy does never fail. Instead, if a conflict arises a new branch is created that diverges from the original branch from the last common commit before the conflict on the branch. This divergence is shown in the lower part of fig. 6.10, each of the commits $\mathcal{B}$ and $\mathcal{C}$ are derived from the same original commit $\mathcal{A}$. In the sequence diagram the new branch is created with the *branch()* method. After the new branch was created the conflicting update operation is committed to the new branch <*Branch'*>.

This strategy allows fire-and-forget operations in a way that the update operation is committed, no matter if it conflicts or not. Also, this strategy allows to postpone a conflict resolution for instance if the correct resolution is not yet known or needs to be found based on a community discussion. This allows a data-centric reconciliation, in contrast to time-based reconciliation, of the conflict using appropriate, e.g. domain specific, merge operations (cf. the next section and section 5.3). Another asset of allowing a versioning log to branch is that it reflects the actual lineage of the update operations and changed dataset. By analysing the version log it is possible to reconstruct in which logical order operations were performed.

Merge

The *merge* strategy is similar to the branch strategy as it creates a new branch to commit the update operation when a conflict arises. In addition it subsequently performs a reconciliation of the diverged versioning log. To perform the merge, a merge method can be selected according to the methods supported by the respective system.

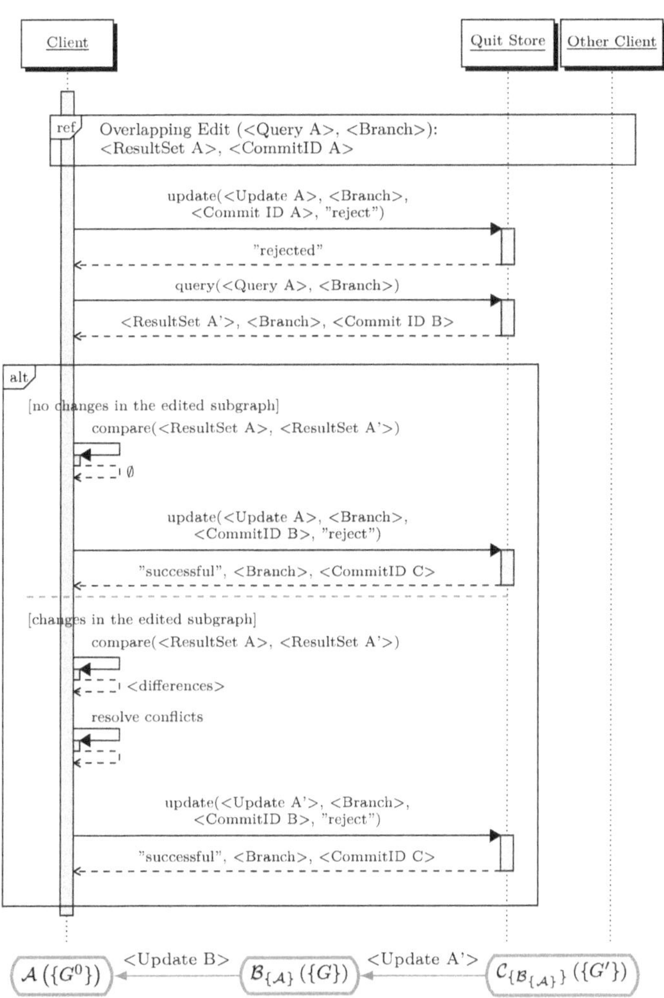

Figure 6.9: Sequence diagram showing the retry of an update operation after it was rejected due to an overlapping update operation.

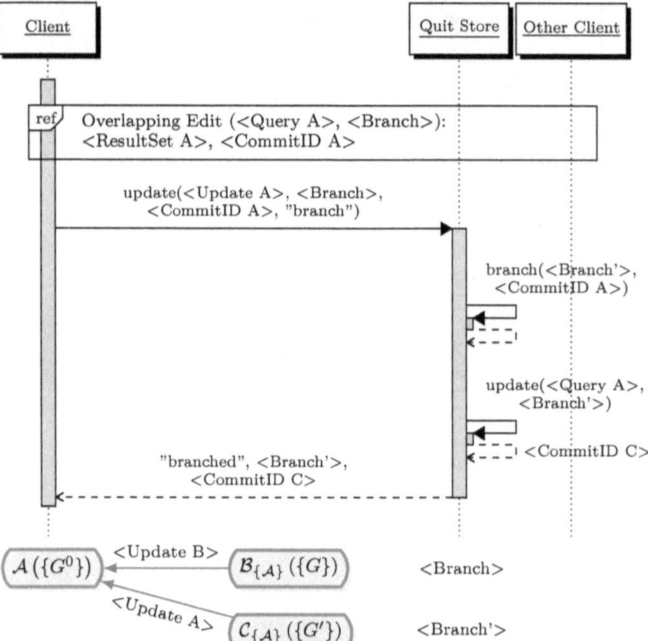

Figure 6.10: Sequence diagram of the overlapping update operation with the resolution strategy *branch*.

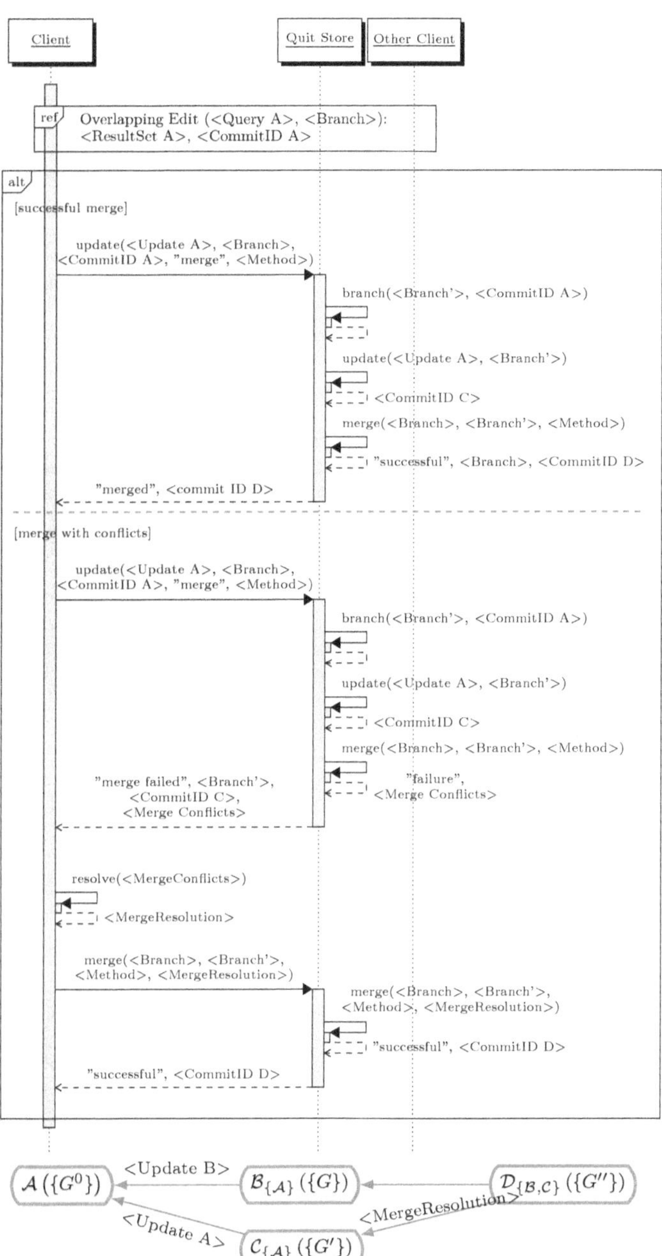

Figure 6.11: Sequence diagram of the overlapping update operations and server side resolution by merging the changes.

The Quit Store has specified the merge methods Three-Way-Merge and Context Merge (cf. section 5.3). The two possibilities for a successful and a failing merge process are depicted in the two alternative blocks in fig. 6.11. The merge is successful in the first case, while in the second case the merge conflicts are reported to the client and need to be resolved on the client side. If the reconciliation is successful, a new commit is created as shown in the lower part of fig. 6.11. The commit $\mathcal{D}$ is derived from the two diverged commits $\mathcal{B}$ and $\mathcal{C}$ and combines the two branches again. If the reconciliation fails, the update operation fails and the system ends up in the branched state. This means that the update operation is committed but the diverged states could not be automatically reconciled. The result of a failed merge operation is the description of the *merge conflicts* and the references to the new branch and commit. The merge conflict now needs to be resolved by the client or can be postponed to a later state. If the merge conflicts are resolved, a new *merge* operation is performed by the client.

A merge method compares the two versions of the dataset as they are produced by the conflicting operations. This comparison takes into account the last common ancestor of the two newly created commits. In our case the newly created commits are $\mathcal{B}$ and $\mathcal{C}$ and the last common ancestor is $\mathcal{A}$. Each of the datasets $\{G\}$ and $\{G'\}$ is compared to the dataset $\{G^0\}$, this allows to break down the conflict from the level of overlapping operations to the actual data in the graphs. Besides the merge methods Three-Way-Merge and Context Merge additional methods can be implemented to reflect special properties of a domain model. This allows a semi-automatic data-centric reconciliation of overlapping operations.

6.3 Conclusion

The usage of the SPARQL 1.1 Query, Update, and Protocol standards allows interoperability across software stacks in different usage scenarios. The Linked Data paradigm allows the exchange of data on the Web in a decentralized way. But these standards are not meant to deal with the problem of collaborative data creation and authoring scenarios. Following from this two questions arise: How can we ensure a controlled state of the SPARQL Store when performing non transactional write operations? And, how can external collaborators of a Web wide collaborative scenario be integrated into the distributed data engineering workflow of a team of domain experts? In the presented collaborative usage scenario we thus have formulated additional requirements on top of the functionality covered by the SPARQL 1.1 standard and by Linked Data.

Defining appropriate interfaces and protocols for the authoring of data allows to structure and guide a collaborative data engineering process. To target the formulated requirements we have presented the Structured Feedback protocol to incorporate external contributors from the Web into a data engineering process of domain experts. And we have presented the Quit Editor Interface Concurrency Control to identify, avoid, and resolve conflicts during concurrent interactions by exploiting the features of the Quit methodology with support of the Quit Stack chapters 4 and 5.

With Structured Feedback we have presented a protocol to give feedback to resources on the Web of Data. The protocol is distributed in a way that resource publishers and comment authors can independently decide on where to host their infrastructure and especially resources. Using Semantic Pingback publishers are informed about newly created comments on the Web and an aggregated Comment Container is created as comment feed for a Web Resource. Further with WebSub it even enables third party agents to subscribe their services to the feed and follow newly created comments (Comment Container). The formulated requirements, *Decentralized Storage of Comment Resources*, *Structured Feedback for Web Resources*, *Comment Container for Web Resource*, *Active Updating of the Comment Container with new Comment Resources Notification for Subscribers* are met by the protocol and implementation.

With the Quit Editor Interface Concurrency Control (QEICC) we have presented a method to identify and avoid overlapping update operations respective conflicts. This is achieved by the possibility for the client to express towards the store which state it assumes to be the most recent respective which is the currently most recent commit on a branch. Preconditions can be verified on the store using a select query and the execution of the update can be ensured to be applied on the same precondition. On top of this we have defined three strategies to handle the conflicts. The presented system allows to strive for a serialized execution of the operations and only diverges if an automatic serialization is not possible. In contrast to conventional systems our system is based on non-linear versioning logs. The branched versioning logs allow us to postpone the serialization of operations (*reconciliation*) and incorporate it into the data engineering process. The reconciliation can happen in a data-centric way that is aligned with the domain model.

Besides using the parameters defined by QEICC for conflict detection on updates the client can store the received values of the current branch and current commit id as the state of the store. This state representation allows the client to detect updates to the store while it performs query operations. This detection allows the client to trigger local updates of the user interface components when the store changes, to always present up-to-date information.

7 Publication and Exploration

Publication of results is an important aspect of sharing for global collaboration. To make results of the collaborative data engineering process available on the Web it is necessary to incorporate a release and publication mechanism. In chapter 1 we have formulated the requirement (g) to provide means to explore and publish the knowledge base. The publication of RDF data on the Web should possibly follow the widely adopted Linked Data principles as formulated by Berners-Lee [Ber09] (cf. section 2.3). This requires appropriate infrastructure to setup and maintain servers and applications to make the Linked Data available. Besides the publication in a machine readable format to make the data available also the accessibility to humans is important. To achieve this accessibility user interfaces are required which provide an exploration interface on the data and can visualize the data with appropriate methods.

In the following we present two systems for different tasks in the process of publishing data from an evolutionary collaborative process. The maintenance of systems for publishing RDF knowledge bases is often challenging or impossible for non technical domain experts. In addition to the complicated setup of such systems the high number of requests for the execution of complex queries on the systems lead to a low availability. With the *Knowledge Base Shipping to the Linked Open Data Cloud* a system is presented in section 7.1 that both supports non technical domain experts in running local system but also supports system administrators or "DevOps" in setting up RDF knowledge base publication systems. Another approach to not only improve the availability but also the accessibility of RDF knowledge bases is presented with the Jekyll RDF system in section 7.2. Jekyll RDF provides a template-based system to generate static sites for the publication of RDF knowledge bases. This allows to publish knowledge bases as machine-readable and human-readable exploration interfaces on the Web.

7.1 Knowledge Base Shipping to the Linked Open Data Cloud

Modelling and representing knowledge using RDF has become an established tool throughout diverse domains. However, the process of publishing and maintaining RDF knowledge bases on the World Wide Web in general and on the Linked Open Data cloud (*LOD cloud*) in particular requires technical expertise. While allocating resources to knowledge engineers who model the domain of interest and create the knowledge bases is easy to justify, making these datasets available as Linked Data is equally important. Although this should be a mere technicality to Linked Data experts, setup and maintenance of knowl-

The results presented in this chapter were first published in Arndt et al.: "Knowledge Base Shipping to the Linked Open Data Cloud" [Arn+15] and Arndt et al.: "Jekyll RDF Template-Based Linked Data Publication with Minimized Effort and Maximum Scalability" [Arn+19b].

edge bases published as Linked Data are time consuming tasks that are often overlooked. These complications become clearer by looking at evaluations of LOD cloud datasets, such as by Schmachtenberg, Bizer, and Paulheim [SBP14], where only 19.47% of proprietary vocabularies were fully dereferenceable and only 9.96% of datasets provided SPARQL endpoints. Another aspect that is affected by the availability of a knowledge base is the reproducibility of experiments performed on or with it.

Properly comparing own approaches to prior research entails working with the same data. However, knowledge bases evolve and public endpoints may either stop serving the data that was originally used in experiments, or they might not be powerful enough to provide the data in reasonable time spans. Finding the data, loading it into a local triple store, and using this local mirror to perform the experiments is the usual way to counter this problem. The publication of a knowledge base to the LOD cloud typically comprises the following steps:

1. Install a triple store

2. Load the data to be published into the triple store

3. Setup of a (publicly accessible) SPARQL endpoint

4. Provide a presentation application to support the exploration of the knowledge base

5. Ensure de-referencability of IRIs occurring in the published knowledge base

6. Maintain the setup and ensure its availability

To perform these steps requires a certain level of technical knowledge and understanding of the individual server components. This often requires a knowledge engineer or knowledge maintainer to either consult a system administrator or to invest a significant amount of time to selectively acquire DevOp-competences that often diverge far from their original domain and core research interests.

To alleviate these issues, we propose the methodology of *Dockerizing Linked Data*[1] (DLD): an approach of a containerized Linked Data publication infrastructure. By using Docker container virtualization, it provides benefits regarding the maintainability and ease of setup, through modularization of individual components following the principle of microservices and separation of concerns [Gan95]; [Gan03]. In addition, it enables easy mirroring of a setup on other computer systems. Apart from the pure presentation of the knowledge base we also taking usage scenarios which require write access into account. A detailed description of the overall architecture is given in section 7.1.2. We specify a way to containerize a triple store together with the used access and management interfaces. Different ways to load the actual

---

[1] *Homepage and description of the DLD project:*

data into a containerized triple store and how to backup the data are presented. We show how to create and attach containers for a HTML representation of the data, in addition to the SPARQL endpoint.

On the subject of Docker containers, Merkel details that Docker containers are a lightweight solution to resolve dependency and security problems as well as platform differences.[2] Docker containers have been explored to enhance reproducible research [CS14d]; [Boe15]. Chamberlain and Schommer [CS14d] detail that software and experimental setups in research are often not documented well enough to provide exact information about the systems they were executed on, hindering reproducibility of experiments. Computational environments are very complex and containerization provides a way to isolate experimental setups from some external variables of the systems they are executed on. Boettiger [Boe15] states that many existing solutions, such as virtual machines and workflow software, provide significant barriers to be adopted by being hard to realize and often not sufficiently low-level to solve the mentioned problems of dependencies and documentation. Both works therefore use Docker as local development environments for reproducible scientific research.

The web service Dydra[3] is a cloud-based managed graph database hosting service on the Web. It offers t o t he u ser t he p ossibility to create graphs, load RDF data and query it using SPARQL. In contrast to our approach the data can not be hosted on a local machine and thus will not give the user control over the availability of the services or the data. Furthermore, in contrast to a local service for a cloud hosting service it is always in doubt whether it is suitable for sensible data. Even though the service provides an authentication mechanism, the full access-control is not in the hand of the user of the service.

7.1.1 Background and Tooling

Container-based operating system virtualization is a technology used to provide an isolated execution environment for multiple individual applications sharing the complete hardware and the host's core operating system components while each container has its own file system [Sch14]. In contrast, with full- and para-virtualization technologies each virtual machine brings its own operating system kernel which increases the resource footprint on the host system. Examples of container-based operating system virtualization technologies are e. g. FreeBSD jail, Linux Containers (LXC), and *Docker*.[4] We have selected Docker as virtualization technology. It is one of the most successful virtualization

---

BSD handbook

technologies, if not even the most successful and can be installed on the three mayor operating systems Linux, Mac OS X, and Windows..[5] Also a huge ecosystem of cloud platforms has evolved around the docker technology.

In Docker, on bootstrapping each container has its own replica of a root file system defined by a *Docker image*. A *Docker image* also groups information about which root process to invoke, potentially required adjustment to the execution environment of the process (i. e. the working directory and environment variables) and which resource limits must be respected. These details are specified in a *Dockerfile*[6] which serves as a recipe to create an image. This *Dockerfile* also allows to declare process invocations and to add additional files to the *base image* to adjust aspects of the configuration in the *base image*. *Dockerfiles* allow a transparent formal description of steps to be performed to obtain a desired initial configuration environment for a process to be executed in a container. With LABEL custom meta-data items can be attached to any Docker image or container as arbitrary key/value-pairs. With *volumes* Docker provides the possibility to mount directories of the host file system or other containers into the file system of a container.[7] Using volumes it is also possible to share directories among containers. Each container receives its own virtual network interface, allowing it to connect to other nodes on the internal virtual network and to the internet through the host. With the EXPOSE keyword a container can select which ports are available to the host system. To allow inter-container connections Docker offers a *linking* mechanism.[8] Containers connected with links can access each other with their host names and via provided ports, further environment variables of linked containers can be accessed. The linking feature was deprecated in the meantime, the network aspect can be substituted by bridge networks while environment variables can not be shared in the same way. To bundle all containers that constitute a service in one network and let them communicate using a private network Docker offers a *bridge network* mechanism.[9] Within a *bridge network* the container names can be used as host names for inter-container communication. It provides a simple but effective way to interchange small pieces of information required for successful orchestration.

Docker Compose[10] (formerly known as *fig*[11]) is a command line tool for configuring and managing complex setups of Docker containers. A setup is declared in a YAML[12] configuration file that declare a set of container configurations. It also specifies the bridge network configuration, shared volumes, and other parameters for the image instantiation. These additional configuration options would otherwise always needed to be manually (re-)specified on the command line interface for the Docker process. Docker Compose coordinates simultaneous starting and stopping of all containers belonging to a Docker Compose-configuration as a group and offers helpful aggregation of the log outputs from member containers. Using Docker Compose it is also possible to make a complex configuration of services reproducible, just as the Dockerfile makes an individual service reproducible.

7.1.2 Architecture

In our architecture we divide the components needed to ship a knowledge base into a number of general types of containers: *store, load & backup*, and *present & edit* components as depicted in fig. 7.1. Each of these components is exchangeable by containers implementing the necessary tasks respective interfaces. The *store* component, in most cases a triple store, can be considered the core of the setup while all other components are reading from it or writing to it. It contains an RDF graph database, is responsible for persisting the knowledge base, and provides interfaces to query and optionally alter the contained data. A *load* component is responsible to load the knowledge base into the triple store if it is not already shipped with preloaded data. *Backup* components are responsible to frequently save the contained data in a secure place to avoid data loss, if write access is implemented in the setup. The *present & edit* components can be any service which provides means to browse and explore the data of the knowledge base. In an authoring use case, these components also provide services to update the knowledge base.

The life-cycle of the containers is organized in three phases, the *configuration phase*, the *data loading phase*, and the *service phase*, which are explained in the section "Container Design and Conventions." During the design of the architecture we followed these principles:

Convention Over Configuration To decrease the amount of configuration items required for a DLD setup we introduce conventions (especially naming conventions) that are expected by the configuration tool to be fulfilled.

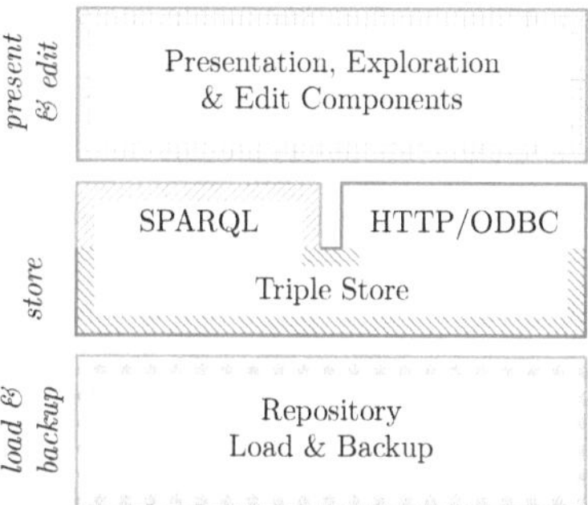

Figure 7.1: Architecture of the containerized microservices to publish knowledge bases

Microservices Whenever possible, create a component image self-sufficient, with little or no assumptions of the modes of operation of other components in a DLD setup.

Programming Language Agnostic Specifications are formulated and data formats were chosen so that a broad choice of programming languages provide the capabilities and libraries to allow the implementation, the configuration, and supervision of components. This should allow for contributions by third parties.

Another simplifying convention in the current state of the project is that at most one *load*, *backup*, and *store* component can exist per setup. These components are referenced by exactly that name in the Docker Compose-configuration. H owever, a n a rbitrary n umber o f *p resent & edit* components is possible.

Storage

A *store* is a graph database management system (triples store) capable of storing the RDF triples of RDF knowledge bases. It usually provides a SPARQL Query [The13] interface which can also be used with SPARQL Update for adding and removing triples. Containers that implement the *store* component typically consist of an executable file t o r un t he D BMS a nd t heir d ependencies t ogether w ith i ts configuration fi les an d a sc ript-based ma nagement pr ocess. Th is process, if necessary, adjusts the configuration fi les pr ior to st ore initialization and supervises the store process, possibly also restarts the store process on (unexpected) termination for basic failover. To ensure the persistent storage of saved triples independent of the lifetime of the store container, data directories for the provided store are kept in a volume (depending on configuration e ither a fi le sy stem lo cation of th e host system or a volume managed by Docker).

For the proof of concept we started with images for the triple store component using the *Open Link Virtuoso*[13] and *Apache Jena Fuseki*

---

[13] *Open Link Virtuoso Open-Source Edition web page:*

2.[14] Other DLD compliant store images can also be provided by third parties if they can be set up in a Linux environment and configured to work according to a small set of conventions detailed later in the section "Container Design and Conventions."

Load and Backup

A *load* component is responsible for pre-loading a triple store with an RDF knowledge base when initialising a container setup. The actual RDF knowledge base file c an e ither b e p rovided a s a fi le on th e host system, can be fetched from an online source, or can be provided from some backup location. During the *data loading phase*, right after the *configuration phase*, a loading container starts to connect to the configured triple store and injects the necessary data, which is then available at the triple store during the *service phase*. A load container can either connect to the triple store via the standard SPARQL interface or use proprietary side-loading mechanisms.

Backup containers serve as a data pump. They frequently query the data of a triple store and store it in a safe location. A backup container has the same life-cycle as the triple store for which it is creating the backup. This can be done by configuring a c ron j ob w hich i s executed in fixed i ntervals t o d ump a ll d ata f rom t he t riple s tore (backup data pump). Components responsible for synchronising different setups also belong to this category of images.

Presentation and Publication

Presentation and publication images are meant to provide exploration interfaces to the knowledge base. This can be any application capable of fetching data from a triple store to provide the user with some generic or special view to the data. In this proof of concept we are providing the generic exploration interfaces pubby ,[15] snorql,[16] and OntoWiki [Fri+15]. OntoWiki also provides the possibility to create very specific exploration and publication interfaces with its Site Extension.[17] This capability allows to provide domain specific v iews a nd e diting com- ponents. A limitation of OntoWiki is that it currently supports the Virtuoso triple store only.

A presentation container is linked to the triple store and connects to the database with the credentials given in the environment variables from the triple store container. It is available throughout the complete *service phase*. Communication with the triple store is implemented in SPARQL or any custom interfaces available. The presentation interface

---

sitory at GitHub:

finally is exposed as HTTP interface (at port 80) which than can be made available to the Web through the host's network.

Container Design and Conventions

```
 1  # VOS7
 2  LABEL org.aksw.dld.type = "store" \
 3         org.aksw.dld.subtype = "vos7" \
 4         org.aksw.dld.component-constraints = {"load": "vos"}
 5
 6  # OntoWiki
 7  LABEL org.aksw.dld.type = "present" \
 8         org.aksw.dld.component-constraints = {"store": "vos[67]"}
 9
10  # VOS load
11  LABEL org.aksw.dld.type = "load" \
12         org.aksw.dld.volumes-from = ["store"]
```

Listing 7.1: Examples for the usage of Docker labels for meta-information on component images for Virtuoso Open Source (VOS) and OntoWiki.

DLD-compatible images expose a set of required meta-data items using the Docker Labels. The DLD labels are used for defining the type, special requirements, and configuration options of an image. Special configuration options for example can be expected environment variables or volumes required to be provided. Label values for DLD keys are JSON strings, which also allow to define Docker Compose configuration fragments to be declared. Listing 7.1 shows some examples of the usage of labels in DLD. Lines 2-4 define the labels for the Virtuoso Open Source 7 component. Line 2 tells it is a triple store, line 3 specifies the type to by a Virtuoso Open Source 7 triple store, and line 4 tells that it can only be loaded with the **vos** component because it requires Virtuoso's bulk loading facilities. Lines 7 and 8 define the type of OntoWiki to be a presentation component and that it requires a Virtuoso Open Source store of version 6 or 7 (the value is interpreted as regular expression). Line 11 and 12 define the VOS load component, which needs to copy data into the file system of the store and for that needs to mount the volumes from the store to obtain a shared part of the file system.

Settings adjusting the behaviour of component containers during their execution are defined by declaring environment variables. This allows for instance load components to be informed about credentials that have been set for the store to gain additional privileges for side-loading operations.[18] Some environment variables like SPARQL_ENDPOINT_URL and DEFAULT_GRAPH are expected by convention for all components and can be defined universally in the DLD configuration file.

Usually the life-cycle of a component is split into a short *configuration phase* immediately after the instantiation, which is followed by an optional *data loading phase* before the container starts serving their encapsulated service in the *service phase*. The configuration phase allows

---

[18] A PASSWORD environment variable from the store e.g. is provided as STORE_ENV_-PASSWORD in the linking load container.

to adjustment the service setup, e. g. set required authentication details for a triple store, which named graph should be presented by default by a presentation component, or the host name under which such a component is exposed to the Web, which is required to ensure correct minting of de-referenceable Linked Data descriptions for resources.

In addition to aforementioned conventions applicable to all components, DLD also builds on some conventions for specific component types. For instance RDF data dumps to be processed by load components are expected to be placed in a mounted volume named /import inside the container.

Provisioning of a Container Setup

The requirements for the presented architecture are the Dockerizing Linked Data (DLD) tools as described at our project web page, a running *Docker* engine installation, and the *Docker Compose* tool. Since the publication of the original paper [Arn+15] the popularity of Docker still kept up and the technology has further evolved. This lead to several changes in the programming interfaces, some of the were used by the original proof-of-concept implementation of the DLD tool. The output of the DLD tool still functioning but since it is making use of the Link feature, which was deprecated in the meantime, also our implementation is deprecated.

```
datasets:
    dbpedia-2015-endpoint:
        graph_name: "http://dbpedia.org"
        location_list: "dbp-2015-download.list"


components:
    store:
        image: aksw/dld-store-virtuoso7
        ports: ["8891:8890"]
        environment:
            PWDDBA: ercesrepus
        mem_limit: 8G


    load: aksw/dld-load-virtuoso
    present:
        ontowiki:
            image: aksw/dld-present-ontowiki
            ports: ["8088:80"]

environment_global:
    DEFAULT_GRAPH: "http://dbpedia.org"
    SPARQL_ENDPOINT_URL: "http://store:8890/sparql"
```

Listing 7.2: A DLD configuration file for a setup with the Virtuoso Open Source triple store, a suitable load component and OntoWiki to present & edit, retrieving DBpedia data via downloads listed in a separate file

Listing 7.2 shows an example of a DLD configuration file. In addition to the specification of components, data to be served by the store can be specified in the datasets section. In the example configuration a separate file is referenced that lists URLs of dataset dumps to be retrieved and loaded. Options to specify the location of RDF data to be imported are `file` a path in the local file system to an RDF dump, `file_list` a file containing a list of local paths, `location` to download an individual RDF data dump from the Web, and, as used in the example, `location_list` specifies a file containing a list of download locations. Based on the example configuration, the DLD configuration tool will perform several tasks to prepare the setup:

1. A working directory is created that will contain the compiled Docker Compose configuration and, if specified, data dumps to be loaded.

2. Referenced images will be pulled.

3. The DLD-specific meta-data labels of the images will be extracted, checks for declared and implicit setup constraints will be performed, and entailed additional Docker Compose configuration items are incorporated to the final setup.

4. Specified Linked Data dumps are downloaded and aggregated into a directory named `models` inside the working directory, augmented with files specifying the named graph URIs according to the conventions of the Virtuosos bulk loader.[19]

5. A Docker Compose file is written that specifies the configured setup.

```
load:
    environment: {DEFAULT_GRAPH: 'http://dbpedia.org',
        ↪ SPARQL_ENDPOINT_URL: 'http://store:8890/sparql'}
    image: aksw/dld-load-virtuoso
    links: [store]
    volumes: ['/opt/dld/wd-dbp2015-ontowiki/models:/import']
    volumes_from: [store]
presentontowiki:
    environment: {DEFAULT_GRAPH: 'http://dbpedia.org',
        ↪ SPARQL_ENDPOINT_URL: 'http://store:8890/sparql'}
    image: aksw/dld-present-ontowiki
    links: [store]
    ports: ['8088:80']
store:
    environment: {MEM_LIMIT: '8G', DEFAULT_GRAPH: 'http://dbpedia.org',
        ↪ SPARQL_ENDPOINT_URL: 'http://store:8890/sparql', PWDDBA:
        ↪ 'ercesrepus'}
    image: aksw/dld-store-virtuoso7
    mem_limit: 8G
    ports: ['8891:8890']
```

Listing 7.3: Docker Compose configuration file compiled by the DLD configuration tool based on the configuration in listing 7.2.

Listing 7.3 shows a resulting Docker Compose configuration, which can either be submitted directly by the configuration t ools t o Docker Compose to start the configured s ervices o r c hecked a nd r evised by the user before a subsequent manual start by invoking `docker-compose up`. The apparent close correspondences between fragments of the DLD configuration a nd t he r esulting D ocker C ompose i s i ntended a s this lowers the entry barrier for new users of DLD with prior experience with Docker Compose and allows to develop an intuition how the final configuration i s c reated m ore e asily. W hen s tarting t he e xample presented, the user can reach OntoWiki at port 8088 and the SPARQL interface of Virtuoso at port 8891 of the host system.

Although not presented in detail in this paper, it should be mentioned that setups without load and backup components are possible as well. A prime example is the usage of a store component that links in a volume with database files t hat c ontain a s election o f R DF datasets already pre-loaded.

7.2 Jekyll RDF

Over the last decades the Web has evolved from a human-human communication network to a network of complex human-machine interactions. An increasing amount of data is available as Linked Data which allows machines to "understand" the data, but RDF is not meant to be understood by humans. With Jekyll RDF we present a method to close the gap between structured data and human accessible exploration interfaces by publishing RDF datasets as customizable static HTML sites. It consists of an RDF resource mapping system to serve the resources under their respective IRI, a template mapping based on schema classes, and a markup language to define t emplates t o render customized resource pages. Using the template system, it is possible to create domain specific b rowsing i nterfaces f or R DF d ata n ext t o the Linked Data resources. This enables content management and knowledge management systems to serve datasets in a highly customizable, low effort, a nd s calable w ay t o b e c onsumed b y m achines a s w ell as humans.

In 2001 Tim Berners-Lee and James Hendler stated: *The Web was designed as an information space, with the goal not only that it should be useful for human-human communication, but also that machines would be able to participate and help users communicate with each other* [BH01]. Now 18 years later we are at the point that a huge amount of data is published as Linked Data as it is apparent in the *Linked Open Data Cloud*[20] with 1,234 datasets and 16,136 links between the datasets.[21] But the RDF data is not suited and meant to be read and understood by humans. On the informal Semantic Web Layer Model the top most layer represents *User Interface & Applications* (cf. section 2.4). A variety of applications exist to visualize RDF

---

[20] *The Linked Open Data Cloud*: h

data. Such applications are table-based triple explorers, like *pubby*,[22] *LOD View*,[23] and *LD Viewer/DBpedia Viewer* [Luk+14]; [LSL14] and visual graph explorers like *LodLive*,[24] *LODmilla* [MTT14], and *Linked Data Maps* [Val+15]. These applications are restricted to a view that is very close to the RDF data model and are thus suited for data experts who understand the concepts of RDF and the respective vocabularies, but not suitable for end users.

Web Content Management Systems (WCMS) are software systems to support the processes to create, manage, provide, control, and customize content for websites [GM09]. Besides the management of the content in a Content Repository, the customizable presentation using templating systems is a key aspect of WCMS. Semantic Content Management Systems (SCMS) extend Content Management Systems with additional functionality to enrich the content with semantic meta-data in a Knowledge Repository. Nowadays we are at the point that the semantic data is not "only" meta-data, but encodes the information itself. The activity to manage the semantic data as information by itself is called Semantic Data Management and gets a lot of attention [BHB09]; [Aue+12]. To make this semantic data available to end users there is a need for semantic templating systems which is experiencing little research so far.

In this work, we present an approach for the generation of static Web exploration interfaces on Linked Data. The approach is based on devising a declarative DSL to create templates to render instance data. The templates are associated to RDF classes and a breath-first search algorithm determines the best-suitable template for any given data resource. To demonstrate the feasibility of the approach, we implemented it as an extension to the popular Jekyll[25] Static Site Generator and CMS.[26] In contrast to dynamic web pages, static web pages are preparatively generated and can be served without further server-side computation, thus providing highest possible scalability. This approach is complementary to the data focused approach of Linked Data Fragments[27] to reduce costly server-side request evaluation. By rendering RDF data to static HTML sites we provide a method to browse the Semantic Web seamlessly integrated with the rest of the Web and close

---

the gap between structured data and human accessible exploration interfaces. To the best of our knowledge Jekyll RDF[28] is the first approach to apply the concept of Static Site Generators to RDF knowledge bases. It does not require programming knowledge from its users, does not need a dynamic back-end, nor is it integrated in an IDE. It is provided as a microservice and as such can be integrated with existing content management and knowledge management workflows. D ue to the modular conception the presented method should be transferable to further Static Site Generators like Next, Hugo, and Hyde or complex frameworks like Gatsby.[29]

In this section we first give an overview on existing RDF publication methods in section 7.2.1. Then we provide an overview on the Static Site Generator architecture with detailed descriptions of the core components in section 7.2.2. An important aspect of the separation of concerns approach is the ability to integrate a tool with larger systems to accomplish high-level tasks. We present the integration of the Static Site Generator in a Linked Data tool chain in section 7.2.3. Finally, we draw our conclusions and outline future work in section 7.3.

7.2.1 Existing RDF Publication Methods

The generic data model provided by RDF allows the publication of data representing various domains and their aspects on the Web. The abstraction of the data model from its representation opens the possibility for arbitrary visualizations of the data. A variety of systems exists that provide ways to access and visualize RDF data [KSN19]; [JDZ16]. Many systems are created to serve a specific p urpose such as visualizing a specific d ataset o r d ata e xpressed u sing a s pecific vocabulary. In the following we focus on frameworks and template-based systems that provide a generic tooling to create custom exploration and visualization interfaces that are usable for any RDF dataset.

Building on the technological stack of the Extensible Markup Language (XML), the Extensible Stylesheet Language Transformation (XSLT) [Bra+06]; [Kay17] is obvious to be used to transform RDF/XML documents to HTML representations. A limitation with this approach is that it requires a strict adherence of the same XML representation of the RDF graph to be able to apply the stylesheet. This makes it inflexible and complicated to use, also it is not easy to incorporate modern web technology when building the HTML representation in such a way.

Templating systems provide a flexible a pproach f or i nserting data into a scaffolding of an HTML page. The *SPARQL Web Pages*[30] sys-

---

[28] *jekyll-rdf*. The jekyll-rdf Repository at GitHub:
[29] *Homepage of the Next.js Framework*:

tem defines a templating language that allows to incorporate data from an RDF graph into HTML and SVG documents. It is shipped with the commercial version of the *TopBraid Composer*. A similar approach is followed by *LESS* [ADD10] which later was integrated with the *OntoWiki* [Fri+15]. The *OntoWiki Site Extension*[31] [FAM16] allows to render RDF resources in HTML views using a PHP base templating language. To serve the required representation of a Linked Data resources the OntoWiki Linked Data server uses content negotiation to dynamically serve an HTML view to web browsers and an RDF representation to Linked Data systems.

A different approach to provide customizable web interfaces to explore and even edit RDF data is presented by Khalili et al. with the *LD-R* [KLH16]. It provides a framework to define *Linked Data-driven Web Components* in JavaScript. With this framework it is possible to reuse existing components and compose new dynamic web interfaces. A similar approach to build *Semantic Interfaces for Web Applications* is presented with the MIRA framework [BS16]. It defines an *abstract interface definition* that composes elements to form a hierarchy of widgets. These widgets can be used in JavaScript applications to build responsive user interfaces.

In summary, the related work of LD-R and MIRA [KLH16]; [BS16] as well as complex frameworks like Gatsby aim at programmers and software engineers. The previous work of LESS and the OntoWiki Site Extension [ADD10]; [Fri+15]; [FAM16] provides a template-based approach. But LESS and OntoWiki Site Extension as well as the application frameworks presented in [KLH16]; [BS16] rely on a server side complex *dynamic* data management system. In this paper, our aim is to provide a *static* approach to maximize the scalability while minimizing the effort by following a template-based approach that can be used without programming knowledge.

7.2.2 The Static Site Generation Architecture

We deceived our system as an extension to existing Static Site Generators. A Static Site Generator translates a set of HTML and Markdown files (*pages*) to a collection of HTML files (*site*) by using structural *templates*. Pages and templates can be conditionally formatted and enriched with tags and filters defined by a markup language to embed data values and alter the presentation. The generated site is served either with an integrated web server or any other HTTP server. To showcase our approach we implemented Jekyll RDF[32] as a plugin for the popular Jekyll system.

The plugin system of Jekyll provides among others the possibility to add a *generator* to create new pages and to implement custom *tags*

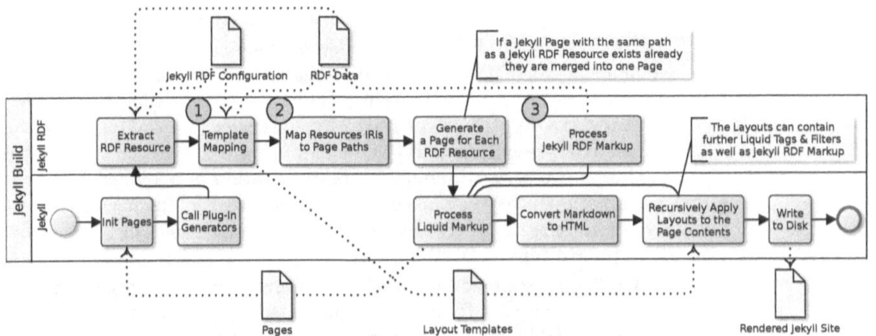

Figure 7.2: The architecture of Jekyll RDF and its interplay with Jekyll.

and *filters* for the Liquid markup language.[33] Jekyll RDF uses this system to provide its main functionalities as depicted in fig. 7.2: (1, 2) generate a Jekyll page for each resource from the RDF graph (cf. section 7.2.2), and (3) extend the markup language by a set of filters and tags to query the RDF graph (*Jekyll RDF Markup Language*, cf. section 7.2.2). *Jekyll* controls the main flow of the build process which is depicted in the lower row. The particular tasks which are relevant for the rendering of RDF data are depicted in the upper row. The process needs several data artifacts namely, the *pages* to be rendered by Jekyll, the *configuration* options which are specific to Jekyll RDF, the *RDF data*, and the *templates* to defined the layout of the pages and RDF resources. The process to generate a Jekyll page for each RDF resource is split into four steps, extract the RDF resource from the RDF data model as specified in the configuration (cf. listing 7.4) and create program objects accordingly, map the resources to templates, map the IRIs of the RDF resources to according page paths, and generate a Jekyll page object for each RDF resource. The template mapping (no. 1 in fig. 7.2) can happen directly per RDF resource or based on the RDF types of a resource, this is described in detail in section 7.2.2. Design decisions required to represent the RDF resource's IRIs in the path system of Jekyll are explained in section 7.2.2 (no. 2). Further, Liquid is extended to the *Jekyll RDF Markup Language* which is presented in section 7.2.2 (no. 3).

In listing 7.4 an exemplary configuration file for Jekyll is provided with the relevant sections to configure a Jekyll RDF setup. Lines 1 and 2 together represent the URL under which a Jekyll site is served. In line 3 the Jekyll RDF plugin is registered. Lines 4 to 13 are the specific parameters to configure Jekyll RDF, the path (line 5) specifies the data source for the RDF data and the restriction (line 6) specifies the list of RDF resources to be rendered. Lines 7 to 13 specify the template mapping and are further described in section 7.2.2.

```
baseurl: "/sachsen/"
url: "http://pfarrerbuch.aksw.org"
plugins: [jekyll-rdf]
jekyll_rdf:
  path: "sachsen.ttl"
  restriction: "SELECT ?resourceUri WHERE {?resourceUri ?p ?o . FILTER
      ↪ regex(str(?resourceUri),
      ↪ '^http://pfarrerbuch.aksw.org/sachsen/')}"
  default_template: "resource"
  class_template_mappings:
    "http://xmlns.com/foaf/0.1/Person": "person"
    "http://purl.org/voc/hp/Place": "place"
    "http://purl.org/voc/hp/Position": "position"
  instance_template_mappings:
    "http://pfarrerbuch.aksw.org/": "home"
```

Listing 7.4: The sections of the Jekyll configuration relevant for Jekyll RDF including base url, data source, selection of resources, and template mappings.

Template Mapping

Jekyll provides a templating system to allow the reuse of components on multiple pages and allow similar pages to look alike. The template for a Jekyll page is specified in a header in the page. During the rendering process Jekyll applies this template to the content of the page. In contrast to a Jekyll page an RDF resources has no "content" and no header and thus we need to specify the representation of the resource. In the following we introduce three mapping mechanisms to determine which template should be applied for a resource. The template assignment configuration is shown in lines 7 to 13 in listing 7.4. In the `instance_template_mappings` section each resource can be directly assigned to a template by specifying the resource IRI and the template name. Further, two indirect options to assign a template are specified. In the section `class_template_mappings` RDF classes are mapped to templates. Each resource that is an instance of a specified class or its subclasses gets this template assigned. The precedence order of the template mappings is: instance-based, class-based, `default_template`.

Other than for the instance-based and default mapping the class template mapping introduces ambiguity as depicted in fig. 7.3. If a resource has multiple classes and each has a template assigned, it can not be decided which template to use for the resource. The template selection can not be limited to the trivial evaluation of `rdf:type` triples as this would not take the assignment of templates to super classes into account. Inferencing along `rdfs:subClassOf` relations would also be no good approach as it introduces more ambiguity and hides precedence information about the most specific class for a resource.

We decided to select the template for an instance according to three rules as depicted in fig. 7.3 (a *candidate* is a class that has a template assigned). (1) Select the closest candidate in the class hierarchy, (2) if more then one candidate exists with different templates but with the same shortest path distance, take the candidate with the most *specific* class, (3) if still no candidate could be selected, produce a warning and randomly select one of the candidates. A class a is considered more *specific* than b if an `rdfs:subClassOf` property path exists from a to b but not the other way around. To implement the template selection we chose a breath-first-search algorithm on the class hierarchy. To avoid cycles, visited classes are marked. Once a suitable templates is selected all classes along the search path are annotated with their distance to the selected candidate and a reference to the selected template. These annotations can be used to prune the search space of subsequent iterations. To optimize the overall process for resources with the same sets of classes we maintain a dictionary of the hashed sorted list of class IRIs and the selected template throughout the rendering process. Using this dictionary no resource that is subsequently rendered with the same set of classes needs to initiate a new template selection process.

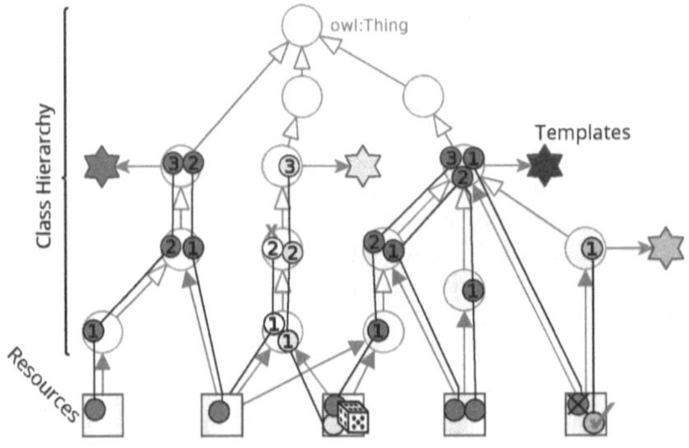

Figure 7.3: Class hierarchy to select a template to render a resource in Jekyll RDF

Resource Mapping and Site Creation

Figure 7.4: Scheme of the selection of page paths based on the configured Jekyll Site URL.

Jekyll RDF is meant to provide an HTML view for Linked Data resources and thus we need to map the resource's HTTP IRIs to file system paths, which is depicted in fig. 7.4. Taking an RDF resource Jekyll RDF matches it with the Jekyll Site URL as it is set in lines 1 and 2 of the configuration in listing 7.4. The matched part is than removed from the resource IRI and the remaining part `ort/3441` is mapped to the file path `ort/3441.html`. A query string in an IRI can be treated in the same way as a path. A fragment part is interpreted and truncated by the browser during a request, thus the second resource IRI ends up at the same IRI as the previous one. As fragment identifiers are typically used to identify anchors in HTML pages, all IRIs with a fragment are added to a list data structure (page.subResources) of the respective non fragment IRI page. All resources that do not match the configured base IRI are rendered with a, currently unstable, fallback solution under the directory rdfsites.

It is possible that a resource created by Jekyll RDF would overwrite a page that was already generated by Jekyll or any other plugin. In this case Jekyll RDF merges the two page object into one page and copies the content of the previously existing page into the content variable (cf. section 7.2.2) of the template selected for the RDF resource. If a template is specified for the Jekyll page, it overwrites the template selected for the RDF resource.

Jekyll RDF Markup Language

Filter	Parameters ([optional])	Description
rdf_get		Get a variable representing a resource from the RDF graph.
rdf_property	IRI, [language, bool]	Get a value of a property of a resource (lines 1, 2, and 7 of listing 7.5). If the last parameter is set to true, an array is returned (line 8).
rdf_inverse_property	IRI, [bool]	Get the value of an inverse property.
rdf_collection and rdf_container	[IRI]	Get RDF collections and RDF containers from the RDF graph as shown in line 4 of listing 7.5.
sparql_query	sparql query	Execute a SPARQL Query on the RDF graph, the passed value is bound to ?resourceUri or to ?resourceUri_n if an array is provided.

Table 7.1: The filters defined by Jekyll RDF and the tasks performed by them.

The Jekyll RDF Markup Language (JML) is based on Liquid and extends it by filters to access the RDF graph from within a template. Liquid provides the concepts of *objects, tags,* and *filters*. *Objects* define placeholders in a template to insert values and are denoted by two curly braces {{ ... }}. The special object {{content}} in templates is a placeholder for the content of the rendered page. *Tags* are used to embed control flow into the template, they are denoted by curly braces and percent signs {% ... %}. The tag {% assign = "some value" %} is used to assign a value to a variable. *Filters* manipulate the output of objects or the value of variables, they are chained and applied from left to right and separated by a vertical bar |. A filter gets a *value* passed from the left and can get *parameters* passed to the right after a colon : and separated by commas.

On every page which is generated by Jekyll RDF the variable page.rdf is present to reference the RDF resource represented by that page. To provide a way to access the RDF graph from within the template Jekyll RDF defines new Liquid filters as shown in table 7.1 and listing 7.5. The usage of Liquid filters allows to chain existing

```
<h1>{{ page.rdf | rdf_property: "rdfs:label", "en" }}</h1>
<div>{{ page.rdf | rdf_property: "dct:created" | date: "%Y-%m-%d" }}</div>

{% assign publicationlist = "ex:publicationlist" | rdf_container %}
<ul>
{% for pub in publicationlist %}
<li>{{ pub | rdf_property: "dc:title" }}</li>
<li>{{ pub | rdf_property: "dct:creator", false, true | join: ",␣" }}</li>
{% endfor %}
</ul>
```

Listing 7.5: A simplified example of template with HTML markup enriched by JML filters.

filters and filters defined by further plugins to the output of the JML filters. The JML filters accept a resource IRI as string or a resource object to be passed as value, they are shown and described in table 7.1.

7.2.3 Integration With Data Publication Workflows

With our approach we follow the microservice principle which recently is gaining attention with the increase of the importance to manage complex software systems. Following this principle, it is possible to integrate Jekyll RDF with existing tools, workflows, management systems, and interfaces to build a full SCMS or to support data engineers to publish RDF graphs as HTML pages. A pragmatic and in software engineering already proven successful approach for coordinating collaboration and exchange of artifacts is the usage of Git repositories, which is taken up by the Quit methodology to manage RDF knowledge repositories. In the following we show two aspects to consider when integrating Jekyll RDF with data management and content management workflows. We present two setups that adapt the continuous integration method from software engineering to build flexible data publication workflows with Jekyll RDF in section 7.2.3. To close the gap between structured data and human accessible browsing interfaces based on Jekyll RDF it is equally important to make the underlying RDF data available. We discuss possibilities to integrate the HTML and RDF publication with each other in section 7.2.3.

Using Jekyll RDF With a Continuous Integration

Continuous Integration (CI) is a concept used in software engineering to automatically test, build, and deploy software artifacts. This concept recently increases in usage for data engineering [MJ16]. With Jekyll RDF it is possible to define a step in a CI system to render and deploy pages whenever the data is updated. Travis CI[34] is a hosted continues integration service used to build and test software projects at GitHub. Using a continuous integration system during the work in a team allows to produce automated builds and feedback during the development process whenever a contributor updates the templates or data in the Git repository. In fig. 7.5 we show two possible setups

---

[34] *Travis CI*. Continuous Integration Platform:

of automatic continuous deployment pipelines to publish Jekyll RDF sites. The setup in fig. 7.5a shows a completely publicly hosted setup that uses the Travis CI service to build the Jekyll RDF site and the webspace provided by GitHub pages to serve the produced Static Site. This setup allows a flexible collaboration system combined with a free of charge deployment without the need to maintain a complex infrastructure. The setup in fig. 7.5b is slightly complexer and allows the differentiation between a stable "master" version and an unstable "develop" version. In combination with Docker it is possible to build ready to deploy system images including the rendered site. Whenever an updated system image is available the deployment restarts the respective service with the updated image.

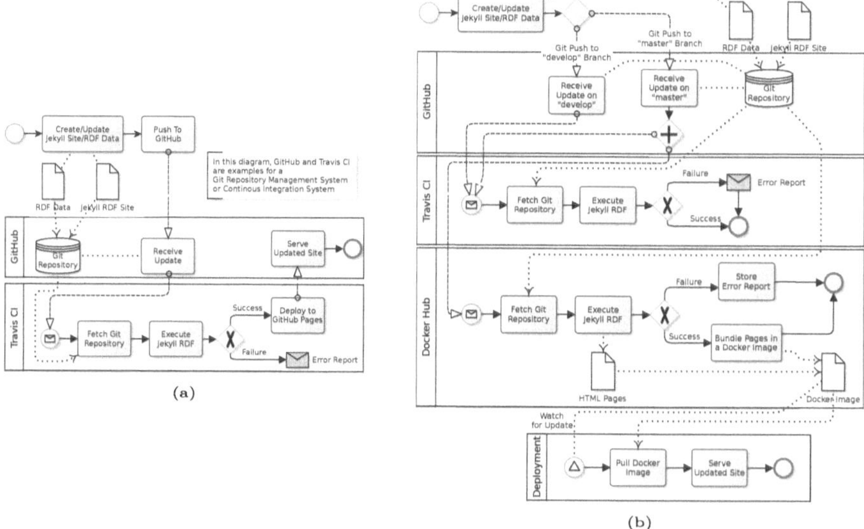

Figure 7.5: Jekyll RDF integrated in two different deployment pipelines.

Integration With RDF Publication

Following the Linked Data principle: *When someone looks up a URI, provide useful information, using the standards (RDF*, SPARQL)* [Ber09] one page is created for each resource in the knowledge graph. Each resource page *provides useful information* in a human accessible format. Since the web page is build based on RDF data, besides the HTML representation, it is also important to make the underlying RDF data available to Semantic Web agents. To achieve this, various methods exist to make the respective data available as needed. In the following we discuss possibilities that have an overlap with the setup of Static Sites.

A way to embed data in a document is to use RDFa properties within the HTML tags. Since RDFa interferes with the surrounding HTML-tags it is not subject to Jekyll RDF. Instead the embedding has to be performed by the template designer. To support the designer this problem could also be subject to future work for building a *Jekyll RDFa* plugin on top of Jekyll RDF. Instead of embedding the RDF data each resource can also be served in a separate file. In this case a script is employed to process the same data source as Jekyll RDF and produce individual Linked Data resource pages. To provide a possibility for an agent to find the respective resource page a link can be set or the HTTP server employs content negotiation. But in many cases, where Static Sites are used, the user has no ability to interfere with the HTTP protocol of the server. In this case the only way is to add an *HTML header link tag*[35] to point to the resource page, this can be embedded directly in any Jekyll template. If the HTTP protocol of the server can be configured, the same link can be set as *HTTP Link header*[Not17]. In this case also *content negotiation*[FR14] is an elegant commonly used way to serve the correct representation of the resource based on the request.

7.3 Conclusion

Setup	#Triples	#Templates/#Pages	#Res. Pages	Avg. Runtime
Open Hebrew Inventory	197,374	4/2	13,426	1952.4 s (32.54 min)
Pfarrerbuch (demo subset)	1,685	4/-	138	8 s
SDA Work Group	27,295	8 (Class) + 49 (Inst.)/2	253	327.3 s (5.45 min)
diggr Vocabulary	221	1/-	1	8 s

Table 7.2: Comparison of the presented Jekyll RDF setups. The average runtime is measured at the Travis CI over the last 10 runs.

Different interfaces for the visualization and exploration of knowledge bases allow editors and other stakeholders in a collaborative knowledge engineering process to get different views on the data. The consumption and exploratory perception of the data is an important aspect in a collaborative scenario to combine existing knowledge and create new knowledge. To allow the publication of RDF knowledge bases with minimized effort we have presented two systems. The Dockerizing Linked Data approach supports administrators and domain experts to provision and maintain RDF publication, and also curation, infrastructures. With the Jekyll RDF system we allow to build templates for RDF classes to render the resources and build a complex exploration interface that can be served with maximum scalability to improve the accessibility of the data.

---

[35] *HTML 5.2: § 4.2.4. The link element.*

With the Dockerizing Linked Data approach we have presented a methodology and procedure to significantly ease knowledge base deployment and maintenance by using *Docker* containers and the principle of microservices. Working with Linked Data one often encounters knowledge bases that face regular downtimes, significant load or completely lack Linked Data publication. The approach together with current proof of concept implementations for pre-configured knowledge base exploration and authoring setups shows several desirable properties. The same setup can be reused for different knowledge bases or under recurring requirements to the software setup, while only the data to load has to be exchanged. On the other hand with the presented modular architecture it is also possible to exchange individual components without major dependencies to other components. One can select different triple store implementations with different advantages and disadvantages in respect to the data to be published and the associated use case. The portability of knowledge base setups is improved by transferring a customized *DLD* specification and optionally the data to load to collaborators. Even though the collaborators might be using different platforms, the presented tool allows them to easily setup a mirror which significantly reduces collaboration overhead. Shipping knowledge bases together with the deployment configuration that was used during experiments also increases the reproducibility of research by eliminating errors in the data setup.

Large, well established and popular Linked Data projects like DBpedia can benefit from the establishment of the presented approach or a similar scheme. It can incentivize a share of users to reduce load on public endpoints by choosing to setup their private mirror which entails further benefits, like stability and faster access. As a result the easy distributed deployment of mirrors can reduce the load on a central infrastructure. We have also shown that small knowledge bases without large community backing can gain from dockerized data deployment. In the future, we want to further improve data deployment by providing a visual front-end for configuration. We further concentrate on reproducibility by enabling data deployment *Docker* recipes to be shipped via DataID. By adding essential configuration properties in a DataID ontology module, dataset descriptions using DataID will be able to provide information on how to set up the data locally. This will make it possible to ship machine readable descriptions of the complete data back-end of experiments and further improving reproducibility. Introducing a common light-weight network message bus infrastructure integrated in all provided images to allow for more detailed queries of configuration and environment parameters for tighter integration as well as status requests appears worthwhile.

With the presented Jekyll RDF system we provide a methodology to close the gap between RDF data publishing and highly customizable publication and exploration interfaces. With our system it is possible to separate the management of RDF dataset from the creation of appropriate templates for the data presentation. Because we piggyback on the successful concept of Static Site Generators a low entry barrier is provided and the system requirements for the HTTP server are low. There is no need for costly dynamic server side computations which often also rely on the availability of a hard to maintain SPARQL endpoint.

With the Jekyll RDF method we have implemented a selection of use cases to build customized data exploration interfaces. The use cases are from different domains and provide very individual user interfaces as shown in chapter 8 in the figs. 8.2, 8.10 and 8.11. Two use cases are from the Digital Humanities, a Current Research Information System, and we eat our own dogfood and present the usability of Jekyll RDF to build vocabulary description pages. In table 7.2 we compare the setups according to the number of triples, defined templates and pages, resulting pages, and execution time. As shown in table 7.2 the system allows the quick publication of small RDF dataset like RDF vocabulary, but also the creation of pages for huge datasets of more then $10k$ pages is possible with just a view templates. Especially, for the publication of highly interlinked datasets the usage of Jekyll RDF has assets as shown by the CRIS use case.

As a Static Site Generator performs the work of creating the HTML pages in advance, the creation and the serving can be separated. The use of computing power is predictable and not affected by the amount of page visits. The separation allows a maximum flexibility in scaling the delivery of the site. It is possible to make extensive use of caching mechanisms such as *content delivery networks* to reduce the workload on the server and increase the availability of a site. In contrast to caching of dynamic pages the maintenance of static sites does not suffer from the problem of cache invalidation which lowers the effort of the publication.

In contrast to the related work of LD-R and MIRA [KLH16]; [BS16] and Gatsby we provide a template-based approach that aims at users without software developing experience. With the JML we minimize the effort of publishing Linked Data without the need to write a single line of programming code. Using JML as domain specific language allows also Web Designers to integrate knowledge from RDF graphs into their work. The template-based approach is similar to our previous work with LESS and the OntoWiki Site Extension [ADD10]; [Fri+15]; [FAM16]. However, the previous work as well as the application frameworks presented in [KLH16]; [BS16] relies on a complex dynamic data management back-end and SPARQL endpoint. With Jekyll RDF we present a static approach to maximize the scalability as it is independent of the availability of dynamic components at runtime.

As we extended Jekyll for our prototype we can benefit from the big ecosystem of plugins to enrich the created site. For the future work the performance of the generation process can be improved by an incremental build process to reuse pages from previous builds. To increase the usability of the presented method as a SCMS a set of predefined themes to be used with Jekyll RDF can support users, as shown by JOD. Looking at the possibilities of this concept in combination with the successful and generic design of RDF we see a good potential for future use cases. Due to the plethora of Static Site Generators we hope to see implementations to adopt our conception and methods to further systems like Next, Hugo, and Hyde.[36] There is no need to decide whether to publish data or a customized human readable interface anymore as the can be server next to each other on a static webspace.

8 Application and Evaluation

The presented method for distributed and decentralized collaborative versioning of evolving Linked Data is evaluated in the following. For the evaluation several case studies, verification tests, and quantitative evaluations are performed. The case studies present the feasibility and practicability of the presented tool stack in different scenarios. The verification tests prove the correctness of the system. The quantitative evaluation investigates the performance of the system and its limitations.

The case studies depend on their purpose, such as requirements of the work to be performed, the organizational structure, and other environmental influences. The case studies are categorized into two groups:

Organizational Data Scenarios for working with organizational data come with an established workflow and well defined roles. Communication and agile collaboration is usually less in the focus then the predefined task to be performed. The organizational structure might be distributed across different collaborating institutions, as typically for virtual organizations. Additionally requirements towards the reliability and failure safety are important and need to be supported by the collaboration infrastructure. Evaluated use cases: THW (Communication in the Emergency Response Staff; section 8.3), amsl.technology (section 8.4.1), aksw.org/sda.tech (Current Research Information System; sections 8.4.2 and 8.4.3)

Research Data For collaboration on creating and maintaining research data the scientific background of the collaborators has to be considered. The background includes the constitution of roles within a team, the level of expertise, and the area of expertise in different domains. The collaboration is either placed in a single common research area or includes multiple research areas. When managing data in a research project typically multiple parties from different institutions collaborate, as in virtual research organizations. The organizational structure is distributed across different collaborating institutions. Also over the time research data is managed by different research projects with changing organizational structure. Workflows within the collaborative scenario might shift in an agile way. Evaluated use cases: MMoOn (section 8.1), Pfarrerbuch and Catalogus Profesorum Lipsiensium are examples for the collaborative research data management (section 8.2), and Vocabulary Documentation (section 8.4.4).

Our overall method is following the microservice principle of individual components. This principle is achieved as each component provides

The results presented in this chapter were first published in Arndt et al.: "Knowledge Base Shipping to the Linked Open Data Cloud" [Arn+15]; Frischmuth, Arndt, and Martin: "OntoWiki 1.0: 10 Years of Development - What's New in OntoWiki" [FAM16]; Klimek et al.: "Creating Linked Data Morphological Language Resources with MMoOn - The Hebrew Morpheme Inventory" [Kli+16]; Arndt and Martin: "Decentralized Evolution and Consolidation of RDF Graphs" [AM17]; Arndt et al.: "Decentralized Collaborative Knowledge Management using Git" [Arn+19a]; and Arndt et al.: "Jekyll RDF Template-Based Linked Data Publication with Minimized Effort and Maximum Scalability" [Arn+19b].

and uses standard access interfaces. This allows use to build complex scenarios in a modular way. Individual methods can be applied as necessary and do not require to impose the complete methodology on a collaboration scenario. Following the Quit methodology we could realize both, light weight and complex scenarios. The light weight scenarios are combinations of only one or two methods to achieve an atomic task while the complex scenarios demonstrate the composition of the complete methodology.

8.1 The Multilingual Morpheme Ontology (MMoOn) Open Hebrew Inventory

The *Multilingual Morpheme Ontology*[1] (MMoOn; [Kli+16]) is an ontology in the linguistics to create language resources of morphemic data for inflectional languages. The ontology is formalized as an RDF vocabulary and is structured in a modular manner consisting of a core ontology which can be extended with language specific terms and concepts (*inventories*). With the Open Hebrew Inventory we created a language specific extension of the MMoOn vocabulary for the Modern Hebrew language. The basis for the inventory data is a manually created vocabulary list organized as table containing vocalized and unvocalized Hebrew words, suffixes, and non-inflecting words annotated with their roots, word-class information, and English, German and Russian translations. This data has been compiled by a Hebrew speaker and, therefore, assures a significant quality of the data. The data has been analyzed, integrated and transformed to the MMoOn Core and the specific Hebrew schema using a custom data integration pipeline. Therefore, the data has been cleaned according to formal criteria. Lexical data entries containing invalid syntax have been removed, e.g. invalid braces, multiple entries in one column, or entries with missing word-class information. This step has been undertaken to achieve a sufficient data quality. After this mostly syntactic cleaning process, from the initial 52.000 lexical entries 11.600 remained for which morphological information is of relevance. These have been mapped onto the established schema ontology and then further processed and transformed to RDF. The dataset consists of $197,374$ RDF Statements[2] describing Hebrew words, lexemes, morphs, and senses. Since this data shall serve as the foundation for an open online dictionary, the dataset will be constantly growing and needs to be maintained.

8.1.1 Properties of the Use Case

To create and further develop the Hebrew morpheme inventory collaborators from a number of domains were involved. Namely, the Hebrew speaker, who compiled the initial dataset, a domain expert from the

---

[1] *MMoOn The Multilingual Morpheme Ontology:* [Web:MMo]
[2] As of February 2020

linguists who devised the morpheme ontology, an expert in the Hebrew Studies and especially morphology, and a data engineer and computer scientist. To structure the further development process of the inventory a collaborative data curation and exploration method and system is necessary. To make the created data available to other researchers and interested users the data needs to be published. Additionally, to incorporate knowledge from visitors of the system some crowdsourcing system has to be implemented to feed back change request to the team of researchers.

Distributed Collaboration System The collaborating parties are coming from different domains and institutes. Contributions by the parties might be unstable or subject to discussion.

Data Curation Interface To add new entries to the inventory and to update existing entries curators need to have some data curation interface. The data curation interface needs support for right to left text, Unicode characters, and internationalized resource identifiers (IRI) as the domain data is using Hebrew characters.

Data Publication and Exploration Interface The morpheme inventory consists of data of various kinds: words (verbs, nouns, adjectives), lexemes, representations of the vocalized and unvocalized lexemes, senses (in English, German and Russian), and morphs (roots, transfixes, and suffixes). The morphological data is expressed as an RDF data set which is not accessible for non-technical persons. This data needs to be represented in a way to be understandable for Hebrew language experts and linguists. Also the purpose of a morphological databases is, the interlinking of the individual morphs of the words. This highly interlinked manner of the datasets requires for an exploration interface that allows to browse through the data and jump between entries.

Crowdsourcing Interface The morpheme inventory is published as Open Data on the Web. This publication should attract people with different levels of expertise to explore our data set. By exploring the data people can learn from the data, but also contribute to the data by reporting errors and suggesting corrections and additions. To allow such contributions a simplified data curation interface is integrated into the publication and exploration interface. Updates performed with the crowdsourcing interface are fed back into the collaborative curation process.

Change Reviewing System Changes to the dataset are introduced through the crowdsourcing interface and by other team members. As contribution are always possible to introduce errors it is necessary to implement a reviewing system. The reviewing system allows to check contributions before they are incorporated into the publicly available reference datasets in a peer-review manner. This allows to maintain a high quality throughout the collaboration process.

8.1.2 The Collaboration Infrastructure

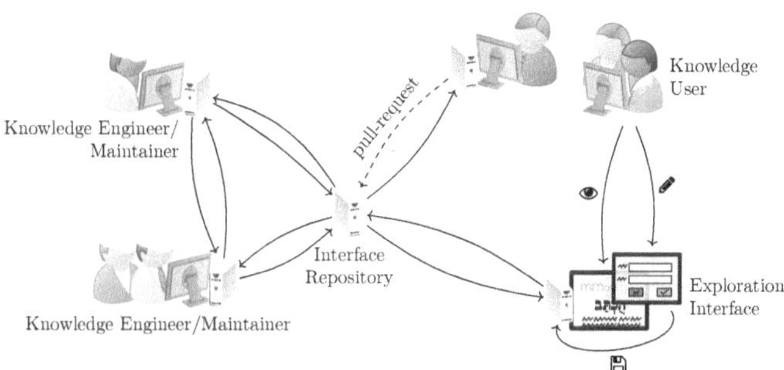

Figure 8.1: The collaboration infrastructure in the MMoOn use case

To support the maintenance of the Hebrew morpheme inventory we have created a setup of a distributed workspace as depicted in fig. 8.1. Each individual curator taking part in the collaborative process has a local workspace setup with a data curation system. With the local workspace the curator can access the data with an RDF editor on the one hand and connect to the distributed workspace on the other hand. The Quit Editor Interface provides a standard SPARQL interface to the data which allows arbitrary RDF editors to access the data in the collaborative setup. With the underlying Quit Store the curators are able create branches to store unstable changes of the dataset and exchange the branches with collaborators to discuss the changes. Using the merge functionality branched states can be incorporated and concurrent changes of remote parties be reconciled.

The individual curation setups synchronize their data data with the *Interface Repository* to allow the interchange with other collaborators. Even though the system enables collaborators to exchange the data directly between instances of the Quit Store, a central Interface Repository allows to maintain a copy that is constantly available, even if individual curation systems are off-line. The reference version of the dataset is published and presented through a customized Jekyll RDF exploration interface, which is explained in detail in section 8.1.3. Within the exploration interface the Structured Feedback System is used to capture contributions from visitors to the dataset. The contributions are then fed back to a Resource Hosting platform which allows curators to review the changes and incorporate them into the development process.

8.1.3 The Exploration Interface

Using the Jekyll RDF system we could create an exploration interface
to the Open Hebrew dataset. The exploration interface is specifically
adapted to the presentation of Hebrew language data.[3] To define the
templates we created a Git repository that consists of four class templates, two overview pages, and the dataset. On each update to the Git
repository the Continuous Integration System (cf. section 7.2.3) executes the Jekyll RDF process to create the exploration interface. The
exploration interface comprises $13,404$ inventory pages, 20 vocabulary
pages, and two overview pages. Figure 8.2 shows the exploration interface at the example of the word הֻכְתַּב (hukhtav). Next to the HTML
interface we created RDF resource pages in Turtle and RDF/JSON serialization. This RDF representation of the data is used to attach a
system for users to contribute to the data through Structured Feedback
(cf. section 6.1). In this way further dynamic elements can be provided
in a static page based on the RDF data.

Figure 8.2: MMoOn ex-
ploration interface showing
the example of the resource
for the Hebrew word הֻכְתַּב
(hukhtav).

8.1.4 Conclusion

With the application of the Quit methodology to the MMoOn project
we are able to provide a flexible knowledge engineering environment for

---

[3] *Open Hebrew.* Explocarion interface of the Open Hebrew inventory:

domain experts from the linguistics. The central interface repository allows collaborators to synchronously access a shared workspace to gain an overview on the current state of the work. With the Quit Store each collaborator can synchronize its local workspace with the current state of the interface repository and perform independently asynchronous work. By connecting each collaborator to the distributed workspace using the synchronization system collaboration is possible throughout the team. Even contributions from the crowd can be integrated using the Structured Feedback system. By using the branching feature a collaborator can prepare changes to contribute to the common dataset which can be integrated using the merge functionality of the Quit Store. The Jekyll RDF setup provides a exploration interface on the dataset that is customized to the needs of the domain experts.

8.2 Pfarrerbuch and Catalogus Profesorum Lipsiensium

The projects *Sächsisches Pfarrerbuch* (German: *Saxonian pastors book*)[4] and *Catalogus Profesorum Lipsiensium* (CPL) [Rie+10a] are research projects in the field of History to build prosopographical knowledge bases. Both projects come with very similar requirements regarding the collaborative nature of the curation processes, the original formats of the data, and the adaption of the user interfaces to the needs of the domain experts. Due to the similar domain of the two projects, the setup of the Pfarrerbuch software system is highly inspired by the Catalogus Professorum Lipsiensium, while the audience is different.

The research group Agile Knowledge Engineering and Semantic Web (AKSW)[5] together with historians from the Herzog August Library in Wolfenbüttel (HAB)[6] run a research project in cooperation with partners from the Working Group of the German Professor's catalogs and the European research network for academic history–Héloïse.[7] The project's aim is to develop a new research method across humanities and the computer science field employing Semantic Web and distributed online databases for study and evaluation of collected information on groups of historical persons focusing on German professors' career patterns during the 18th and 19th centuries. The project deals with many challenges as individual datasets have been developed by those different communities, some of them are more than 600 years old as the *Catalogus Professorum Lipsiensium*. The *Catalogus Profesorum Lipsiensium* collects all professors who have taught at Leipzig University from its foundation in 1409 to the presence.

In the Pfarrerbuch project we build a Research Data Management system for historians to create a database of all pastors who served in Saxony, Hungary, the Church Province of Saxony, and Thuringia since the reformation in 1517. The data sources are differing in their expressiveness and structure as the data was collected with various aims. Some data is available in structured relational databases containing foreign key relations while other data is contained in word documents, where the structure is expressed by the formatting. The Pfarrerbuch dataset contains $1,366,380$ RDF statements, $807,647$ in the dataset from Saxony, $130,440$ in the dataset from Hungary, and $428,293$ in the dataset from the Church Province of Saxony and Thuringia.[8]

Both communities, the professor's catalogs and the Pfarrerbuch communities, have different singularities that make the development and management of a common vocabulary very challenging. For instance, the German professor's dataset of the state of Saxony contains a list of as much as six working places and respective positions of each professor across time as well as a detailed description of the archive where the information were extracted from. These information were not available in previous published datasets and therefore they would cause a vocabulary change. However, in order to perform the changes, there is a need of (a) creating an independent vocabulary or (b) to implement the changes over a mutual agreement among the different research groups. Creating independent vocabularies (a) in the individual working groups would not help to integrate the datasets among the working groups. Due to the organizational distribution of the individual research groups, a common vocabulary expressing a mutual agreement among the groups (b) can only be the result of a collaborative process. Based on the origin of the individual datasets, their diverse granularity, and structure the individual discussions have varying starting points. Most of the data was imported into the collaboration environment in a rudimentary way using customized scripts. This description of an application domain is exemplary for other interdisciplinary projects in fields as the digital humanities, but can also stand for many other collaborative scenarios.

8.2.1 Properties of the Use Case

Distributed Collaboration   The collaborators in the projects are affiliated with different institutions. As there is no broadly accessible collaboration infrastructure available in the history domain collaborators need to build an infrastructure for the purpose of the collaboration. The system needs to support autonomy of the individual collaborating parties at distributed locations, while still an exchange of the data is necessary to reach a common data model and interlink the individual datasets. While some collaboration arrangements are subject to a formal coop-

---

[8] As of February 2020

eration agreement with temporarily shared infrastructure other collaborations are on their way to be established and are organized in an ad hoc manner. Thus the systems need to support distributed collaboration between the individual parties. But also in projects with formal cooperation agreement the partners need to retain access to the collaboratively curated data when the project ends and the common infrastructure is shut down.

Customized Exploration and Authoring Interfaces To deal with this heterogeneity of the original data models and the agile development processes the systems used throughout the process need to be adjustable to changing vocabularies. In the two projects presented, especially when working with domain experts like the historians, we see a need for customized and easily accessible user interfaces. The domain experts are no knowledge maintainers and are not trained to deal with the technical aspects of the RDF knowledge representation format.

Continuous Publication of a Subset The curatorial work on the datasets is performed to make the data available to the public. Nevertheless, some of the datasets contain data about currently living persons. This data needs to be kept back from being published to the Web to preserve personal rights, while it still needs to be available in the internal system for the researches. Thus the continuous publication system can only publish a subset of the data.

Feedback by Citizen Scientists Since the data is publicly available citizen scientists and hobbyists are attracted by the data and inspired to undertake independent research activity. Especially if the citizen scientists are related to the person of interest or are living at place of activity of a person, they have access to expressive sources. The results of such activity might be of high value for the researchers as the sources are complicated to take into account for the researchers in the first place. To enable citizen scientists to provide their research results to the scientists a feedback system needs to be able to capture the relevant information in a structured way.

8.2.2 Wiki System Architecture

The architecture of CPL is based on a protected Web interface for the project team and two public interfaces as can be seen in fig. 8.4. The architecture is making highly use of the Wiki approach, with the OntoWiki system, to support the collaboration on the data. OntoWiki is not only a stand-alone application for curating and exploring RDF datasets but also the OntoWiki Application Framework, it was used to implement very different use cases throughout the years. One mechanism to enrich OntoWiki's behavior is its extension system, which allows for a modular approach of introducing new features. In some cases it was extended mainly in its functionality, in other cases it has completely changed its appearance. In the Pfarrerbuch and Catalogus Profesorum Lipsiensium systems OntoWiki is used as data curation and exploration platform especially for data scientists and domain experts in the respective historical domain. Different entities with various properties, such as persons, places (churches, schools, universities), events with personal relations, staffing and attendance relations can easily be managed with the flexible RDF data model and editing interface in OntoWiki. Using the OntoWiki Site Extension[9] allows for a template-based publication of RDF resources resulting in easy to explore HTML Web pages (in addition to the default OntoWiki SPARQL endpoint and Linked Data Server). Also OntoWiki's support for multiple languages helped to implement a German and a Hungarian version of the Pfarrerbuch in one system. Further the wiki approach supports distributed groups of researchers and data scientists to flexibly collaborate on a common dataset. Figure 8.3a depicts an example page showing the resource of Pfarrer Christian Friedrich Ernst Führer[10] with various properties and relations retrieved from the RDF data model. In the upper right corner one can see the search interface, which queries the OntoWiki SPARQL endpoint in real time to allow easy navigation. Below the search interface the links can be used (from left to right) to access the default OntoWiki UI, edit the currently displayed resource, create a new instance of the currently selected class and change the UI language between German and Hungarian. Due to the extensible architecture of the OntoWiki we could attach customized data curation interfaces which allow domain experts to curate the RDF data model without knowledge of RDF. The editor interface is shown in fig. 8.3b. The editor interface is customizable with shape description of the data to be updated and reads and writes the data using a SPARQL 1.1 interface. By using the approach of the containerized Linked Data publication infrastructure we can reuse most of the containers among the two projects while still loading different datasets to the triple stores.

8.2.3 Distributed System Architecture

Even though the wiki approach that we were following was successful in helping the researchers to curate the dataset, we were facing several problems. Wiki systems consist of a shared database and a generic editing interface that is used to create, updates, and explore resources. As we have extended the system with template-based publication and customized edit interfaces we have extended the wiki system towards an agile content management system. But the maintenance of the database with the SPARQL endpoint and the dynamic front-end made the whole curation and publication system error-prone and hard

(a) The entry of Pfarrer Führer from Leipzig in the Pfarrerbuch database

(b) The customized editing interface for the entry of Pfarrer Führer from Leipzig in the Pfarrerbuch database

Figure 8.3: The exploration and editing interfaces of the Pfarrerbuch curation system.

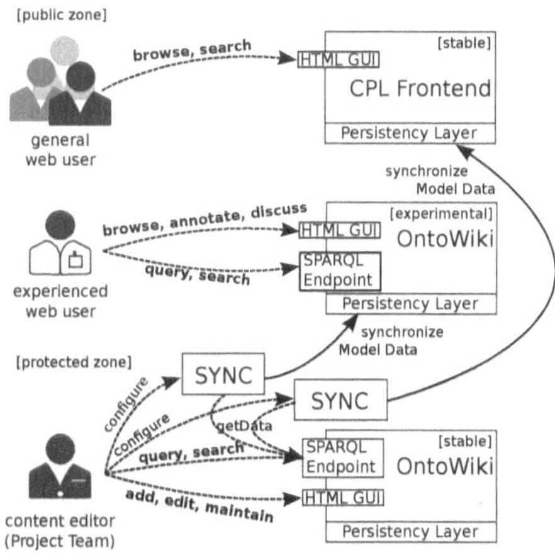

Figure 8.4: Architecture of the Catalogus Profesorum Lipsiensium (cf. [Rie+10a])

to maintain. Further, the dense coupling of the components did not allow to update individual components as they ware outdated.

To overcome the problem we have started to build a distributed architecture of individual microservices. The distributed architecture is attached to the original wiki-based curation system as this is still well accepted by the domain experts. The modular approach allows us to separate dynamic components from components which can be served as static artifacts. The extended architecture is depicted in fig. 8.5. Additionally, we are able to distribute components and thus spread the workload. In addition to the wiki and content management approach we now follow the Quit methodology for knowledge engineering that is inspired by DVCS as used in the field of software engineering.

The DVCS approach is attached to the legacy wiki system though a chronological export of the dataset. During the export, the dataset is normalized and imported into an internal Quit repository. This Quit repository can be used with a local Quit Store instance for the curation, independent of the wiki system. From the protected Quit repository a subset is synchronized with a public repository that serves as basis for the crowd curation process. The excerpt of the already curated data that is publishes is currently very limited to make sure that no personal rights are infringed. On top of the public repository we implemented the Jekyll RDF method to build a customizable exploration interface that can be served with minimum effort. By improving the structure to reach more clarity by building on top of a well established templating language we could reduce the effort for building templates. By building on a static site generation system we could increase the scalability and flexibility of the system to serve a browsing interface. The published web page is extended with the Structured Feedback system to allow citizen scientists to report errors, update the data and create new entries. The feedback that is collected through the Structured Feedback system is lead through the QEICC system using the branch strategy. With the branch strategy thus a new branch is created for each update in order to separate the individual contributions. Parallel to the Jekyll RDF based exploration interface we serve a dynamically generated web page, which is based on Java Script and SPARQL.

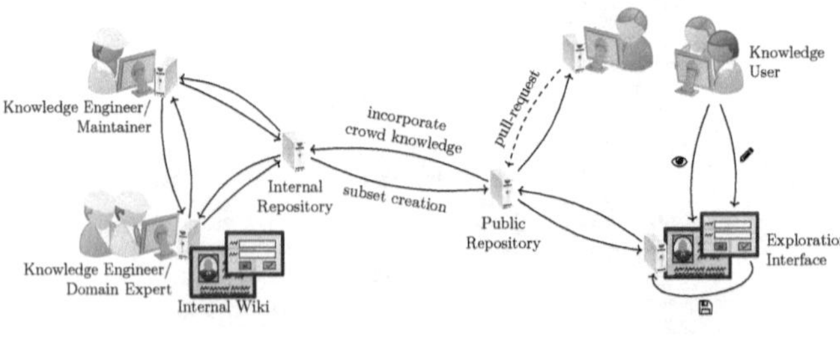

Figure 8.5: The distributed curation and publication system of the Pfarrerbuch

8.2.4 Conclusion

By following the Quit methodology we were able to separate individual tasks in the infrastructure. In contrast to the previously chosen synchronization system to distribute data to several access layers as depicted in fig. 8.4, with Quit we are able to perform duplex synchronization of the data. The duplex synchronization as depicted in fig. 8.5 allows to incorporate changes from the public space into the protected curation process. In addition with the branching system of the Quit Store we are able to separate individual contributions and track the provenance of all data throughout the process. Compared to the first approach using the wiki method implemented in the OntoWiki we could make the collaboration process more flexible using the Quit methodology. The use of Quit allows different researchers to develop their datasets in a local workspace while sharing core components to the distributed workspace. This allows to locally perform experiments on the data and transformations of the data by applying tools that are not supported by the OntoWiki. These local changes can be performed independent of the daily data curation workflow by utilizing the branching feature. The branches can be merged into the common dataset, once the transformation task is finished and there is a consensus to do so. Quit also made it easy to explore differences across the different dataset versions by using the `diff` feature that previously had to be performed manually. Further, it was possible to detect issues regarding the incorrect use of name spaces during the conversion process of the Hungarian Pastors dataset by using the provenance functionality. As a result it is now possible to solve an issue by reverting the respective changes on the dataset and by deploying the updated dataset version. Further, using the synchronization mechanism it was possible to implement a backup strategy that made the whole process more robust with regard to server faults.

With the flexible synchronization system in combination with Jekyll RDF we can provide a highly customizable exploration interface for a subset of the dataset. Using our custom SPARQL editor extension we can provide an editing interface usable for the domain experts to update RDF data. A subset of the data is synchronized to a public repository to let the public benefit from the curated data while ensuring personal rights. With the Structured Feedback system we can even feed the changes performed by citizen scientist back to the domain experts' protected curation system.

8.3 Communication in the Emergency Response Staff

The Federal Agency for Technical Relief (Bundesanstalt Technisches Hilfswerk, THW) is an authority controlled by the government of the Federal Republic of Germany and is subordinated to the Federal Ministry of the Interior. The tasks of the THW are to supply technical relief (cf. [Bun90]):

- as part of the national civil protection and disaster relief act,

- in abroad on behalf of the government,

- and in case of fight against disasters, public emergencies, and large-scale accidents upon request of the according authorities responsible of the hazard prevention.

The THW is operated by 80,000 volunteers and 1,300 full-time employees. It has more then 1,400 rescue units (Bergunggruppen, B1/B2), around 1,000 special units (Fachgruppen, FGr) organized in 715 technical platoons (Technische Züge, TZ) stationed in 668 local sections (Ortsverbände, OV). A technical platoon consists of a platoon troop (Zugtrupp, ZTr), two rescue units, and a special unit.[11] In addition to the special units organized in technical platoons the THW has the special units lead/communication (Fachgruppe Führung und Kommunikation, FGr FüKom) and logistics (Logistik, FGr Log). For special operations the THW is also maintaining rapid deployment units (Schnelleinsatzeinheiten).

In case of large accidents or other large missions the special unit lead/communication (Fachgruppe Führung und Kommunikation, FGr FüKom) is responsible for leading multiples units i.e. two to three technical platoons. For this purpose the special unit lead/communication is a staff unit and operates an implementing agency (Führungsstelle) which acts as operational (sub-)area mission control, local mission control, or technical mission control. Textual communication within an implementing agency is organized in a very strict workflow which is as well used throughout different emergency response forces in Germany, such as fire brigades and ambulance. A principal item in this work-flow is the *4-Fach-Vordruck* or *Meldezettel*, a form with 4 layered carbon copy.

Together with the *THW Fachgruppe Führung und Kommunikation* (FGr FüKom) we have analyzed the current workflow used for emergency communication. Its properties are: paper based, high response time, highly fault tolerant with regard to the persistence, but fragile to faults with regard to the hand writing style, easy accessibility, low requirements to the tool stack (pen and paper), organizational robustness.

8.3.1 Communication Workflow in an Implementing Agency

The communication workflow in an implementing agency is standardized across emergency response forces in Germany. The workflow spans across the implementing agency and a signaling center (Fernmeldezentrale) attached to the implementing agency. It involves five roles, on the side of the signaling center: a radioman (Fernmelder) and a head of the signaling center (Leiter der Fernmeldezentrale) and on the side of the implementing agency: a reviewer (Sichter), the area managers (Sachgebietsleiter, S1-S6), and the head of situation (Sachgebietsleiter

---

[11] *THW at a glance.* German Federal Agency for Technical Relief - An Overview:

Lage, S2). The *Meldezettel* as message carrier is manually handed over between the individual persons in the workflow. The workflow of composing and processing a Meldezettel is depicted in fig. 8.6. As the Meldezettel is a 4 layerd carbon copy it is possible to process it in parallel. At the parallel gateways the carbon copies are separated and distributed to the respective roles. In fig. 8.6a the reception of a new message at the implementing agency is depicted. In fig. 8.6b the composition and transmission of a message from within the implementing agency is depicted. The incoming and outgoing messages are transmitted via radio to subordinated platoon troops or a superordinated staff agencies. To archive each message that was transmitted by the signaling center the LdF is responsible of putting a *Nachweis* on file.

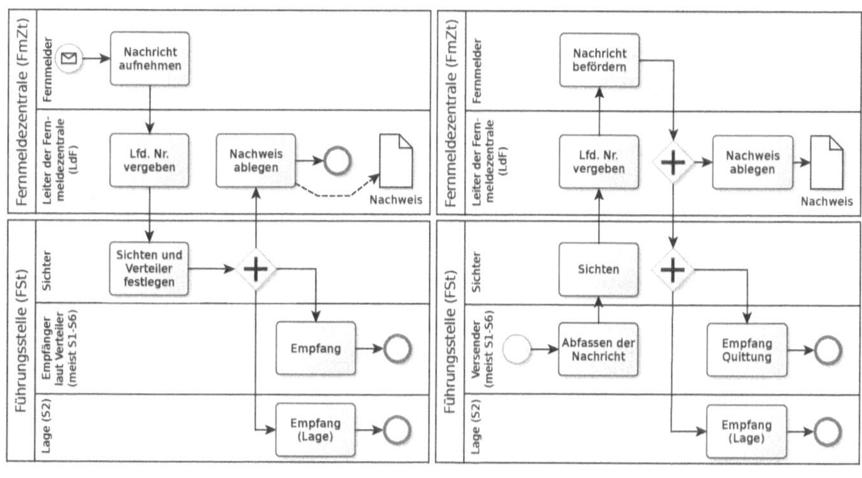

(a) Inbound message flow

(b) Outbound message flow

Figure 8.6: The workflow for processing messages in an emergency response staff

8.3.2 Properties of the Use Case

Following the Given Standards   The Meldezettel and the attached workflow is used throughout different emergency response forces in Germany. Keeping a staff open for colleagues from different units and forces for exchange and reinforcement of staff is an important concept for a sustainable organization. For this purpose a digital solution must stay as close as possible to the paper archetype and workflow as possible.

Backward Compatibility   The used technology needs to be backward compatible to the existing workflow. It is not possible to introduce or remove any steps which would break the well established workflow used with the paper forms.

Backup and Fault Tolerance Software introduced for supporting emergency response needs to be fault tolerant, robust, and redundant. In case of hardware failures it is necessary that the system can provide a failover strategy. Backup systems need to periodically perform dataset backups for instance by synchronizing them with a remote system. A version controlled backup system also allows to restore data even after faulty changes. Further, a backup of the work of each collaborator allows other parties to continue the overall work, even if collaborating parties quit. Providing means to backup data, helps to avoid content loss and reduces time on restoring the system. A transparent integration in a tool to track the changes of the data and submit the data to a safe location into the daily work of the data creator, avoids gaps in the backup and distraction from the main tasks.

Reproduce the Communication Flow After an operation the THW is obliged to archive all documentation material produced during the operation. This archive is searched in case of disputes with regard to decisions made during an operation. The system needs to archive the communication data and needs to preserve all necessary information to reproduce the communication during the operation.

Multiple Simultaneous Collaborating Clients An emergency response staff consists of around 8 persons with different tasks at different positions. All of these positions are frequently working with the messaging system, 4 positions are even constantly working with the messaging system. The system is required to allow simultaneous read and write access to the current state of the database.

8.3.3 The Vocabulary

The software stores its data using an RDF vocabulary. The current vocabulary is kept very rudimentary and represents the individual entry fields of the original form in a straight forward manner. To design the system in a way to be extensible with additional components like a situation map and unit outline the data model needs some rework. As there is currently no standard and not such components available to be attached we follow the simplicity concept of extreme programming to develop a for the presence rather then an envisioned future.

The vocabulary consists of two classes, `thw:document` for the Meldezettel messages and `thw:operation` for the Operation. Each field in the meldezettel form corresponds to one property in the vocabulary. Additionally, each message is associated with the current operation through the `thw:inOpperations` property. The vocabulary is subject to improvement, once additional components to link with are implemented.

8.3.4 Message Organization Interface

The user interface for the message organization completely hides the RDF vocabulary from the user. Instead it reproduces the form as it is given by the existing *4-fach Vordruck* and thus does not require additional training for the users. Additionally the interface provides a virtual desk which serves as combines in-box of incoming and outgoing messages. The virtual desk shows an overview list of messages which can be filtered using the faceted search functionality in the sidebar.

8.3.5 Conclusion

With the presented system for digitalizing the communication workflow in the THW emergency response staff we could demonstrate the usability of the Quit methodology in this scenario. The presented system allows to introduce the advantages of a digital system while integrating it into the existing paper driven workflow. The usage of the Quit Store allows a digital archive which preserves all changes happened during a communication flow due to the underlying Git system. The Git system also ensures the fault tolerance of the system by synchronizing the repository to a backup location. Because the organizational data workflow in an emergency does not give room for complicated consent finding processes as they are possible in a knowledge engineering workflow, we are able to maintain a permanently consistent and reconciled repository using the QEICC re-submit strategy. As an advantage, the RDF vocabulary allows the possibility of faceted search systems on the data set which brings more clarity into the communication and the handling of transported messages. The combination of the Quit methodology and the RDF vocabulary allows to extend the message-based communication system with further systems of an emergency response staff, such as force overview and situation map. Due to the design which is structured similar to the *4-fach Vordruck* the system also serves for training purposes.

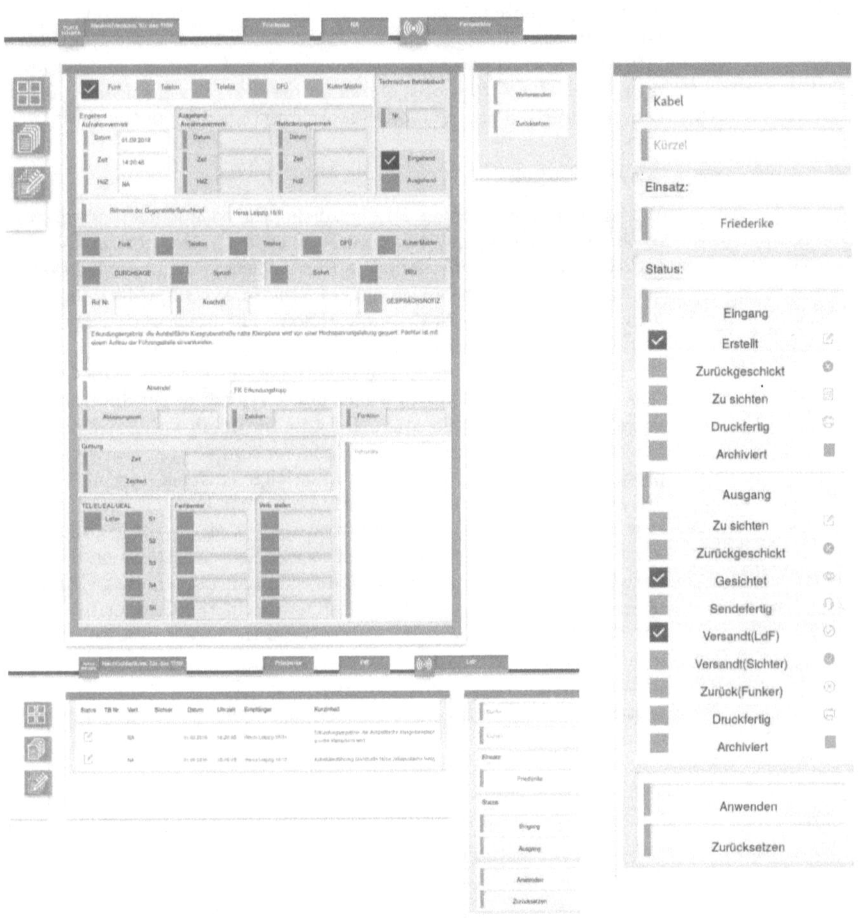

Figure 8.7: The user interface for the communication in the Emergency Response Staff. (a) User interface as seen by the radioman for composing a new message and sending it to the head of signaling center. (b) User interface as seen by the head of the signaling center with an overview of messages coming in from the radioman. (c) User interface of the faceted search for filtering incoming and outgoing messages according to several relevant properties including a free text search.

8.4 Agile Use Cases

Besides the complex use cases consisting of multiple steps of a collaborative knowledge management workflow, as presented in the last sections, we were also able to implement some break out use cases. These break out use cases only apply a portion of the methods presented in this theses. The application of the partial methods is possible due to the modular microservice design of the Quit methodology. This allows the agile implementation of small distinct use cases, but also the extension of larger use cases only with part of the methodology presented in this book.

8.4.1 Electronic Resource Management System

- Arndt et al.: "AMSL: Creating a Linked Data Infrastructure for Managing Electronic Resources in Libraries"

- Nareike et al.: "AMSL: Managing Electronic Resources for Libraries Based on Semantic Web"

In the *amsl.technology*[12] project an Electronic Resource Management System is developed based on OntoWiki. amsl.technology is targeted to support libraries and other players in the library domain to manage not only physical resources, such as books, journals, CDs/DVDs, but also electronic resources (e.g. e-journals, e-books or databases). Especially challenging in this use case are new licensing and lending models which have been introduced by publishers, such as pay-per-view, patron-driven-acquisition, short term loan or big deal. The existing infrastructure is not yet prepared for managing those electronic resource's lending and licensing models. Even worse, software that is developed to meet those requirements is likely to be outdated once new media types or licensing and lending models are introduced. The amsl.technology application benefits f rom O ntoWiki's fl exible an d ag ile da ta management capabilities as well as from its features for curating, exploring and annotating resources in a collaborative way. Also the development of amsl.technology brought back many improvements to OntoWiki due to its Open Source development model. A demo system, as depicted in fig. 8.8, is available on-line.[13]

8.4.2 AKSW Research Group

The website of our research group[14] (AKSW) is backed by an OntoWiki with an extension to publish websites based on templates and data from a triple store. This sophisticated extension is called the *site extension* and it extends OntoWiki towards a CMS. Since the AKSW research

ge of the AKSW research group run by OntoWiki:

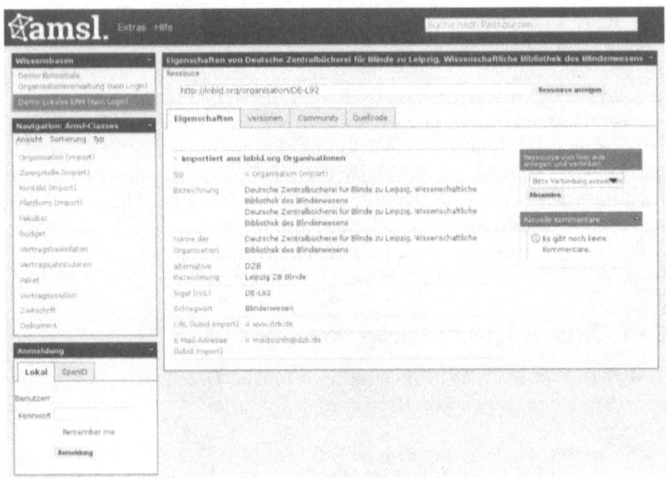

Figure 8.8: An entry in the amsl.technology customized OntoWiki

group has become quite large recently (the website currently includes more than 50 team members and a large number of different projects) a CMS is indispensable. On the other hand a large amount of the information that needs to be presented is very structured (e.g. information about team members, project abstracts, etc.) and should be reused on different pages. In addition lists of resources of a certain type (e.g. project and team lists) should be maintained automatically. Within this use case OntoWiki (without further modifications) is used to author and maintain the data including page content in literals written in Markdown syntax. The site extension then retrieves this data and renders it according to a set of templates and SPARQL queries. Another benefit of the site extension is the ability to automatically publish the raw RDF data next to the rendered HTML content as Linked Data. Every web page created with the site extension has a related resource URI that can be used to retrieve RDF data or the HTML page using content negotiation.

Figure 8.9 depicts the page of the OntoWiki project on the AKSW website. This page is dynamically composed from very structured information fragments (e.g. title, abstract, team members, publications, screenshot, etc.). Based on the well structured data and the team setup of the research group we plan to implement the Quit methodology in the future. The transition can happen through a hybrid setup consisting of the OntoWiki and the Quit Store in a similar way as for the Pfarrerbuch project. We could already implement a data pump that periodically performed backups from the OntoWiki setup to a Git repository. This repository is synchronized with an interface repository

Figure 8.9: Page of the OntoWiki project on the AKSW website.

on GitHub.[15] From this repository a continuous integration job builds
a static version of the work group page using Jekyll RDF.[16]

8.4.3 Smart Data Analytics Work Group

The Smart Data Analytics research group (SDA[17]) investigates machine learning techniques (*analytics*) using structured knowledge (*smart
data*). Machine learning requires sufficient data as training datasets.
SDA investigated techniques which could help also to build such a
dataset to depict the organizational structure and entities representing SDA. The SDA knowledge graph contains entities about persons,
groups, projects, and publications as well as their relations. It is used
for question answering, faceted search, data mining, and analysis for
better decision making based on the data. Using Jekyll RDF and the
Linked Data principles helps to reuse the existing knowledge graph to
build the work group homepage. In this way it is possible to publish a
Current Research Information System (CRIS) with Jekyll RDF based
on the SDA knowledge graph on the Web as shown in fig. 8.10.

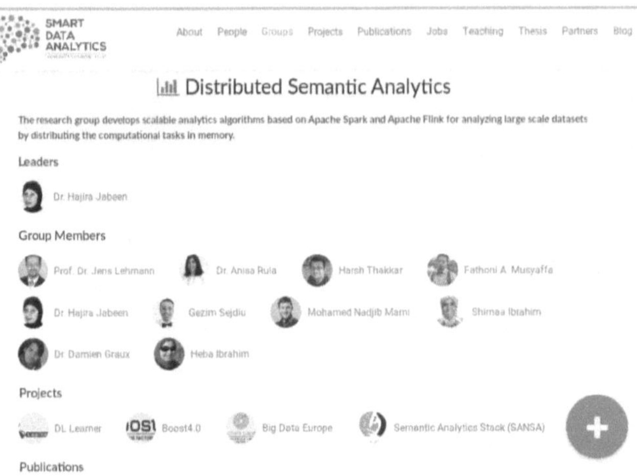

Figure 8.10: A work group
page generated with Jekyll
RDF showing the members
and projects

8.4.4 Vocabulary Documentation

One of the major advantages of using RDF to describe resources is the universality of the model and the ability to describe the schema resources as part of the same graph as the described data. This enables consumers and producers of the data to use an exploitable, executable, and metadata rich knowledge framework. eccenca[18] is a European enterprise based in Germany with a strong vision how semantic vocabularies and Linked Data can be used to integrate project data and data management. An important aspect of semantic data integration are vocabularies which capture essential concepts from the customers domain. These vocabularies build the foundation for a semantic data landscape which interlinks all customer datasets into an exploitable graph. In order to communicate the results of an ontology specification work, it is necessary to visualize and document the vocabularies. Existing ontology documentation tools lack the ability to extensively customize the result. Using Jekyll RDF we could build a set of templates for all major ontology classes and publish it as a theme called Jekyll Ontology Documentation project (JOD).[19] However, fetching OWL constructs is problematic with graph access based on SPARQL alone and also complex functionality such as the generation of a Manchester Syntax description is currently missing. It can easily be integrated in an existing RDF vocabulary project as shown at the example of the diggr Video Game Vocabulary project[20] performed by the Leipzig University Library. The deployment of Jekyll RDF with the JOD theme and a CI/CD pipeline in order to create the vocabulary documentation was straight forward. The user interface of the vocabulary documentation is shown in fig. 8.11.

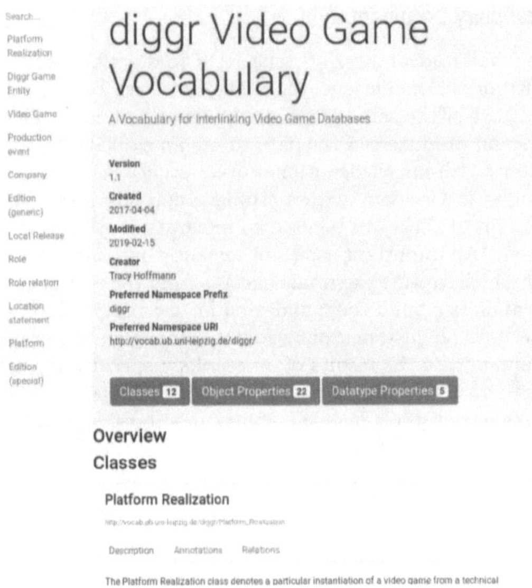

Figure 8.11: The documentation page generated with Jekyll RDF for the diggr OWL vocabulary used to model the interplay of games and publishers in global game culture research.

8.5 Verification and Quantitative Evaluation

To evaluate the methodology presented in this book we examin the correctness of the methodology regarding the recorded changes and the performance, memory, and storage footprint. In order to perform this task we have taken our implementation of the *Quit Store*.[21] This currently is a prototypical implementation to prove the concept and support the application of the methodology, thus we are not aiming at competitive performance results. The hardware setup of the machine running the benchmarks is a virtual machine on a Hyper-V cluster with Intel(R) Xeon(R) CPU E5-2650 v3 with a maximum frequency of $2.30GHz$ and $62.9GiB$ of main memory. As operating system Ubuntu 16.10 (yakkety) 64-Bit is used.

Listing 8.1: The BSBM generate command with its argument.

```
$ ./generate -pc 4000 -ud -tc 4000 -ppt 1
```

As benchmarking framework we have decided to use the Berlin SPARQL benchmark (BSBM) [BS09], since it is made to execute SPARQL Query and SPARQL Update operations. The initial dataset as it is generated using the BSBM, shown in listing 8.1, contains 46370 statements and 1379201 statements to be added and removed during the benchmark. To also execute update operations we use the *Explore and Update Use Case*. We have executed 40 warm-up and 1500

---

[21] *Quit Store.* The Quit Store Repository at GitHub:

query mix runs that resulted in 4592 commits on the underlying Git repository using the testdriver as shown in listing 8.2. The setup to reproduce the evaluation is also available at the following source code repository:

```
$ ./testdriver http://localhost:5000/sparql \
  -runs 1500 -w 40 -dg "urn:bsbm" -o run.xml \
  -ucf usecases/exploreAndUpdate/sparql.txt \
  -udataset dataset_update.nt \
  -u http://localhost:5000/sparql
```

Listing 8.2: The BSBM testdriver command with its argument.

8.5.1 Correctness of Version Tracking

To check the correctness of the recorded changes in the underlying Git repository we have created a verification setup. The verification setup takes the Git repository, the initial dataset, the query execution log (run.log) produced by the BSBM setup, and a reference store. The repository is set to its initial commit, while the reference store is initialized with the initial dataset. Each update query in the execution log is applied to the reference store. When an effect, change in number of statements,[22] is detected on the reference store, the Git repository is forwarded to the next commit. Now the content of the reference store is serialized and compared statement by statement to the content of the Git repository at this point in time. This scenario is implemented in the verify.py script in the evaluation tool collection. We have executed this scenario and could ensure, that the recorded repository has the same data as the store after executing the same queries.

8.5.2 Correctness of the Merge Method

The functional correctness of the Three-Way-Merge method (cf. section 5.3.3) was verified using a repository filled with data using the graph generated by the BSBM. Since the Three-Way-Merge is conflict free it can be evaluated in an automated manner. To create the evaluation setup and run the verification of the results, a script was created. This script takes a Git repository and creates a setup of three commits. An initial commit contains a graph file that serves as base of two branches. Each of the branches is forked from this initial commit and contains an altered graph file. The files in the individual commits contain random combinations of added and removed statements, while the script also produces the graph that is expected after merging the branches.

After creating the two branches with different graphs they are merged using git merge. The result is then compared statement by statement to the expected graph and the result is presented to the user. We have

---

[22] Since the Quit Store only creates commits for effective changes it is necessary to identify and skip queries without effect. This heuristic does not effect the result of the actual comparison, because still all queries are executed on the reference store, to which the content of the Quit Store is compared in each step.

executed the verification 1000 times and no merge conflict or failure in the merge result occurred.

8.5.3 Context Merge

To demonstrate and evaluate the conflict identification of the Context Merge, we have created a repository that contains two branches holding the data as depicted in fig. 5.3. Further, it contains a second graph with a resource which a label is added on the *master* branch, while the same resource is moved to a different namespace by renaming it from to in the *develop* branch. The output of the Context Merge method is depicted in the screenshot fig. 8.12.

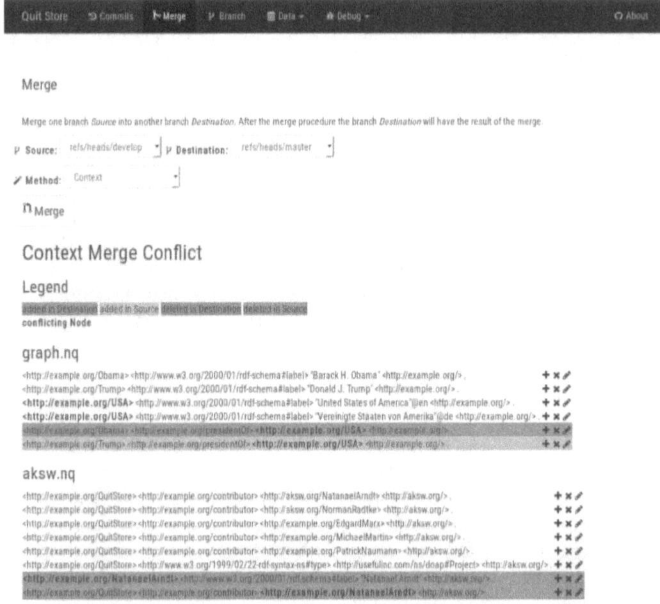

Figure 8.12: A merge operation on the Quit Store using the context strategy with identified conflicts.

The merge method identifies in each of the graphs two statements that have been added or deleted and overlap at a common node. An overlap of statements is, when two different statements involve the same IRI at subject or object position. The respective IRI is highlighted in all other statements to let the user identify it easily in order to decide how to resolve the conflict. This heuristic, to identify overlapping changes from different branches, allows in the first graph to identify two contradicting statements and in the second graph and otherwise abandoned label.

8.5.4 Query Throughput

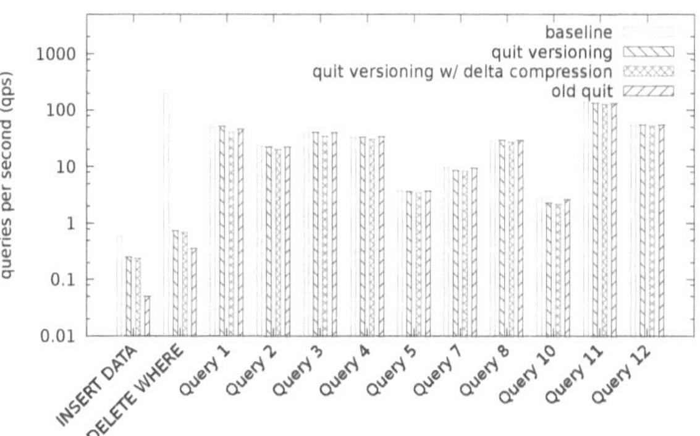

Figure 8.13: Execution of the different BSBM queries.

The query throughput performance of the reference implementation was analyzed to identify the bottlenecks in the design of our approach. In fig. 8.13 the queries per second for the different categories of queries in the BSBM are given and compared to the baseline. For the comparison we use four store setups. Our baseline without version tracking is the *Ad-hoc light weight SPARQL endpoint* (adhs),[23] a simple RDF store implemented using the Python RDFlib and a SPARQL interface implemented using Flask. To add support for quads we have adapted *adhs* accordingly, the source code can be found on GitHub.[24] The Quit Store implementation is executed in three configurations. In the first configuration (*quit versioning*) the plain quit versioning system is executed. In the second configuration (*quit versioning with delta compression*) additionally the delta compression is enabled, that introduces garbage collection runs (cf. sections 5.2 and 8.5.5). In the third configuration (*old quit*) the are executing an older version of the Quit Store at an intermediate state of development as published in an early paper [AM17]. After the "old quit" we have introduced a reworked architecture, which is presented in chapter 5, and a number of optimizations based on profiling results, especially by reducing I/O overhead.

As expected the versioning has a big impact on the update queries (INSERT DATA and DELETE WHERE), while the explore queries (SELECT and CONSTRUCT) are not further impacted. We could reach $247QMpH$[25] with Quit's versioning (*quit*), $235QMpH$ with additionally enabled delta compression, and $641QMpH$ for the baseline. With the present implementation we could reach an improvement of $3.7\times$ for the query throughput over the speed of the old implementation of $67QMpH$ (*old quit*).

8.5.5 Storage Consumption

During the executions of the BSBM we have monitored the impact of
the Quit Store repository on the storage system. The impact on the
storage system is visualized in fig. 8.14. We have measured the size of
the repository on the left y-axis, and the size of the graph as well as the
number of added and deleted statements on the right y-axis and have
put it in relation to the number of commits generated at that point
in time on the x-axis. We compare the execution of the BSBM on a
Quit Store without using Git's delta compression and with the delta
compression enabled (cf. section 5.2).

The benchmark started with $46,370$ initial statements and grew finally to $1,196,420$ statements. During the commits between 12 and
776 statements were added to the graph, while between 1 and 10 statements were removed. The fragment-based storage system, which stores
snapshots of each graph, was expected to increase severely as the stored
dataset increases, which could be confirmed during our evaluation. The
repository has increased from initially $12.4MiB$ to a size of $92.6GiB$
without delta compression at the end of the benchmark. One of the
disadvantages of this setup is also visible in fig. 8.14 towards the end of
the evaluation run. Starting at about commit 3500, while the dataset's
growth slows down, the repository is still growing by a copy of the
changed graph plus the added statements. Enabling the compression feature during the benchmark could compress the repository to
$18.3GiB$. This is a compression rate of 80.2% at the end (at commit
4593). During the run of the evaluation the compression rate fluctu-
ates like shark fins, starting of course with 0% it is between 76.9% at
commit 4217 and 94.5% at commit 4218 at the flank near the end of
the evaluation run.

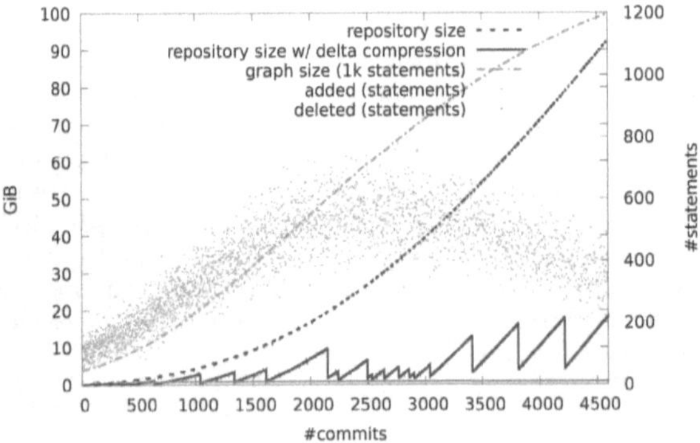

Figure 8.14: Storage consumption and number of
commits in the repository
during the execution of the
BSBM.

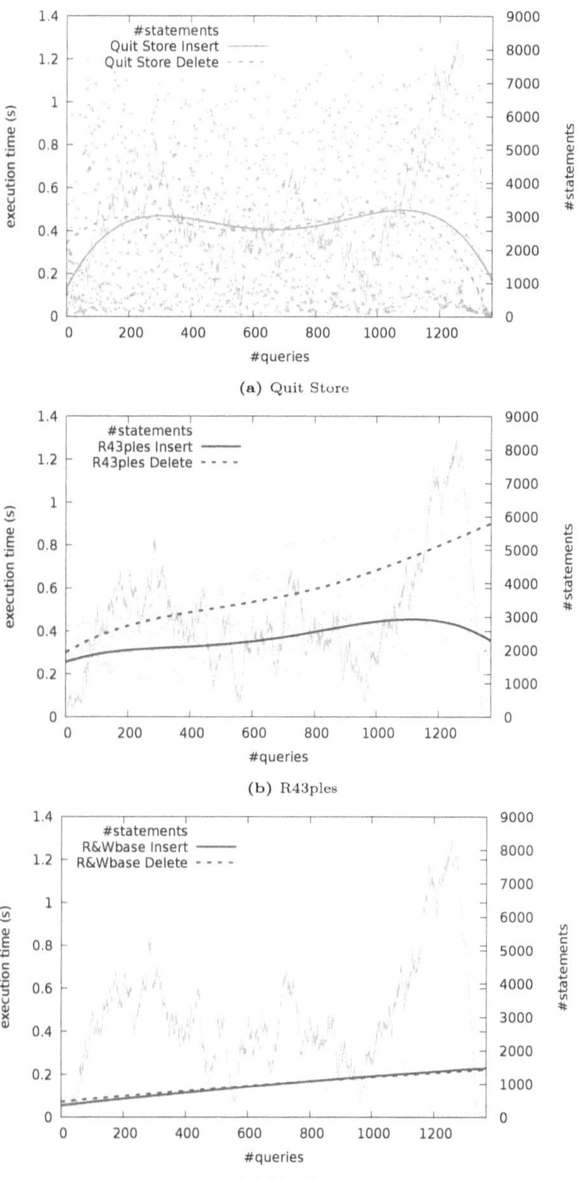

(a) Quit Store

(b) R43ples

(c) R&Wbase

Figure 8.15: Query execution time of the Quit Store and the related work systems R43ples and R&Wbase with INSERT DATA and DELETE DATA queries and the number of statements (right y-axis).

8.5.6 Update Comparison

To compare our prototypical implementation with other RDF versioning approaches we have selected the implementations of the R43ples Store and the R&Wbase (cf. section 3.5.4). To run the R&Wbase, the R43ples Store, and the Quit Store we have created Docker images for all systems which we also have made available at the Docker Hub.[26] We have tried to execute the BSBM on the R43ples Store, but the queries were not actually executed and no revisions were created by the store during the run. We have also tried to execute the BSBM on the R&Wbase Store, but for each update query the generated version identifier of its predecessor is needed. This identifier has to be queried from the versioning graph before each new update query. This is not supported by the BSBM. Thus we have decided to create a custom comparison setup to measure the execution time of INSERT DATA and DELETE DATA queries. The comparison setup takes the dataset_-update.nt file, which is generated by the BSBM, and randomly creates update queries. The system performs three steps, (1) generate a query log of INSERT DATA and DELETE DATA queries, (2) execute the generated queries on the store currently under testing, and (3) execute SELECT queries on a random sample of commits on the store under testing (cf. section 8.5.7). The system is available in our QuitEval repository (as mentioned above). On our system R&Wbase terminated after between 900 and 1900 commits for several query log configurations with the message: *Exception during abort (operation attempts to continue: Cannot abort a write lock-transaction*, when trying to query the versioning graph. Even after several attempts with exponential delay up to 1024 seconds, the system did not recover. We have found a setup that works for all stores. The setup creates update queries with 50000 total triples. Each generated update query inserts or deletes a maximum of 200 statements. This setup results in 1370 update queries that produced 1370 versions on each store.

The measured query execution times are depicted in figs. 8.15a to 8.15c. We could show that the Quit Store's query execution time is related to the number of statements added resp. deleted. The R43ples Store's insert query execution times draw a similar picture as the Quit Store, because of its approach to keep the latest version as full snapshot in the revision log. In contrast the R43ples Store's delete query execution times and R&Wbase's insert and delete query execution times increase with the size of the repository.

8.5.7 Random Access

After executing the update comparison we have tested the systems with respect to the availability of the stored revisions. For this we took the

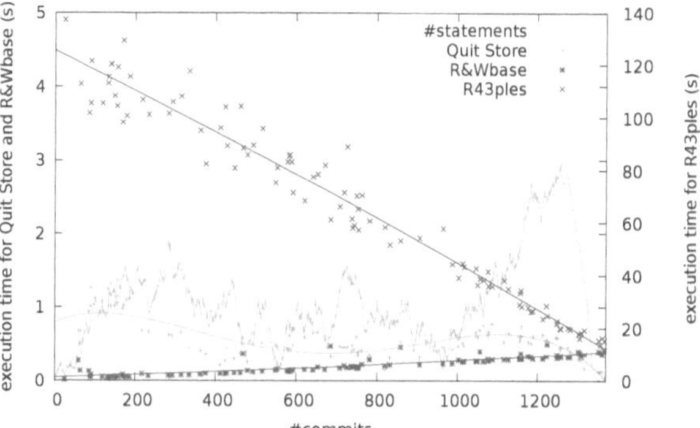

Figure 8.16: Query execution time comparison of Quit Store, R&Wbase, and R43ples (right y-axis) with SELECT queries on a random sample of revisions. (The number of revisions is just for illustration, for its scale please fer to figs. 8.15a to 8.15c.)

resulting stores with all revisions and performed a random access query execution comparison between R43ples, R&Wbase, and Quit Store. We have executed a simple select query as shown in listing 8.3 on a random sample of 100 of the recorded revisions on each store. The queries were executed in a random order on different revisions. The results of this comparison are depicted in fig. 8.16. The execution times of R43ples were significantly higher than the execution times of R&Wbase and Quit Store, we thus have decided to plot the results for R43ples on a different scale on the right y-axis. Due to the change-based approach followed by R43ples and R&Wbase, these stores have high costs to retrieve old revisions (in case of R43ples), respective new revisions (in case of R&Wbase). The Quit Store with its random access query interface can execute standard SPARQL queries on the store at the status of any revision. The execution time is not related to the position of the revision in the repository but is dependent on the size of the dataset at the respective revision.

Listing 8.3: SELECT query used for the random access comparison.

```
1 SELECT ?s ?p ?o WHERE {
2     GRAPH <urn:bsbm> {?s ?p ?o .}} LIMIT 1000
```

8.5.8 Conclusion

To verify the correctness of our system and test its performance 7 scenarios were executed on the implementation of the Quit Store. The scenarios are based on the Berlin SPARQL Benchmark (BSBM) as it provides support to generate both SPARQL Query and Update requests. First, an evaluation regarding the correctness of the model was performed in sections 8.5.1 to 8.5.3 followed by an examination of the performance of our implementation in sections 8.5.4 to 8.5.7.

The feasibility of the theoretical foundations could be confirmed by testing the correctness of the version tracking in section 8.5.1 and the merge strategy in section 8.5.2. In addition to the Three-Way-Merge, with the Context Merge strategy we are able to identify possible conflicts and bring them to the users attention. This was demonstrated in section 8.5.3 with an example of two branches with conflicts in two graphs of the dataset.

The performance and storage consumption of the system was examined in four scenarios. The query throughput tests in section 8.5.4 show an impact on the update requests, while the query requests are only marginally impacted. With the improved implementation we could even reach a $3.6\times$ improvement of the query throughput over the speed of the old implementation, at the state of development as published in our previous paper [AM17]. While the results show an acceptable performance the comparison to the base line shall be an incentive for improvement.

The Quit Store uses a fragment-based repository data structure, which was examined in section 8.5.5. The snapshots of the graphs were expected to increase severely as the stored dataset increases, which could be confirmed during our evaluation. The garbage collection could make up for the growth of the repository and we could show that the snapshot-based approach does not necessarily put a high load on the storage requirements. Further we could show that the impact on the query execution performance was negligible (cf. section 8.5.4 and fig. 8.13). The evaluation of more advanced compression systems for the stored RDF dataset or the employment of a binary RDF serialization format, such as HDT [Fer+13] is still subject to future work.

To position our approach in relation to the related work we have compared the Quit Store with the R&Wbase and the R43ples implementations. The comparison was performed with respect to the execution time of update requests in section 8.5.6 and with respect to explore queries in section 8.5.7. As the setup that works commonly for all stores and allows a comparison is quite limited we can not draw good conclusions about the general limits of RDF data versioning. Furthermore, we were able to identify different characteristics in the behavior of the systems for different kinds of requests as it was expected for the selected storage systems. For R43ples, the approach to extend the syntax of standard SPARQL queries by custom keywords makes it hard to integrate the store with existing tools and systems. The necessity to query the versioning graph separately before creating a new version in R&Wbase, does also hinder its usability with standard tools. For both systems we have seen that it is very complicated to find a configuration that lets us compare the selected stores under common circumstances. Using docker as virtualization system allowed us to encapsulate the steps necessary to get each system running without interfering with the other setups. With the virtualization system it was possible to provide each store with is required execution environment, also the docker setup allows us to make these steps reproducible.

9 Conclusion and Future Work

In this book research work for the Quit methodology, to improve the collaborative knowledge engineering process on RDF knowledge bases in a distributed setup, is presented in detail. The conceptual properties are to support the collaboration on datasets in a distributed process. Groups collaborating on datasets need to synchronize their workspaces, but also independence, means to express dissent, and the possibility to produce a single consolidated version of the dataset are needed. To support these properties the Quit methodology provides asynchrony, synchronization, dissent, and reconciliation. These aspects were visualized in fig. 1 .1. Based o n t hese a spects a s et o f r equirements was specified: t o d evise a *d istributed w orkspace* (a) w ith s upport f or *dissent* (b) and *asynchrony* (c), a method to *synchronize* (d) asynchronous workspaces, a method to *reconcile* (e) dissent knowledge bases, methods to *create and author* (f) data, *publish and explore* (g) data, and track and publish *provenance information* (h). The approach chosen for the Quit methodology is to combine methods from the Semantic Web and software engineering. We adapted the methodology of DVCSs from the field o f s oftware e ngineering a nd i ntegrated i t i nto t he Semantic Web Stack. With the Quit methodology we now provide a generic approach to support distributed teams to collaborate on RDF datasets with support for the specified requirements.

The *distributed workspace* is constituted by a network of multiple workspaces running the Quit Store implementation as an RDF quad store with support for dataset versioning. By recording commits of changed data it is possible to track the contributions made to a dataset, by branching the evolution of a dataset different p oints o f v iew and *dissent* can be expressed. Diverged branches can be *reconciled* using the merge operation while the user can select between different merge strategies. This postponed reconciliation of the data development branches allows to separate the role of the knowledge maintainer from the knowledge engineer. The Quit Store can be setup as multiple instances in distributed locations which can be used *asynchronously* by the collaborators. Using the push and pull operations of the Quit Store different i nstances c an *s ynchronize* t heir c hanges a nd m ake the contributions available to collaborators in the distributed setup.

By following the UNIX philosophy to "make each program do one thing well" [Gan03] we could implement an architecture of microservices with separation of concerns. By providing the standardized SPARQL 1.1 Query & Update interface the system provides a clear point of integration for applications to *create and author* and *publish and explore* the data. This allows to incorporate various tools into the knowledge engineering process. With the Quit Editor Interface we extended the

The results presented in this chapter were first published in Arndt, Radtke, and Martin: "Distributed Collaboration on RDF Datasets Using Git: Towards the Quit Store" [ARM16]; Arndt, Naumann, and Marx: "Exploring the Evolution and Provenance of Git Versioned RDF Data" [ANM17]; Arndt and Martin: "Decentralized Evolution and Consolidation of RDF Graphs" [AM17]; and Arndt et al.: "Decentralized Collaborative Knowledge Management using Git" [Arn+19a].

SPARQL Update interface with a transparent and fully backward compatible possibility for concurrency control. This enables us to provide specific interfaces to participants with different background and in different scenarios of an application. With the Structured Feedback interface we are able to integrate crowd contributions into the knowledge creation and authoring process. The *Knowledge Base Shipping to the Linked Open Data Cloud* system allows to build and bundle releases of knowledge bases and publish them using a ready-to-deploy microservice architecture. With Jekyll RDF customized domain and human adapted exploration interfaces can be generated using a templating system. These exemplary implementations of authoring and exploration components demonstrate that the Quit methodology, in contrast to the wiki approach, does not provide a shared workspace as a "one size fits all" interface. Moreover, collaborators are able to use workspaces that are customizable, can be adapted to the personal needs and are separated from the workspaces of the collaborators but still allow to be synchronized as needed.

During the knowledge engineering process the system automatically keeps track of the data's versioning and *provenance information*. Exploiting Git's commit system the Quit Store attaches metadata describing the performed actions along with other versioning information in the repository. This enriched commit meta-data can be processed and used semantically through a SPARQL 1.1 Query interface. Using the provenance graph we could also show that the concept of `git blame` can be transferred to semantic data. With the presented system we can provide access to the automatically tracked provenance information with Semantic Web technology in a distributed collaborative environment.

Even though we aim for systems to support collaborative processes it is also possible to apply the Quit methodology and its tools to support single users in performing knowledge management and engineering processes. To organize individual and group engineering processes based on the Quit methodology it is possible to build knowledge sharing platforms similar to collaborative source code sharing platforms like GitHub, Bitbucket, and GitLab. Such a platform can play the role of a hub to interconnect data engineering activity and provide interfaces, tools, and visualizations specially suited for data scientists and knowledge engineers. Concepts like issue trackers, forking, and individual contributions as pull requests (even from outside of a community) can be adapted to the knowledge engineering process.

The generic conception of the Quit methodology allows to apply it to various use cases and use it with appropriate domain specific vocabularies. Also the focus on SPARQL 1.1 as a standardized data read and write interface allows its application in various environments. We expect, that based on the Quit methodology the implementation of further methods to support the knowledge engineering workflow are enabled or can gain support from our system. In the following three fields of application are presented.

Custom Merge Methods and Continuous Integration   With the Three-Way-Merge a basic possibility for merging RDF knowledge bases is provided, which does not produce any conflict reports. In software engineering a goal of a good merge strategy is to highlight inconsistencies in the source code that might result from conflicting change operations. With the Context Merge strategy we are able to identify possible conflicts, based on the structure of the RDF graph, and bring them to the user's attention. An aim of the Semantic Web is to formalize relations within the data and allow automatic reasoning, which can be used for consistency checks on a semantic level of the data. For these formalizations and expressions of semantics, specific vocabularies and ontology systems are employed. To incorporate this semantic level in the Quit methodology it is possible to extend the system with custom merge algorithms. In the domain of software engineering additional measures are undertaken to avoid conflicts in the source code base. Employing continuous integration is already widely used in the Git ecosystem and can now also be adapted to RDF knowledge bases. The knowledge maintainer can define rules specific to the application domain, for instance by using ontological restrictions or rules (e. g. with OWL [W3C12], SKOS [MB09], or SHACL [KK17]). Support to ensure adherence to special semantic constraints, application specific data models, and certain levels of data quality is provided by continuous integration systems on the Git repository as presented in [Kon+14a]; [Kon+14b]; [MJ16].

Tracking of Evolution Patterns   The provenance tracking system of the Quit Store allows to relate the changes on the RDF representation to the actually executed update operation. These performed actions allow users to get a deeper understanding of the performed changes. This is demonstrated by storing the SPARQL Update operations along with each commit that was created. The system is not limited to SPARQL but can be extended to other operations and evolution languages. Tracking evolution patterns like EvoPat [Rie+10b] can help knowledge maintainers to comprehend for which purpose specific update operations were performed and could thus provide a better solution for merge conflicts. Also the tracking of the evolution of a schema, ontology, or mapping (cf. [Pal+12]) allows to identify complex change operations (cf. [HGR10]; [HGR12]), identify evolution trends and unstable regions in graphs (cf. [Har+09]), align evolving schemas and mappings, and support the migration of instance data, which can help to avoid inconsistencies like schema drift. In this way in addition to the versioning of the pure RDF structure of the data also the originating performed evolution operations and patterns can be added to the provenance meta-data.

Collaboration Workflows   In the domain of software development different work-flows have evolved in using Git to improve the quality of collaboratively developed software [SBZ12]; [PSW11]. Examples are Subversion-Style Workflow, Integration Manager Workflow, Dictator and Lieutenants Workflow, Gitflow, Git Feature Branch Workflow, and Forking Workflow.[1] These work-flows are also called branching strategies. They define models of when to create branches, how to name them, and when and into which branch they should be merged. This allows to delimit areas of development based on the responsibility with personalized branches or based on organizational measures such as introduction of new features, refactoring, hot fixes, releases, and development versions. Halilaj et al. [Hal+16a] have proposed a branching model for RDF vocabulary development, built on top of the *Gitflow* model. Currently the application of these work-flows premise that the participants are familiar with the respective software engineering tools. Using the Quit methodology these branching work-flows can be integrated in a knowledge engineering workflow by using Semantic Web tools. This setup can enable complex worldwide distributed collaboration strategies. As there is a big ecosystem of further methodologies and tools around Git to support the software development process, the Quit Store can support the creation of such an ecosystem for RDF dataset management.